Network Forensics

Network Forensics
Privacy and Security

Anchit Bijalwan

CRC Press
Taylor & Francis Group
Boca Raton London New York

CRC Press is an imprint of the
Taylor & Francis Group, an **informa** business

A CHAPMAN & HALL BOOK

First edition published 2022
by CRC Press
6000 Broken Sound Parkway NW, Suite 300, Boca Raton, FL 33487-2742

and by CRC Press
2 Park Square, Milton Park, Abingdon, Oxon, OX14 4RN

© 2022 Taylor & Francis Group, LLC

CRC Press is an imprint of Taylor & Francis Group, LLC

Library of Congress Cataloging-in-Publication Data
Names: Bijalwan, Anchit, author.
Title: Network forensics : privacy and security / Anchit Bijalwan.
Description: First edition. | Boca Raton : Chapman & Hall/CRC Press, 2022. |
Includes bibliographical references and index. | Summary: "Network
Forensics: A privacy & Security provides a significance knowledge of network forensics in different functions and spheres of the security. The book gives the complete knowledge of network security, all kind of network attacks, intention of an attacker, identification of attack, detection, its analysis, incident response, ethical issues, botnet and botnet forensics. This book also refer the recent trends that comes under network forensics. It provides in-depth insight to the dormant and latent issues of the acquisition and system live investigation too"— Provided by publisher.
Identifiers: LCCN 2021027908 (print) | LCCN 2021027909 (ebook) |
ISBN 9780367493615 (hardback) | ISBN 9780367493646 (paperback) |
ISBN 9781003045908 (ebook)
Subjects: LCSH: Computer crimes—Investigation. |
Computer networks—Security measures. | Computer security. | Forensic sciences.
Classification: LCC HV8079.C65 B55 2022 (print) | LCC HV8079.C65 (ebook) |
DDC 363.25/968—dc23
LC record available at https://lccn.loc.gov/2021027908
LC ebook record available at https://lccn.loc.gov/2021027909

ISBN: 978-0-367-49361-5 (hbk)
ISBN: 978-0-367-49364-6 (pbk)
ISBN: 978-1-003-04590-8 (ebk)

DOI: 10.1201/9781003045908

Typeset in Palatino
by codeMantra

Contents

Part B   Network Forensics Acquisition

Preface

It gives me immense pleasure to introduce this book for all the students, academicians and professionals around the globe. The book is a sincere attempt to foster quality education and awareness on the subject of network forensics and the unfolded contemporary issues thereof. The book aims to fulfill the requirements of technical, cyber world, forensics and professional education students at the undergraduate, post graduate, and research levels.

Network forensics is a very important subject and emerging terminology in these times when people are tormented by the different kinds of fraud they may encounter while using internet. Network Forensics is a science that starts after crime happens in the network. It helps in reading the behavior of attackers and can be useful in preventing the same kind of future attacks. Network forensics investigates all kind of attacks through the pattern that comes from all egress and ingress traffic.

This book strictly adheres to the scientific teaching learning pedagogy as all twelve chapters are designed on the predefined learning objectives which are tested in the learning outcome section at the end of every chapter. The book tries to explain the topics covered from the theoretical and practical aspects. Additionally, case studies are presented for the better understanding of the various topics. Similarly for nurturing the student's decision-making skills, real-life scenarios are given at the end of chapters. For a quick synopsis of the chapter, a summary is included at the end of every chapter. For making the topics more interesting and easier to understand different types of figures, tables, and photographs are utilized.

I hope that the book will help the students and professionals to develop a better understanding of the subject matter and will be useful to academicians in imparting the quality education.

Organization of This Book

The book is divided in three parts. Part one of the book is about network forensics which enlightens the significance of network forensics in different functions and spheres of the security. It provides complete knowledge of network security and the cyber forensics, differentiates between network security and network forensics, defines the terminologies of digital forensics and compares computer forensics and network forensics. It further describes the different cybercrimes, attack intentions and the types of the attacks. In Chapter 3 all recent trends that come under network forensics are discussed. It shows the process model and the framework in detail. Part one ends with the classification of network forensics in which payload, signature, decision tree and ensemble-based classification techniques are explained.

Part two of the book presents acquisition of crime from multidimensional angles. It provides in-depth insight to the dormant and latent issues of the acquisition. It starts with the different tools used to acquire the clues followed by all the conventional and advance network forensics techniques. It further explains the process of identification and detection of vulnerabilities and its attacks.

Part three is about the attribution of network forensics. It explains the analysis of detected vulnerabilities, evidences and its incident response, botnet attacks, system investigations with various challenges, highlighting the contentious issues hampering ethical behavior in the business world and possible solutions of those issues. Finally, this section of the book explains the different theories and opinions of ethics from various scholars and intellectual clan of the society.

Author

Dr. Anchit Bijalwan is an academician, researcher, consultant, and mentor with 18 years of teaching experience for graduate and post-graduate students, and Ph.D. scholars. He is an Associate Professor in the Faculty of Electrical & Computer Engineering, Arba Minch University, Ethiopia. He also handles projects from various funding agencies. He has authored books and published more than forty research papers in reputed international journals and conferences. He is also working on various international research and community service projects. His specialization is in Privacy and Security. His interest areas include network forensics, botnet forensics, Industry 4.O, Internet of Things, and machine learning. Dr. Bijalwan has chaired the technical sessions for IEEE international and Springer conferences, served as a committee member for other conferences, and was a keynote speaker at conferences El Salvador, Central America, and India. He is a reviewer for Inderscience, IGI Global, and many other publishers.

Acknowledgments

I would like to thank almighty God for bestowing his blessings on me.

I would also like to mention special thanks to my wife Dr. Jyotsna Ghildiyal Bijalwan for her positive feedback, motivation, and extended support. I would therefore like to dedicate this book to my wife for her unconditional love and encouragement throughout. I would like to thank to my beloved family for their sacrifices and encouragement.

I am thankful to my Ph.D. guide Dr. Emmanuel S. Pilli, Malviya National Institute of Technology (MNIT), Jaipur, India for his guidance and motivation, both on the personal and professional fronts, and to Prof. R.C. Joshi, Chancellor, Graphic Era University, Dehradun & Ex. Prof. Indian Institute of Technology (IIT), Roorkee, India for his guidance.

I am grateful to Arba Minch University for formalizing my knowledge and allowing me to experience various aspects of security analysis. I extend my sincere gratitude to Dr. Alehmehu Chufamo, Academic Vice President (AVP), Arba Minch University, Ethiopia for developing and nurturing the research environment and for encouraging the quality education in the university. I am also thankful to the Scientific Director Dr. Muluneh Lemma, Dean Faculty of Electrical & Computer Engineering, Satenaw Sando, and Chair Computer Stream, Afework Tademe, for having faith in me.

I am grateful to Shikha Garg and Aastha Sharma from CRC Press for making this book possible. Last but not least, I am thankful to all my friends, well-wishers, and extended family for their love and support.

Part A

Network Forensics Concepts

1

Introduction to Network Forensics

LEARNING OBJECTIVES

This chapter focuses on imparting the knowledge about introduction to network forensics. It gives the basic concepts and definition of network forensics and differentiates among network security, computer forensics, and network forensics. After reading this chapter, you would

- Have knowledge about the in-depth concepts of network forensics.
- Have knowledge about the concept of network security.
- Understand the concept of digital forensics.
- Understand the differences between computer forensics and network forensics.
- Have knowledge about the differences between network security and network forensics.

1.1 Introduction

The Internet has experienced tremendous growth in conventional attacks in this decade which ravage the features of network security such as confidentiality, integrity, and availability of many services. These attacks target the users alongside the enterprises and the organizations too. This causes exploitation of the security related to the internet systems and its services, e.g., web, cloud, etc. These attacks cause economic loss to businesses and have a very bad impact on internet-related business, security, and infrastructure.

The Internet has made a remarkable impact on people's life; especially if we look at the last two decades, it has become an indispensable part of our lifestyle and work culture. The role of the Internet has become very dominant and pretty evident in the lives of common and special people. Its impact can be witnessed in all spheres of life, let it be space technology, defense, education, banking, trade and commerce, industry, health, hospitality, or the entertainment industry. Its continuous use has made the transfer of information faster and efficient, which further led to space and time utility. Especially, in the case of stock exchanges, it has brought a revolution in the stock markets. By facilitating quick exchange of the information about market prices, it enabled the traders, arbitrators, and dealers to make quick money through trading in goods, money, stock, currencies, and other financial instruments. By providing massive database and storage, it has brought

DOI: 10.1201/9781003045908-2

a revolution in the social media, and with quick access to information, it has also aided the internet marketing. It has become easier for the students, researchers, and scientists to get information on their research areas at a less cost and time. The Internet has become a significant part of modern lifestyle. It is basically a group of computers that communicate with each other or a system which connects with World Wide Web. It has become a connecting pool between people, which facilitates sharing and exchange of information and ideas. The Internet has overcome time bounds, geographical boundaries, and sociocultural dynamics and connected people globally for the better at large. The efficiency of the Internet greatly depends on the strength of the protocol utilized for connection. The attackers target loopholes in the protocols which put the security of the system at stake. A system with vulnerable protocols is an easy prey for the attackers as the security system can be easily compromised. Exchange of information over networks can be a risky affair if the security part of the designing protocols is taken up in a casual manner. As the Internet has become a core means for exchange of information and communication, some nasty elements try to mulch it for their personal gain; for example, antisocial elements such as black hat communities get engrossed in malicious activities and try to steal the personal information of the users so that they can mint the money by using that personal information. To attain their self-centered goals, they use spams, pushing and probing, denial of service attack, click fraud, etc. as their weapons. The malicious software are distributed with the help of compromised machines and networks. Attackers connect their malicious software on compromised systems that enable attackers to steal the relevant information and make them part of the malicious activity and continue with them for further attacks.

Network forensics has become a very important topic as well as emerging terminology nowadays particularly when people are tormenting with different kinds of fraud using the Internet. Network forensics is the science that starts after crime happens on the network. It helps to read the behavior of attackers and prevent the same kind of attacks in future. Network forensics investigates all kind of attacks through the pattern that comes from all egress and ingress traffic.

On September 28, 2018, there were 50M accounts that had been attacked by hackers. The breaches were found after a few days. Users were affected when they relogged into their account on the same day. Later on, Facebook officials revealed that the app which the users were taking for a login, not looking like it is already compromised by the attackers. These kinds of issue were caused by the attackers several times in yesteryears. The attackers exploited the vulnerability to get the Facebook code which is related to one of the features such as "view as". This feature is designed for the users to see how their profile looks like on others' account. As and when the user accesses this feature, the attacker will be able to steal the access token of your account, and he will be able to compromise your Facebook account.

Network forensics enables the analysis of modus operandi of the attack that has occurred and the duration of the attack, and by this, it helps in finding the people involved in the attack and the method used for the attack. Network forensics implementation is like using a network time machine that allows you to go back to a particular time point and regenerate the series of events that showed at the time of a breach. Network forensics is used as a tool for monitoring the activities, specifying the source of attacks and analysis, and detecting them. Various network forensics tools can be used to capture the packets and analyze and investigate them. Network forensics is an extended phase of the network security. Network security protects the system against attacks, while network forensics mainly focuses on recording the evidence of the attack. The deep learning technique is also the best possible way for intrusion detection.

It is obvious that we ought to take detailed information about few old terminologies that refer us to build our core concept stern. Network security is one of the major topics we ought to fathom.

1.2 Network Security

It is an established fact that security is a major concern for all people to protect their valuables, both tangible and intangible assets. For instance, while cobbling the house safety and security is given apex significance, the boundaries are constructed so that the outsiders cannot directly barge into the vicinity. Doorbell alerts us that a person wants to enter our house. CCTV shows the owner all the surrounding activities. Hence, we can protect our house directly from all intruders' entry.

Similarly, network security is protecting our network from outside anomalies. None of the users can directly intrude through the network. Its overall goal primarily surmises the internal network that should be intact from ingress traffic, and it completely hinges upon the internal trusted network and the tool deployed inside the premises. Network security means to provide the unremitting transmission of information through stopping, preventing, detecting, and correcting the security violations, and hence, it can also be referred to as a defensive mechanism. According to the National Institute of Standard and Technology (NIST), it is "the protection afforded to an automated information system in order to attain the applicable objectives of preserving the integrity, availability, and confidentiality of information system resources". Network security protects the confidentiality, maintains the integrity, and ensures the availability of the network.

1.2.1 Evolution of Network Security

Before the Internet was widespread, in the days of Bulletin Board Systems (BBSes) from the late 1970s to the early 1990s, malicious intruders came looking for notoriety. Attack methods were naïve as were countermeasures. Usually simple programs exploited basic security flaws that were easily preventable if unsafe features were avoided or passwords were protected. Connections were limited to local communities, and people connected to others via the local telephone lines. The advent of TCP/IP protocol interconnected and integrated the scattered government and academic nets around the globe. Noncommercial use restrictions were abandoned, and the Internet began to grow rapidly. A wide scope description of security protocol-level issues in TCP/IP appeared first in 1989, and 15 years later, the same author published a retrospective view of that paper. Before the computers became interconnected as today, the viruses spread when infected files were transferred using floppy disks and other data storage media. Unlike today, the hustle and bustle of virus activation triggered alarms causing annoyance and rising even to the most inexperienced user. The *Morris Worm* was the first worm distributed via the Internet in 1988. It is usually reported that this worm infected 6,000 UNIX machines. Techniques evolved, and more than 10 years later, a major worldwide epidemic was caused by a virus called *Melissa*. Greed for notoriety, naïve viruses and overt attacks became less attractive, being replaced by stealth and complex attacks motivated by economic and political factors.

1.2.2 Importance of Network Security

The evolution of network security and its related tools paves the way to users to secure their network as well as confidential information by preventing malicious ingress traffic. It is an important aspect when users are working over networks. It is no matter whether the user is using a small network through LAN or working in a bigger network internally alongside, and it also doesn't matter how much is the user's business capacity. Network security is mainly important due to the following reasons:

1. Network security helps the user to protect the network from all the outside vulnerabilities.
2. It helps the workstations to protect themselves from all viruses.
3. It helps to secure all data and information.
4. It ensures all data should be kept secure.
5. The efficient network security system provides security to all clients from any kind of theft.
6. Efficient network system helps to reduce the risk of victimization of businesses.
7. It helps to reduce any kind of attack such as impersonation attack, interruption, modification, and fabrication.
8. Eavesdropping is also a kind of breach of network security objective. It can also be prevented by various levels of security aspects on network security tools.
9. Network security also provides the reliability between the parties through continuous monitoring of any suspicious transaction.
10. Network security provides good protection to home internet that can be connected with umpteen wireless routers that can be exploited very easily. An efficient system helps to reduce data theft, disrupt, and data losses.
11. It helps many important organizations around the world such as defense organizations, airports, railways authorities, etc. It makes their work smooth by protecting their valuable data and by maintaining the confidentiality, authenticity, and integrity of the data.

1.2.3 Basic Terminology for Understanding Network Security

In order to understand network forensics in a better way, it is a must to have the knowledge of its basic terminologies. This information helps in gaining in-depth knowledge about network forensics.

1. **Threat**: Threat is a probable risk that might exploit the vulnerability. It is a probable loss that can be in physical, mental, or financial terms. This is a violation of security that can further cause harm.
2. **Vulnerability**: Vulnerability is the sensitive user, network, or other event that can be easily exploited for malicious purposes.
3. **Attack**: Attack is a potential threat that converts into harm. The vulnerable system is a threat of network exploited through different methods or techniques. It is a breach of security services that is violated by the outsider.

4. **Exploit**: Exploiting means taking gratuitous deliberate advantages from other systems or networks specifically from vulnerable sources for intruders. It refers to the act of making an attack successful.

5. **Attack Vector**: Attack vector is a technique to compromise the particular system. This is a kind of method for unauthorized access of a system or network. It can also be a former employee of the organization. This can be a malicious program, pop-up, virus, malicious web page, message, or email link.

6. **Attacker**: Attacker is an intruder who wants to compromise a system or network for his own agenda.

7. **Target**: Target means aiming at an appropriate system or network through which maximum information can be retrieved.

8. **Compromise**: Compromise means taking over something, either the targeted machine or network.

9. **Defender**: The expert who sorts out the network deformity and makes systems or network intact.

10. **Malware**: Malware is a computer program that is made for harming others.

11. **Trojan**: Trojan is a kind of malware that deceives its intention from others and works as a legitimate software.

12. **Worm**: A worm is a standalone program that itself replicates and generates the service demand from itself in order to spread it to other systems.

1.2.4 Features of Network Security Services

The main features of network security services are the following:

1. **Confidentiality**

When both the parties, i.e., sender and recipient, mutually agree to exchange the information between them, it necessitates the network to ensure the confidentiality of the data exchanged. Network security ensures that the confidential data should not divulge to maintain unauthorized person. Confidentiality also refers to maintaining the privacy. Individual person has his own will on what information should be stored and where and what information to disclose. For instance, we all have an email account where we store umpteen confidential data and information. Somehow, we also communicate our daily basis conversation through its chat box. All this is done to keep our data and information confidential. Just imagine, if a channel is vulnerable, what will happen. The trespasser will use this information for malicious purposes or to make us compromise at any case. Similarly, all we have a bank account where all transactions remain safe through a secure channel. What if all transaction details are compromised by the intruder? This feature of network security assures and provides a confidential platform to make the process flawless, i.e., without any hindrance.

2. **Integrity**

Data integrity means the information that is forwarded to the recipient side should be reached intact. Data must arrive in the correct form as well as length to the recipient side as it broadcasts through the sender. For instance, user A transfers

$5,000 to user B; however, user B received only $500. It shows the abysmal blunder of the communication network.

Similarly, system integration refers to all the components having capacity to run without outside flaw and compromise through others by unauthorized access.

3. **Availability**

It assures that the system will give prompt information as and when required. It also ensures that the service will not be interrupted to all the authorized people. All the system-related assets should be available to authorized parties. Both sender and receiver follow the nonrepudiation of message.

4. **Authenticity**

Impersonation attack is an example of violating the authentication feature of network security. When people interact and share their information online, there is a chance of compromise by an unauthorized person. Authenticity is a crucial feature after data integrity. The recipient knows all ingress information is from a reliable source. Source identity must be known to receiver so that receiver can easily interpret the source of information and can weed out the derelict user. User or network should be identified prior to interaction with the system resources.

For instance, when someone accesses net banking of a bank, it should be authenticated by his/her user id and a strong password. If login declined after using three attempts, the system asks few confidential questions to get in again. Malicious users fail to authenticate through this process and can prevented from accessing the data.

5. **Accountability**

Accountability term can be understood by the word accountable that means reliable or explicable. It exhibits the responsibility of taking over all the process safely during network interaction. It fixes the accountability of all the actions taken by individuals.

1.3 Types of Network Security Attacks

Although network security experts dig up all the possibilities to make their network secure, the black hat community keeps trying to breach these networks. They use different tools and techniques to get into the network of vulnerable users. These illegitimate intruders pretend like a legitimate user; as and when they find passage to enter others' network, they start working their problem. It is obvious that everyone should acquire knowledge about these attacks. Majorly these attacks can be bifurcated into two types. The types of network security attacks are as follows.

1.3.1 Active Attack

When attackers try to modify the content of information for their own purpose, it is often called an active attack. It means that the alteration of messages is possible here, and due to alteration, system halt can occur during the active attack. These possibilities show the changes in system resources. In such cases, there is an impact on integrity and availability characteristics of network security. Integrity suffers here as the information is distorted

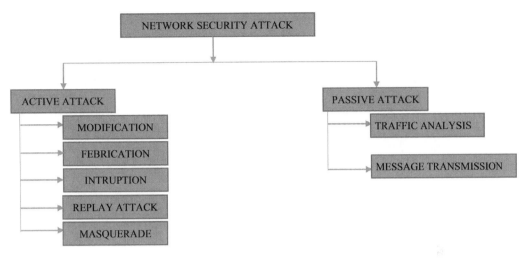

FIGURE 1.1
Network security attacks.

during channel, whereas system resources face failure due to not following the availability features of network security. These active attacks can be of the following types (Figure 1.1).

1.3.1.1 Modification

Modification means to tamper something. This is the best example of violation of the integrity feature of network security. When user A interacts with user B, an unknown user takes over the network at bang on dot, modifies the messages, and then transmits them to the user B; this is referred to as modification. In the above example, user B does not get a wind of modified messages. This includes the altercation of legitimate messages, altercation of programs, and changing the order of messages.

1.3.1.2 Fabrication

This attacking type violates an authentication feature of network security. In this type of attack, illegitimate users add spurious content with the messages and further retransmit the entire message to the recipient. The examples of fabrication active attacks are email spoofing, sql injection, user counterfeiting, etc.

1.3.1.3 Interruption and Denial of Service

Interruption violates availability features of the network security. In this type, legitimate use of the network is made unavailable. An example is communication line blockage. In denial of service, attack results into erratic or complete inaccessibility of an Internet service. Due to this attack, the user of the services does not get access to the Internet service and resources.

1.3.1.4 Replay Attack

Replay back attack is also referred to as playback attack. In this type of attack, repetition of messages or message delayed can be done by the attacker. So the data retransmission may be possible because of the masquerade attack by IP substitution. This kind of attack creates confusion to the recipient side as the originator message is retransmitted by an illegitimate user.

1.3.1.5 Masquerade Attack

Masquerade attack means the deception to a targeted system that pretends like an originator. Masquerade attack is an unauthorized access to a system's information through spoof network identification.

1.3.2 Passive Attack

The attackers continuously reconnaissance individual's messages for extracting it from the network. This retrieved information is further used for their own malicious intends. This entire malicious act is executed in such a secret way that the user does not get a wind of it as there is no change in his messages. This type of attack is also known as passive attack. Passive attack breaches the confidentiality feature of network security as here, eavesdropper can read the entire messages and use them for malpractices; however, system services remain the same. In passive attack, eavesdropper monitor the ordinary user's system or communication, when they find any vulnerability, they try to obtain the information from being transmitted messages. Passive attack follows the presumption of "prevention is better than cure" as this kind of attack is obtuse to detect from the network. It is not like any alteration or modification or replaying of the messages; rather, it is a clandestinely extraction of information that victim cannot get the wind of. In these attacks, intruders perform different activities to extract the information. They look into vulnerability-intended network. They may find passwords through the trash folder from the system or other network devices. They may enter through pretending like a legitimate user and then launch different algorithms to extract some information.

1.3.2.1 Traffic Analysis

Attackers use cryptanalysis tool to decrypt the information through the traffic. The traffic analysis can be done by monitoring the traffic length, rate, type, duration, etc. Network traffic monitoring refers to keeping a close eye on the traffic movement or inflow or outflow of all the packets on the network and looking for the abnormal behavior and analyzing the traffic behaviors so that the potential threat to network security, if any, can be detected in its advanced stages. It protects the efficiency of the networks. The technologies facilitating network traffic monitoring are as follows: firewalls, intrusion detection and prevention system, network monitoring, managing and performance software, and antivirus.

1.3.2.2 Message Transmission

When intruders capture all the confidential data during transmission but source as well as recipient do not know about it, this kind of scenario is known as message transmission passive attack. In this process, exchange of information does continue. The confidential data can be captured through telephonic conversation, transfer of file, email communication, etc.

1.4 Network Security Tools

It is obvious that network security tools are necessary to install in organizations. These tools are the backbone of the organization as they prevent from outside vulnerabilities. They not only control all the ingress and egress traffic but also secure all the devices on the network. These network security tools are the following.

1.4.1 Intrusion Detection System

Intrusion detection systems are used to detect intrusions, i.e., malicious attacks or abnormal behavior in a system. It responds by giving an alert. Data are collected from two main sources which are traffic passing through the network and the hosts connected to the network. Therefore, according to their deployment, IDSs are divided into two categories: those that analyze network traffic and those that analyze information available on hosts such as operating system audit trails. They can be broadly classified as follows (Figure 1.2).

The current trend in intrusion detection is to combine both host-based information and network-based information to develop hybrid systems.

1.4.1.1 Knowledge- or Signature-Based IDS

In knowledge- or signature-based IDS, the incoming packets are compared with known patterns of attacks, which are used to detect malicious threats, and if matches are found, then the alert is generated. The basic motive is to measure how close a behavior is to some previously established standard of misuse or normal behavior. Depending on the level of a priority or domain knowledge, it is possible to design detectors for specific categories of attack (e.g. denial of service, user to root, remote to local).

1.4.1.2 Behavior- or Anomaly-Based IDS

In this method, the incoming traffic that does not match the normal or expected behavior is alerted to be an intrusion. Intrusion detection systems can be implemented at network-, host-, or application-level IDs that work effectively in this type of level. Intrusion detection

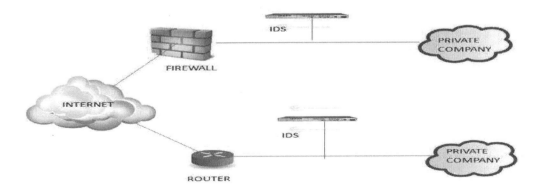

FIGURE 1.2
Intrusion detection system.

systems assist by generating alerts, which can enable investigation process in network forensic systems. The basic functionality is just detection not investigation.

Sometimes intrusion detection systems can give wrong alerts, i.e., false alarms; we call it either false positives or false negatives. False positive refers to flagging of an alert, even though an attack has not occurred. And false negative refers to inability to flag an alert, even when an attack has occurred. The anomaly detection first requires the IDS to define and characterize the correct and acceptable static form and dynamic behavior of the system, which then can be used to detect abnormal changes or anomalous behaviors. An IDS is shown in Figure 1.2.

1.4.2 Firewall

The firewall is a network security system that controls the incoming and outgoing network traffic based on a set of rules. It can either be hardware or software and acts as a barrier between the trusted networks and other untrusted networks like the Internet or less trusted networks.

It actually prevents the malicious attacks from entering the protocol unit by the rules that control the access in and out flow. Although the firewall detects some attacks and viruses, it also has some limitations. The firewall becomes weaker and less effective as the attack model of the attacks changes day by day. The attacks occur as they are generated in the local network, and firewall can just filter the packets from the WAN, as shown in Figure 1.3. The firewall is installed between the WAN and the LAN. The firewall can be bifurcated into three ways as follows (Figure 1.4).

1.4.2.1 Network-Level Firewall

It is also called Packet filters. This operates at a relatively low level of the TCP/IP protocol stack, and thus prevents packets to pass through the firewall unless they match the established rule set. It is of two types: stateful and stateless. The stateful firewalls maintain the information about the active session and use that state information to speed up the processing of the packets. The stateless firewall needs less memory and can be faster for simple filters that require less time to filter than to look up.

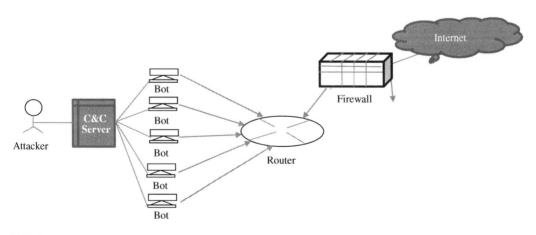

FIGURE 1.3
Firewall.

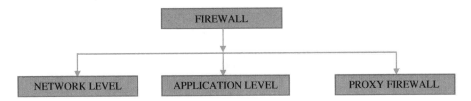

FIGURE 1.4
Types of firewall.

1.4.2.2 Application-Level Firewall

It works at the application level of the TCP/IP stack and may intercept all packets that travel to and from an application. They function by determining whether a process should accept any connection. They filter connections by examining the process ID of data packets against a rule set for the local process involved in the data transmission.

1.4.2.3 Proxy Firewall

Proxy server may act as a firewall by responding to input packets in a manner of an application while blocking other packets. It is a gateway from one network to another for a particular network application, in the sense that it functions as a proxy on behalf of the network user.

1.4.3 Antivirus

Virus is a category of malware that, when executed, tries to replicate itself into other executable code, and when it succeeds, the code is said to be infected. When the infected code is executed, the virus also executes. A computer virus is a kind of bad software code (*"malware"*) that, when runs, multiplies by reproducing itself (copying its own program code) or *tainting* other computer programs by editing them. *Corrupting the* computer programs also includes data files or the "boot" sector of the hard disk.

1.5 Security Issues

The aim of network security is to protect the network from ingress traffic alongside protecting systems within the network. It also prevents the data as well as information while being processed on the network. It consists of both hardware and software components that take all preventive measures to protect the data and information. They work as an armor for organization that stops unauthorized access, interception, fabrication, interruption, modification, etc. Network security mainly relies on three major components that are software, hardware, and cloud services. Different software that contain different software antivirus applications are installed among the nodes or devices on the network. A software-aided network helps to detect and overcome the threat. The hardware appliances are installed mainly on server or installed at that emanate point of ingress and egress traffic. The cloud services add on hardware services by scanning the threats and detects the clue from it.

The various types give us the broad knowledge on network security.

1.5.1 Network Access Control

Network access control refers to the whole system by providing point-to-point security through antivirus, authentication protocol for user alongside systems, intrusion prevention, and procurement of all kinds of vulnerabilities. It provides the solution for the network devices through appropriate authentication protocols. It means that the set of protocols with well-defined policies makes all devices stern when it interacts with the network node. It ensures authentication, authorization, and accountability to the user. The main benefits using network access control are as follows:

1. It reduces the vulnerabilities.
2. It provides authority, accountability, and authentication of connection.
3. It prevents all end stations from accessing other networks in which there is lack of proper antivirus, and intrusion prevention software is not installed.
4. Different policies can be implemented by operators through network access control. It can be accessing network areas, types, and roles of computers.

There are two basic types of network access control that are the most important aspects of network security (Figure 1.5).

1. **Preadmission**: In this type of network access control, end user devices will get access once users prove that they are authorized to access the network. The user will get entry only when they match their corporate security policies for the network.
2. **Postadmission**: This type of network access control works after getting the accessibility by end users. It works within the networks when preadmission network access control fails to recognize illegitimate users; it controls the post movement inside of network and mitigates the damages by the attackers. In the postadmission, users must authenticate multiple number of times for all requisition to visit any part of network.

1.5.2 Application Security

Application security is a process of building, detecting, and preventing applications from the outside security vulnerabilities against all the unauthorized accesses. In today's scenario, applications are made available through networks, and these networks are also connected with the cloud. It is obvious that the availability by networks makes these applications more squeamish. It is highly prone to breaches by the intruders, so getting rid of unauthorized accesses with all breaches, security features are indispensable to apply for

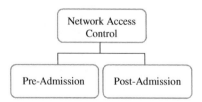

FIGURE 1.5
Network access control types.

FIGURE 1.6
Life cycle of application security.

the application. These application securities are required at different stages of the life cycle of an application (Figure 1.6).

Application security works at different phases. It may deploy in different areas such as mobile application security, web application security, and cloud application security.

1.5.2.1 Application Security Process

Application security process refers to the expertise for applying a systematic approach to make application secure. The process of application security are as follows:

1. Authentication
2. Authorization
3. Encryption
4. Log files

1.5.2.1.1 Authentication

When users get to interact with any application, it is very essential to know the probity of a user. The experts have to add on features with user id and the password to make an application more secure. They may provide more security features on different pages for prevention from unauthorized access.

1.5.2.1.2 Authorization

Authorization is the next phase of making application secure after authentication. Authenticated user further authorizes to set authorization pages inside of application pages. Authorization can be done by checking all authorized user lists. Authorization phase prevents application from unauthorized access and unauthorized modification.

1.5.2.1.3 Encryption

Efficient encryption techniques make application more secure. All authenticated authorized users may exchange their information through secure channel. They trust very easily on the applications. Various intruders actively reconnoiter the vulnerable applications; hence, to prevent outsiders' attack, it is very important to encrypt the data while exchanging.

1.5.2.1.4 Log Files

Log files help applications administrator to check, detect, fix, and test the security features through log file records. These records can prevent applications from all security breaches.

1.5.3 Email Security

Email is the best way of permeating fraudulent desire by the intruder. Black hat communities use emails as a weapon to launch their malicious script for their own interest, so it is indispensable to make email more secure preventing from these anomalies. Spamming and phishing attacks are common examples of attacker's intended desire through which they engross in crime. Email security is a set of processes of protecting email content and accounts from all unauthorized access and modification through various tools and techniques, and thus, these email security services work with all security measures alongside the rest of the network security types such as application security, web security, network access control, etc. cordially. Email security contains all security measures such as strong password, strong encryption algorithm, firewalls, intrusion detection, and prevention systems.

Email security is an extensive term that subsumes the umpteen tools and techniques to prevent from unforeseen contingencies as well as for securing email services. To create email services sturdier, there is requirement to set regulations for users' perspective alongside the email service provider. The user has to follow certain points as follows:

1. Antivirus application on system
2. Spam filters
3. Antispam application
4. Strong password
5. Password rotation.

1.5.3.1 Antivirus Application on System

Antivirus application weeds out all existing ingress malware from the user's system. The user has to ensure installing efficient software so that the virus cannot enter inside of the system. The user also has to ensure that they not only update these antivirus application at appropriate time but also to install the new version of applications.

1.5.3.2 Spam Filters

The spam filter is a program for preventing inbox from spurious mails. It makes all undesired messages filtered and prevents them from entering the inbox of particular mail. The service providers set the algorithm in which it watches the specific line of the subject message, segregates it, and sends it to another folder.

1.5.3.3 Antispam Applications

Antispam application is a tool that blocks all messages to enter a system. This application may be a process, software, or hardware that prevents the system from anomalies. It is a set of protocols that stop all the unwanted messages from entering the system.

1.5.3.4 Strong Passwords

Strong passwords help users to secure their email id from illegitimate and nefarious people. Black hat communities always try to crack users' password on networks that are more susceptible to email. Strong passwords convolute to the illegitimate people to get into users' account.

1.5.3.5 Password Rotation

Users have to change their password at least in a month so that the illegitimate users cannot get the wind of it. Frequent changes on password makes it more secure.

Email service providers also ensure the stringent network framework for the users so that it cannot be cracked easily. They provide efficient access control mechanisms to prevent unauthorized access. Strong firewall protects email services from unauthorized ingress and egress traffics. Spam filtering application also filters and sends suspicious mail to the spam folder through which inbox folders receive mails from the genuine sender.

1.5.4 Wireless Security

As everyone is aware that if there is wireless internet connection, then network can be accessed at places where it is impossible to bestow through wires. Wireless security is a specific kind of services that protect computers, wireless routers, and other wireless devices from unauthorized access. Wireless-related crimes also suffused over the period of time with the popularity of wireless services. Still there is carelessness and ignorance which jeopardizes the user's work when they interact with these kinds of services.

Wireless security refers to the security for all kinds of wireless communications that may represent wireless media such as Wi-Fi communication, mobile communication, Bluetooth communication, and satellite communication. Although they use different architectures, they share the same wireless platform. These wireless devices can be computers, laptops, smartphones, smartwatches, smart televisions, or any smart home appliances that can access the Wi-Fi services.

The routers that work as connectivity providers also need security, specially the ones that utilize wireless controller (WLC), service set identifier (SSID), cell, channel, and antennas and also access Wi-Fi-protected access (WPA).

1.5.5 Firewall

The firewall is a network security system that controls the incoming and outgoing network traffic based on a set of rules. It can either be hardware or software and acts as a barrier between the trusted network and other untrusted or less trusted networks like Internet.

It actually prevents the malicious attacks from entering the protocol unit by the rules that control the access in and out flow. Although the firewall detects some attacks and viruses, it also has some limitations. The firewall becomes weaker and less effective as the attack model of the attacks changes day by day. The attacks occur as they are generated in the local network, and firewall can just filter the packets from the WAN, as shown in Figure 1.7; the firewall is installed between the WAN and the LAN.

1.6 Digital Forensics

Digital forensics is the science that starts after crime takes place in the network. It helps to read the behavior of attackers and can help to prevent the same kind of attacks in future. Network forensics investigates all kinds of attacks through the pattern that comes from all egress and ingress traffic.

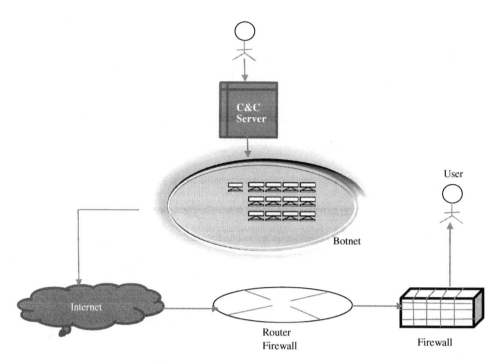

FIGURE 1.7
Processing of firewall.

Digital forensics is a branch of forensic science that involves finding out the clues, investigate them, and utilize incident response of a crime in digital devices. Initially, digital forensic was known as computer forensics, but due to the limitations of computer forensics, later on it was called digital forensics. The term digital forensics has a wide scope for the investigation of all digital devices that are capable of storing the bunches of data. Digital forensics is a process that involves preservation, identification, extraction of data, documentation, and finally interpretation of digital evidences for the analysis. These process finds out all the evidences in the digital media. These digital media can be a smart phone, computer, laptop, server, or a network too. The experts of digital forensics are well equipped and well trained by the latest tools and techniques through which they process it magnificently. The subbranches of digital forensics are network forensics, malware forensics, botnet forensics, email forensics, mobile forensics, and somehow computer forensics too.

1.6.1 Digital Forensics Evolution

Before 1980, there were certain laws that covered the crimes related to the computers, but it had several loopholes. The lame cyber security laws paved an easy escape for the criminals committing cyber-crimes. The legislation was made for all illegitimate altercation of data on a computer system, but these provisions were unable to deal with gradually increasing computer-related crimes.

The USA law authorities received the first forensic service lab which was set up in 1932. In the late 1970s, Florida Computer Crime Act got the first computer-related crime. During the 1980s, umpteen law enforcement acts and related expert team enacted which were specifically from US, Canada, and Britain. In 1992, the term computer forensics was coined in many academic literature studies. During the 1990s, many organizations' technical detectives as well as experts had started investigation through fingerprinting. DNA testing was also initiated by these technical experts. They had started following the process of digital forensics such as preserving, identifying, seizing, and analyzing the evidence. The first FBI regional computer forensic laboratory was established in 2000. The first book *Best Practices for Computer Forensics* came into existence in 2002, which was published by a scientific working group on digital evidence.

1.6.2 Digital Forensic Types

Generally, the subbranches of digital forensics are often called the types of digital forensics. These types are the following:

1. **Malware Forensics**

   Malware forensics is the analysis of malware. It is directly associated with the malicious activity that causes distributed denial of services, phishing, spam, etc. The forensic investigation is needed to get rid of this problem. For this purpose, behavioral analysis of the malware is needed.

2. **Mobile Forensics**

   Examination and analysis of all mobile-related devices come under this type of digital forensics. Nowadays, umpteen crimes are taking place through mobiles. People keep all their valuable data in their mobile phones. They do exchange transaction through mobile banking. These phones consist of both software and hardware that work like a small-scale computer, so there are much chances to fall prey to malicious traps.

3. **Email Forensics**

   Email forensics is the subbranch of digital forensics that involves analysis of content and source of mails as an evidence. It also focuses on recovery of the mail through many email investigation techniques such as server investigation, header analysis, software investigation technique, network device investigation, sender mail fingerprints, etc.

4. **Network Forensics**

   Network forensics involves capturing (fetching) the network traffic, retrieving the data in reconnaissance from multiple devices, systems, processes, and other resources. The information given by network forensic is utilized to strengthen the security tools by understanding the modus operandi of the attacks. The available observations can be utilized in future also to prevent a potential threat to network security.

5. **Computer Forensics**

   Earlier the term computer forensics was used for digital forensics, but gradually, computer forensics was widely used specifically for computer-related crimes. It started with the law enforcement to tackle all computer-related data. It consists of a five-phase process to complete the tasks such as preservation, identification, extraction of data, documentation, and finally interpretation.

6. **Wireless Forensics**

   Wireless forensics is a subbranch of digital forensics that involves tracing out all anomalies from the network. In this process, all data are to be captured first, and subsequently, the network events on network are analyzed to find out the anomalies.

7. **Botnet Forensics**

Botnet forensics is the technique that assists to ameliorate the system through an analysis of the bot attacks and their detection. It focuses on the preservation and acquisition of the digital evidence from the various sources that is further utilized for investigating the botnet attack. Botnet forensics is of great importance nowadays, as it assists and prevents the organizations from the outside and inside network attacks. It helps to detect the attacks and to mitigate the damage occurred by determining who is responsible for an attack and also can determine the path from an affected network or system to the point from where an attack originated. So to identify where an attack originated and the method used, traceback and attribution are performed.

1.7 Computer Forensics

Computer forensics is the subterm of digital forensics that involves preserving, identifying, extracting, documenting, and finally interpreting the facts to get rid of the problem. Computer forensics deals with static data only. This computer information is handled only by law enforcement. Computer forensics experts always get better position than the intruder as they have better tools and techniques than the attacker.

The dependency on computer has tremendously increased due to which the spread of cyber-crime inevitably soars across the globe. However, it is widely associated with the investigation of computer crimes which is in line with the civil proceedings. There are well-prepared guidelines to handle these crimes from the initial investigation to interpretation of crimes. Computer experts use different tools and techniques to resolve these issues. These techniques can be live forensic analysis, deletion of files, cross-drive analysis, and steganography and may be through stochastic forensics.

In live forensics analysis, experts investigate all volatile data that reside in random access memory, computer registries, or cache. When the system is in active mode, experts extract the information before the power cut. Herein, they use different tools to recover the data. Before the power goes off, prior content can be traced through the RAM as memory cells retain electrical charge for a while. Experts use the same technique to get these volatile data for further analysis. Many organizations provide different tools, and experts also get these tools from an open source for investigating the computer-related crime.

1.7.1 Computer Forensics Process

Computer forensics process refers to all the phases through which experts recover the information from a machine. The phases of computer forensics process are as follows:

1. Preservation.
2. Identification.
3. Extraction.
4. Documentation.
5. Interpretation.

The details of all phases of computer forensics are explained in detail as below:

1. **Preservation**

   Various network security tools like intrusion detection system, packet analyzers, and firewalls are deployed at various points on the network. They must have access to the sensitive data on the network.

2. **Identification**

   The data are identified and captured by using the available tools in identification phases. There are various tools that may be used for data recovery.

3. **Extraction**

   All identified resources further keep separated from other sources in extraction phase.

4. **Documentation**

   It is obvious that the systematic process also fulfills the criteria with legal requirements. All the information is recorded in the documentation phase. Crime-related scene mapping, all photography, sketching, etc. are kept as evidence.

5. **Interpretation**

   Interpretation of computer forensics phase describes the findings and the reports by detailed comparison of actual and final evidences. Evaluation of evidences also takes place in this phase.

1.8 Network Forensics

Network forensics is the field of research that tremendously expands with the tendency to help in arbitrating, capturing, and detaining the exponential growth of the cybercrimes. With this expansion, the field of network forensics is still not clear and is uncertain.

1.8.1 Definition

Network forensics is a very important and emerging terminology nowadays when people are tormented with different kinds of network attack. Network forensics is the science that starts after crime happens on the network. It helps to read the behavior of attackers and can help to prevent the same kind of future attacks. Network forensics investigates all kinds of attacks through the pattern that comes from all egress and ingress traffic.

There are many definitions for the term network forensics since its existence by Marcus J. Ranum in 2012, and all researchers have shown greatly a gamut since then. Schwartz in 2010 coined network forensics as "The reconstruction of network event to provide definitive insight into action and behavior of users, applications as well as devices". Network forensics contains the utilization of scientifically and experimentally proven techniques to identify, collect, detect, acquire, corroborate, examine, analyze, and present the document via using digital information from live network sessions.

The network forensics process can be done through collecting all the ingress and egress traffic from the various resources, devices like servers, firewall, honeypots, and various browsers. These proactive and reactive processes investigate the attack intention and recover the clues from an intrusion. The ultimate goal of this field is to give law enforcement and security tightening perspective. It refers to finding out the level of attack intrusion so that the network can be intact, secure, and strengthened with evidences.

Network forensics is used as a tool for monitoring the activities, specifying the source of attacks, and analyzing and detecting them. Various network forensics tools can be used to capture the packets and analyze and investigate them. Network forensics is an extended phase of the network security. Network security protects the system against attacks, while network forensics mainly focuses on recording the evidence of the attack.

Network forensics deals with the capturing, retaining, and analyzing the network traffic. Packet mining, packet forensics, or digital forensics terminology can be taken for network forensics. All are having the same concept with the objective to register each and every packet and the data that it contains which were moving throughout the network and storing them for some period of time. Network forensics can be used as a powerful device to unlock the mysteries found within the network, i.e., capturing the digital evidence before any specific event takes place. A network forensics analyzer commonly called a network recorder captures and stores all the traffic so that it can be retrieved later for the further analysis.

Network forensics focuses on two issues. The first one is related to the security which involves detecting the traffic and identifying the intrusions. The second one is related to the law enforcement which shows capture and analyzes the traffic and can include various tasks such as searching for the keywords and reassembling the transferred files. The tendency of network forensics is to make attackers busy on the network and involve them to spend much time and energy to trace the track and scenarios go more costly.

1.8.2 Taxonomy of Network Forensics Tools

Garfinkel et al. classified the network forensics systems into catch-it-as-you-can terminology and stop-look-and-listen terminology. Catch-it-as-you-can term takes all the packets as much as possible which cross through a certain traffic point and store further. In these kinds of tools, analysis is done in the batch mode. This type of process, therefore, needs a huge amount of space. In stop-look-and-listen term, each packet is analyzed in a minimum necessary way in memory. Some information is preserved for the future acquisition. Speed processor is needed to check the path of ingress traffic especially in this approach. Quite a bit space is needed to store for updating the new information from the old in both the approaches (Figure 1.8).

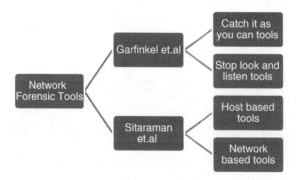

FIGURE 1.8
Network forensics concept.

Sitaraman et al. described the whole network as host based and network based. The host-based networks collect and analyze the packet that comes from a specific host. It relies on a single host and helps to understand network activity.

1.8.3 Network Forensics Mechanism

The different components of the network forensics analysis have been shown in Figure 1.9. It shows the various stages through which the clues will be evaluated.

The architecture of analysis mechanism for the network forensics is shown in Figure 1.9. The first module of this architecture is evidence collection module. The first module collects intrusion clues from many hosts and the network, and preserves them for investigation which are further forwarded to the evidence preprocessing module that parses certain types of clues such as intrusion alerts into required structure and reduces the repetition in low-level clues by aggregation. The second module is attack knowledge base module. It is a separate module that provides prior knowledge of known exploits. The second separate module is asset knowledge base that provides prior knowledge of the networks and hosts under investigation. The first and the second separate modules merge and produce output sent to the evidence graph manipulation module which generates and updates the evidence graph by retrieving intrusion defense in the repository. Further, automated reasoning will be performed in attack reasoning module. This reasoning is based on the evidence graph. It is followed by all the visualization of evidence graph, and reasoning results are passed to the analyst in analyst interface module. The final analysis and the feedback are sent for both graph generation and attack reasoning modules.

This architecture itself reveals that the identified source will be collected for further investigation. Here, all the real-time tools should work efficiently. This collected evidence is sent for preprocessing. The entire preprocessed evidence is further stored in the depository. The attack knowledge base ensures the entire alert to graph generation module. Asset knowledge base gives information about the number of hosts under investigation, combined with attack knowledge base which further merges in the graph generation module. The graph generator module also retrieves information from evidence depository, and refurbished information is sent to the depository. This graph generator module sends all revamp data to interface module. Graph generator module also forwards all the investigated evidence to attack reasoning module. The analyst interface module gives their

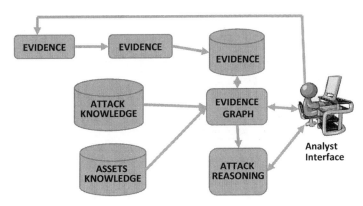

FIGURE 1.9
Network forensics analysis design.

expertise comments without band information by "edit the evidence graph directly" and another "send queries to extract specific evidence". The updated evidence graph is finally sent to the attack reasoning module for improving the results.

1.8.4 Network Forensics Process

Network forensics is the process of investigating the attack that describes how an incident happened and the involvement of the parties in this process. The network forensics investigation of the digital evidence has been employed as the postincident response for an activity, but it is definitely not an incident that complies with the organization's terms and policies. Therefore, there are various frameworks and techniques proposed in order to investigate the digital evidence. Pilli et al. showed in their work about ubiquitous research on network forensics and proposed a generic framework for the network forensics investigation. This framework describes many of the phases that already have been proposed in the various digital forensics models, but some new phases have been included specifically. Figure 1.10 describes the proposed framework and the detailed description about those phases later. The attack intention and types can be further analyzed according to their malicious intent.

1.8.4.1 Authorization

In this stage, background is set toward the higher ground tasks. Various network security tools such as intrusion detection system or intrusion prevention system, firewalls, and the packet analyzers are deployed at a number of points on the network, and also they require taking the access of the sensitive data on the network. Trained staff is required in order to handle these tools and ensure collecting the quality evidence to facilitate the acknowledgment of network security attacks. Required legal warrants and authorization must be obtained in order to ensure that the privacy of an individual and the organization is not violated.

1.8.4.2 Collection of Evidences

Various tools including software and hardware are deployed to capture logs as much as possible. The various sensors are also installed to reconnoiter the activities. Network evidences are collected by the various NFATs employed such as TCPdump, Wireshark,

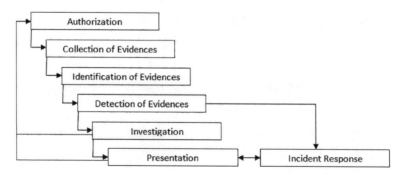

FIGURE 1.10
Generic process model for network forensic investigation.

TCPflow, Snort, SiLK, PADS, and bro. As the incoming traffic changes very rapidly, and also it is not possible to retrieve exactly the same traces at the same time, and therefore, it is critical to analyze at that point or stage. The network must be monitored, and the integrity of the captured traces must be maintained as well to identify the future attacks. Sometimes, the large amount of memory space is required to keep the logs intact. Logs are more in quantity, so the system must be able to handle it in a proper manner.

1.8.4.3 Identification of Evidences

Data collected in the previous stage is identified by the network forensics specialist for further investigation. This stage also makes it sure to preserve the copy of the network data so as to facilitate legal requirements, and as soon as the process is repeated on the original data, the results obtained after investigation are proved to be the same. Without modifying the original data, a copy of the data is analyzed, and also a hash of data is preserved. Bijalwan et al. showed the UDP flooding approach in their work through the randomizer approach.

1.8.4.4 Detection of Crime

In case of eccentricity, alerts have been generated by the deployed security tools like TCPdump, Wireshark, PADS, bro, snort, etc. These tools help to detect the security breach and the privacy violation. These eccentricities are further analyzed for the various parameters in order to persuade the presence and the nature of the attack. To determine the attack or for further analysis, a quick validation process has been carried out. This process decides whether to continue or ignore the alert as false alarm. If the analysis goes on, then it performs two actions: collection of the clues and incident response of the clues. Network traffic is classified through SVM for multiclass classification.

1.8.4.5 Investigation

The data we get in the previous stage may consist of the reluctant data or are referred to as contradictory data. Therefore, in this stage, an examination is made, and a mythological search is conducted so that no crucial information is lost. The data collected are classified and clustered into the groups to reduce the stored volume of data into manageable portions. The highest possible evidence and the data containing the least information are identified to remove the redundancy. After examination, these evidences are analyzed to identify network intrusions. Data mining and soft computing technique are used to search the data and correlate the attack patterns. To understand the nature and the workability of the attackers, the attack patterns are then put together. The attacks are further reconstructed and replayed. Few important parameters related to network connection establishment are operating system fingerprinting, DNS queries, packet fragmentation, and protocol. Validation of the suspicious activity is the final outcome of this phase. The information obtained from the previous stage is used to check who, where, when, how, and why of the incident as it helps in the source traceback, attribution to a source, and reconstruction of the attack scenario. The result of the previous phase further observes to see the way from where the attack emanates. It is observed from any intermediate systems and through communication pathways. The data for incident response and prosecution of the attacker are the final outcome of this phase. Attackers hide themselves using two simplest approaches: stepping stone attack and the IP spoofing. Similar and anomaly-based approaches are used to detect these attacks. The approach of the investigation depends on the type of the attack.

1.8.4.6 Presentation

In this phase, the process model presents observations in a required format. It provides the explanation of the various procedures to reach at the conclusion of the investigation process. The conclusions are drawn from the visualizations so that they can be easily understood. Here, the system documentation is also being done to meet the legal requirements. A detailed review of the incident is done, and countermeasures are recommended to prevent the similar incidents in the future. The entire case documentation is done for the future investigations and network security.

1.8.4.7 Incident Response

For detecting the security attack, the response is initiated depending upon the information to be collected for validating the incident. This response is predicated on the nature of the attack identified. It is governed by the organizational policy, legal and business constraints. For preventing the future attacks and getting rid of the attacks, an action plan is performed. The decision is also taken at the same time to proceed for investigation and to trace collection. This phase is applicable where the attack is still in progress and investigation is already being initiated.

This is an anatomy of network forensics which works both in real-time and postattack scenarios. The real-time network traffic is shown in the first three phases. The authorization phase ensures that all observing tools are well in place, and the collection phase captures the network traces ensuring integrity of the data. The detection phase helps in the discovery of the attacks. Suitable incident response hinges upon the nature of the attacks finally. The last two phases are the same for both the real-time and postattack scenarios.

Investigation and presentation phases exhibit the postattack investigation, and various sources identify the attack and give input to this phase. Attack patterns are classified using various data mining, soft computing, or statistical approaches in the analysis phase. The traceback technique, the attribution and the final presentation phase result exhibit the hideous intention of the attacker. The exact in and out of the attacker divulge in investigation phase.

1.9 Computer Forensics vs Network Forensics

The term computer forensics was widely used earlier, but lately, digital forensics became the broad term for computer forensics. We may refer now computer forensics and network forensics as the subbranches of the digital forensics where the detailed investigation of computer-related crime is taken up in computer forensics while finding out all the clues and investigating them on a network referred to as network forensics.

The main differences between computer forensics and network forensics are the following.

1.9.1 Computer Forensics

The main characteristics of computer forensics are as follows:

1. It deals with preservation, identification, extraction, documentation, and interpretation of computer-related data.
2. It helps to find out the intention behind the attack but is unable to identify the main culprit.
3. Handling of computer data is in line with the guidelines of civil procedures.
4. The technical expert is always in better position than the attacker.
5. It is comparatively easy to find the clues for experts.
6. It follows the chronological sequence of custody and analysis of physical evidence and preserves this evidence.
7. It acquires, preserves, and interprets the evidences.
8. Skills of experts are better than the attacker.
9. It helps you to identify all evidences quickly.

1.9.2 Network Forensics

The main characteristics of network forensics are as follows:

1. Capturing, recording, and analyzing network clues to investigate the attacks.
2. It helps to find out the source of attack and intention of the attack too.
3. It is related to investigating through different security tools such as IDs, firewalls, etc.
4. The skills of technical experts and the attacker are at the same level.
5. To find the clues for experts is comparatively difficult.
6. It is all about finding the clues through different tools and techniques.
7. It is the incident response of the crime.
8. Skills of experts are sometimes lesser than the attacker.
9. It takes comparatively more time to identify all evidences than computer forensics.

1.10 Network Security vs Network Forensics

In recent times, the network forensics has drawn tremendous significance for ensuring the organization's network security. Network forensics facilitates the detailed analysis of both the outside attacks as well as the insider's abuse. By investigating both kinds of attacks, it ensures its detection of attacks and their prevention in the future, which saves financial loss and the reputation of the organization.

In spite of focused research and development on the network forensics for a long time, there are many questions unanswered, with one problem or another issue popping up.

Network security and network forensics are two different technologies. Network security is a wider term, which includes network security. Security products are utilized for avoiding intrusion and providing data for forensics analysis and investigations. Unlike network forensics, the network security prevents the attack on the system. Network security has a proactive approach as it keeps a close observation on the network and is constantly looking for the abnormal behavior in the context of potential security attack. It is a preventive measure to avoid the malicious activities by the Bots. Network forensics is a reactive approach, in which the investigation is usually done after the attack. It is like an autopsy, i.e., postmortem investigation. Most often, it is observed that it is specific and focused on the type of attack and addresses only the issues related to the attack. The main difference between network security and network forensics are as follows.

1.10.1 Network Security

The main characteristics of network security are as follows:

1. Network security requires in real time.
2. It mitigates the probable risk to come inside of network.
3. It works round the clock to watch the network.
4. It is a continuous process.
5. It is a well-established field in computer science.

1.10.2 Network Forensics

The main characteristics of network forensics are as follows:

1. Network forensics works after crime happens.
2. It is a post-mortem of an attack.
3. It works when it is required, i.e., when a crime is notified.
4. It is a time-bounded activity.
5. It is a nascent science.

Questions

Q.1. What do you understand by network security? Explain the evolution of network security.

Q.2. How can you say that network security is an important issue? Explain in detail.

Q.3. Explain the types of security issues.

Q.4. Explain the features of network security services.

Q.5. What are the types of attacks? Explain in detail?

Q.6. Explain the life cycle of application security.

Q.7. Explain the difference between the modification and fabrication attacks.

Q.8. What do you understand by denial of services attack?

Q.9. What is replay attack? Is there any difference between playback attack and replay attack?

Q.10. What do you understand by masquerade attack? Explain with examples.

Q.11. Write the details of some security analysis tools.

Q.12. Explain the process of application security.

Q.13. What do you understand by network forensics? Explain the difference between network security and network forensics.

Q.14. Write down the network forensics process in detail.

Q.15. What do you understand by computer forensics? What are the differences between computer forensics and network forensics?

Bibliography

A. A. Ahmed, "Investigation Approach for Network Attack Intention Recognition," *International Journal of Digital Crime and Forensics*, vol. 9, no, 1, pp. 22, 2017.

V. Baryamureeba and F. Tushabe, The Enhanced Digital Investigation Process Model. *Proceedings of the 4th Digital Forensic Research Workshop*, Maryland, USA, 2004.

A. Bijalwan, and P. Emmanuel, "Crime Psychology Using Network Forensics," *Journal of Computer Engineering & Information Technology*, 3, p. 2, 2014.

A. Bijalwan, S. Sando, and M. Lemma, "An Anatomy for Recognizing Network Attack Intention," *International Journal of Recent Technology & Engineering*, vol. 8, no. 3, pp. 803–816, 2019.

A. Bijalwan, M. Wazid, E. S. Pilli, and R. C. Joshi, "Forensics of Random-UDP Flooding Attacks," *Journal of Networks*, vol. 10, pp. 287–293, 2015.

E. Casey and G. Palmer. "The Investigative Process," in Casey, E. ed. *Digital Evidence and Computer Crime*, Elsevier Academic Press, 2004.

S. Ó. Ciardhuáin, "An Extended Model of Cybercrime Investigations," *International Journal of Digital Evidence*, vol. 3, no. 1, 2004, 2004.

T. Dubendorfer and B. Plattner, "Analysis of Internet Relay Chat Usage by DDoS Zombies," Ph.D., Department of Information Technology and Electrical Engineering, Swiss Federal Institute of Technology Zurich (ETH), 2004.

S. Garfinkel, "Network forensics: tapping the Internet," http://www.oreillynet.com/pub/a/network/2002/04/26/nettap.html.

C. Y. Liu, C.-H. Peng, and I.-C. Lin, "A Survey of Botnet Architecture and Batnet Detection Techniques," *International Journal of Network Security*, vol. 16, no. 2, pp. 81–89, 2014.

E. S. Pilli, R. C. Joshi, and R. Niyogi, "Network Forensic Frameworks: Survey and Research Challenges," *Digital Investigation*, vol. 7, pp. 14–27, 2010.

N. Shone, T. N. Ngoc, V. D. Phai, and Q. Shi, A Deep Learning Approach to Network Intrusion Detection, *IEEE Trans. On Emerging topics in Computational Intelligence*, 2017.

A. C. Shorren, C. Partridge, L. A. Sanchez, C. E. Jones, F. Tchakountio, B. Schwartz, S. T. Kent, and W. T. Strayer, "Single-Packet IP Traceback," *IEEE/ACM Transactions on Networking*, vol. 10, no. 6, pp. 721–734, 2002.

S. Sitaraman and S. Venkatesan, "Computer and network forensics," in *Digital Crime and Forensic Investigation in Cyberspace Book*, IGI Global, Hershey, 2006.

A. Yaar, A. Perrig, and D. Song, "Pi: A Path Identification Mechanism to Defend Against Ddos Attacks," *Symposium on Security and Privacy*, IEEE 2003.

2

Cyber Crime

LEARNING OBJECTIVES

This chapter discusses about all crimes on the network. It also discusses about attack intention of attackers. It also defines different terminologies of crimes such as malware, phishing, cyberstalking, child pornography, web jacking, data diddling, etc. After reading this chapter, you would

- Have knowledge about the concepts of cyber-crime.
- Understand the attack intentions and terminologies such as phishing, malware, child pornography, web jacking, data diddling, etc.
- Understand the various terminologies related to crime such as virus, worm, zombie, rootkit, Trojan horse, logic bomb, etc.
- Understand the types of attacks.

2.1 Introduction

The Internet is almost used by every person for one or the other purpose such as learning, sharing ideas with other people, entertainment, sharing resources, etc. Only the legitimate or responsible use of the Internet will be advantageous for the people in using its services. The moment the Internet is used in an indecent or illegal way, it may start bouncing back the user in the most undesired manner, and it may go up to such an extent which he has not even dreamt of. Social websites that are used all over the world such as Facebook, Twitter, Instagram, and many more allow people to communicate with each other, but at the same time, a large number of malicious activities also take place on such social media websites. Facebook dissipated its first viral attack on July 10, 2014. As per Facebook sources, countries such as India and developed countries from the west are the worst hit by malicious activities on the Internet. Industry analysts Sullivan et al., on October 8, 2014, made a new report mentioning Damballa's capability to focus on advanced cyber threats such as zero-attack and APT (advanced persistent threat). It has been realized by most enterprises that it is not enough to detect the malware by using a single approach. Rodriguez stated that bot detection system must draw a clear line of distinction between good bots and infected ones. With the advanced malware that is well equipped and has different techniques of escaping from being detected, it has become very risky to depend completely on the virtual computing environment for the identification of advanced persistent threats. Attackers' new practice of renting their networks has further complicated the problem. They rent their network from 200 to 300 dollars per hour. This is giving fuel to the rising problems of frauds, extortion, and other cybercrimes. Though continuous efforts are being made to overcome these issues, new methods have evolved which can trace the origin of the bot master.

In 2002, attackers targeted some large companies like Yahoo, eBay, and Amazon using distributed denial of service. The attackers caused interrupted services and a huge loss on finance. In 2003, an attacker named Clark in Oregon in the U.S. used more than 20,000 zombie computers to launch a DDoS attack against the eBay website. In April 2008, due to its refusal to post, a mainland Chinese private game server ad, the Bahamut website suffered a DDoS attack in which it was deluged with hundreds of data packets per second by more than 1,000 computers from all over the globe and paralyzed its services. In August 2009, the social networking site Twitter was also exploited by hackers as a tool to issue botnet control instruction. After the biggest attack in history on March 27, 2013, there was a slowdown in global internal. London and Geneva-based group 'Spamhaus' was attacked over a week in this cyber-crime. An international cyber police team comprising five countries was given the charge. As per the CEO 'Spamhaus', Steve Linford, the scale of the attack was unprecedented. According to the investigators, the tactic used by the attacker was DDoS. DDoS has a prominent feature that it makes the target unreachable by flooding it with huge traffic. In this incident, the attacks were peaking at 300 Gbps (Gigabit per second).

Distributed Denial of Services (DDOS) attacks are besetting today's growing economy alongside the user's capability toward producing more output. These DDOS attacks on social media such as Twitter, Facebook, etc. are recent headlines. In July 2014, the arbor network produces global DDOS attack data retrieved from its collection and illustrations, threatening and monitoring the infrastructure, and its shows a flood in measuring and determining the initial half annual attacks in 2014 with over 100 attacks larger than 100 GB/s were reported.

According to NSFOCUS, high-volume and high-rate DDOS attacks were increasing tremendously in the first half of 2014. Most of the attacks hit industry and media by the DDoS attack traffic. The senior VP and general manager in security, Stuart Scholly at AKAMAI states on 21st May 2014 that distributed denial of services proliferators' contingent rarely upon conventional botnet infection which was hinge upon reflection and amplification techniques. According to them, instead of using the network of zombie computers, DDOS attackers abuse the internet protocols that are available on the servers as well as the devices. According to Ameen Pishdadi, founder of DDOS protecting leader GigeNET on September 23, 2014, the most popular attacks that were seen are DNS reflection and NTP. NTP attacks were very huge at the beginning of the year and were actually larger than normal.

PLXsert on May 23, 2014 has spotted 14 SNMP DDOS attacks undertaken targeting umpteen industries including hosting, consumer products, gaming, and software-as-a-service (SaaS) as well as infrastructure as a service mostly in the US (49.9%) and China (18.49%). On February 11, 2014, according to a Twitter post by Cloudfare CEO Matthew Prince, the full volume of the DDOS attack has exceeded 400 GB/s which made this maximum distributed denial of service attack ever recorded till that time. This attack uses the NTP (network time protocol) reflection. It is exactly the same process as attacks took that time for gaming sites.

DDOS attacks are quickly becoming serious threats and the pain point for the industries. DDOS attacks are becoming more effective and causing major disruption and sometimes bring down the organizations for the entire working days. If the organizations and enterprise want to provide the uninterrupted service to their customers, they need to take this threat very seriously.

2.2 Attack Intentions

Growth in the multiple sources of attacks provides a platform for malicious activities. It has become a serious cause of concern for almost all the countries around the world. According to Amorso (2012), the following possible motives are behind the cyber-attacks.

2.2.1 Warfare Sponsored by the Country

It is similar to the physical warfare between two countries in which the attacking country aims at the critical resources of the other country. In this case, also, the bot masters from the attacking country target the national infrastructure of the opponent country. The intensity of such attacks largely depends upon the intention and resources of the attacking nation. To stand by the nation and for strengthening the national resources, the citizens sometimes donate their computing powers. This plays a very significant role in such kind of cyber-attack facilitated by peer to peer network.

2.2.2 Terrorist Attack

The terrorist groups execute this type of attack to accomplish their evil goals. In this type of attack, a normal internet user can help terrorists attack simply by donating his computer equipment to them. It simply means involving in a terror attack without acquiring any formal training expertise, knowledge, or skills.

2.2.3 Commercially Motivated Attack

Such cyber-attacks are motivated with the intension of hampering the market reputation and finances of the rival company. In such attacks, the competing company attacks the cyber infrastructure of the rival company. Such attacks are more evident in the e-commerce business.

2.2.4 Financially Driven Criminal Attack

Such attacks intend to harm the user financially. In such type of cyber-attacks, the attacker targets the financial data such as particular's banking details, mode of making payments online, and other similar financial services. Such attacks depend on individual attacker where they target to the companies as well as by giving them threat for their online infrastructure.

2.2.5 Hacking

Hacking is the practice by an individual or a group seeking pleasure from such notorious activities and looking for some extra attention on the Internet. There are two contradicting terms hacking and cracking that can make people in a catch-22 situation. The hacking term actually refers to constructive things, whereas the cracking word is used to refer to the destructive. The definition of hackers changes over the days. It is mistakenly taken for the people who just engross in malpractices, but the definition revolves around the attempt to compromise the system or network for malicious purpose. Hackers are the maven people who self-design and control the whole network independently. They are well tech-savvy, efficient, and expertise in their work. Generally the hackers can be categorized by white hat, grey hat and black hat categories that are defined separately in the common terminology section.

2.2.6 Cyberstalking

Cyberstalking is a kind of crime that involves observing, reconnaissance, collecting information espionage, identity theft, threats, blackmail through a groundless allegation, traduce, culmination and provocation for sex, etc. over the Internet. The purpose can be changed as per the person's motives. It can be corporate cyberstalking, headliner cyberstalking, politician's cyberstalking, gender-based cyberstalking, etc., although cyberstalking is also a heinous crime in various countries and the stalkers are continuously engrossed proliferating for their own or someone's purpose.

2.2.7 Child Pornography

Child pornography is one of the most sensitive and heinous crimes among all cybercrimes. It is a kind of child sexual exploitation through Internet whether they contain images or any videos. Child pornography is strictly prohibited by law in many countries if the child is less than 18 years old. As the number of users on the Internet is increasing, the percentage of porn users is also rapidly thieving round the clock. Presently, around 30% of internet bandwidth consumes by watching porn videos on the Internet by cyber users. Cyberspace is a good and easy platform for child pornography for trading or a matter of enjoyment. The perverted kind of people use these platforms for a sake of minting money by suffusing their images or videos alongside connecting with their agents for making business. It also allures for sexual activities with pedophiles toward their side. These videos and images easily can be sold to pedophiles through the Internet. Subsequently, these pedophiles also involve visiting their online chat box through which they offer minors interaction with them. Despite several rules imposed for child pornography, this industry is permeating rapidly all over the world. However, lawmakers are forming many rules to restrict the proliferation of this industry as well as abolish this process. Many children are forcefully prey to pornography.

2.2.8 Web Jacking

Web jacking is a term that refers to stealing the web. It is a kind of cloning of the website which is highly susceptible to compromise through the malicious link that is placed there. The spoof website looks somehow similar to the original website. When the user of the website clicks on the spoof site link, malicious web servers take control, which means losing complete control over the original website. The reason for making clone and acquiring access may be a demand for ransom or may be identity theft or may be their self-moto.

2.2.9 Data Diddling

Data altercation is the best example of data diddling. It is a kind of cybercrime where attacker use the forging, fraudulent, or misrepresenting data as a weapon to launch their motto to the vulnerable user. The attacker engrosses in modifying the data so that the inaccurate information harms the individual. This process may devastate the user's credibility partially or entirely as per the attacker's intention.

2.2.10 Counterfeiting

The term counterfeiting means replica of something. Somehow the counterfeiting is purloining, destroying, or replacing the original for using it for their own purpose. This replica is unequivocally similar to originals and can work equally like the originals. For instance, the person printing any currency at home is a kind of counterfeiting in which the replica of original currency is created outside.

2.2.11 Phishing

Phishing is a form of social engineering which relies on the victim clicking on a link usually in an email, the result of which can have several consequences. It may then attempt to trick the victim into parting with some valuable information such as passwords and bank account details, or it can also lead the victim into downloading malware leading to the infection of their computer. Phishing attacks can be generated by an attacker using all social engineering techniques toward the user. For instance, users may receive a mail with a certain link of getting expiration of password of email or bank account. Once the user clicks on that, it certainly redirects it to their own website which look like the legitimate site where the users insert their confidential information that can be traced through social engineering techniques.

2.3 Malware

Malware, short for malicious software, is comparatively a new subject, but is not a new name in the research field. With respect to its inherent nature, malware is a collection of unfriendly, invasive, or bothersome software or program codes created to secretly access a computer system without the owner's permission.

2.3.1 Definition

The term malware is coined by the term malicious software, and it is defined by some eminent researchers and scientists as follows:

> Malware or malicious code is software that intentionally exploits flaws in working programs and makes a computer do something the owner did not want or exists without the user's knowledge, taking over partial control of the computer.

> **(Pfleeger & Pfleeger 2012)**

The short form for malicious software, malware refers to software programs designed to damage or do other unwanted actions on a computer system. In Spanish, "mal" is a prefix that means "bad", making the term "badware", which is a better way to remember it.

> Malware is a variety of hostile, intrusive or annoying software or program code designed to secretly access a computer system without the owner's informed consent.
>
> **Roughua Tian**

> Malware is a programming code used to destroy or interfere with computer operations.
>
> **Christopher C. Elison**

> Malware is a software used or created by attackers to disrupt computer operation, gather sensitive information, or gain access to private computer systems. It can appear in the form of code, scripts, active content, and other software.
>
> **Wikipedia, Malware, Internet**

These days, malware is a concern for everyone who directly or indirectly uses the computing devices. A huge amount of money is wasted each year throughout the world just because of malware. However, an exact amount is impossible to state, but it may be estimated to be hundreds of billions. Many of the most visible and grave problems faced by the internet community now a days depend upon a broad presence of malicious software and tools. Spam, phishing, denial of service attacks, botnets, and worms largely depend on some form of harmful code, commonly referred to as malware. Malware is generally used to cause infection to the computers of unsuspecting victims by exploiting software vulnerabilities or tricking users into running the code with malicious intent. To be aware of this phenomenon and how the hackers or attackers use the backdoors, key loggers, passwords stealing, and other malicious activities is becoming quite difficult and a problem deserving high attention.

Defining the concept of malware for the virology of computers has always been a great problem. Basically, this is a malicious program or file that attacks, infects, and harms other software. By acknowledging the difference between intended and actual behaviors, the harmful attack of the malwares can be easily observed. This observed attack can easily exhibit the main difference between the actual and intended behaviors. This can also be defined as follows: the malware is malicious software which enters the system without the consent of the owner and basically intrudes the computer to create damage. Different types of malwares are viruses, Trojans, worms, spywares, etc. It is software that intentionally harms the computer fulfilling the hazardous intentions of the attacker. The similar harmful of malicious behavior is exhibited by worms, Trojan horses, and viruses.

The formal definition of malware concept in a model logic language is defined malware in abstract formulation. It is independent apart from being abstract and can be applied to the malware manifestations which are concrete. A general and formal definition of benware, medware, and anti-malware are derived from the malware formulation. The benware is the benign software, anti-malware is the antibodies that are developed against malware, and the medware is the software for medical in better terms. It is a sort of medicine that is provided to the software that is affected. For the purpose of the malware's classification along with the classification of its derivatives including their detection and comparison, they have offered various tools and techniques both theoretical as well as practical. The main intention of all the black hat community is to proliferate malware on

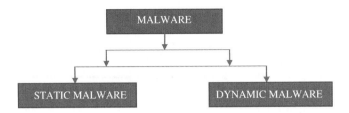

FIGURE 2.1
Types of malware.

the network and make a zombie network. The influence of malware somewhere it is necessary to prevent otherwise, the infection will get worsen day by day and all over the world will engross an epidemic from the infection of malware.

Types of Malware: The malware can be further bifurcated into two types of the malware analysis: the static and dynamic malware analyses (Figure 2.1).

For analyzing the malware, the dynamic malware analysis is preferably used over the static malware analysis as static analysis has some limitations. There are an unlimited number of tools available for the analysis to be performed using the dynamic malware analysis.

2.3.2 History of Malware

The term malware was coined by an Israeli professor named Yisrael Radai in 1990. Before Yisrael Radai coined the term malware, malicious programs were collectively referred to as computer viruses. Computer viruses are self-replicating programs that suffuse from one host to another. History of malware can be bifurcated into different categories which also represent the time frame in which the events from that category happened. According to Nikola Milosevic, the history of malware can be divided into five categories. The first category is the early phase of malware. The second phase is the early Windows phase. The third category is evolution of network worms. The fourth category is rootkits and ransomwares, and the fifth category is virtual espionage and sabotage (Figure 2.2).

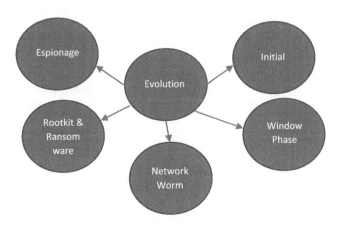

FIGURE 2.2
Evolution phases of malware.

In the beginning or the early days of malware, the malicious programs were mostly file infectors and self-replicators. In 1982, the first computer virus known as Elk Cloner appeared and was written by Rich Skrenta in Pittsburgh, Pennsylvania when he was studying in ninth grade. At that time nobody knew what to call it. This situation had continued till 1984 when Dr. Fredrick B. Cohen finally introduced the term Computer virus. There were umpteen malwares for other platforms before 1986 though in 1986, the first malware for PC appeared. It was called Brain virus which was compatible with IBM pc. It was developed by two Pakistani brothers Basit and Amjad. After the virus Brain, there were other viruses such as Omega, Michelangelo, V-Sign, Walker, Ambulance, Casino, mutation engine, etc. ravaging at various places.

In the 1980s, the evolution of an Internet gave the whole world at one place or we can say 1st January 1983 is considered the official birthdate of an Internet and connected University computers to each other to facilitate extensive research. The network was quite vulnerable to pure worms, and it was proved by a young scholar Robert Morris. The first big malware incident that occurred possibly was the Morris worm in Nov 1988. It was based on UNIX which knocked out almost all computers on the Internet which had attracted the attention of a lot of media also.

In the computing industry, creating and distributing malware is of interest to those people and companies which have unethical or illegal intentions. The nature and behavior of malware include the following:

- Deletion of important files on a computer to make them unusable without a recovery process.
- Recording every keyboard input to keep track of what the users type.
- Stealing personal or professional information or files from a computer.
- Using computer system's resources for the purpose of the malware, e.g., sending spam emails, DDoS (Distributed Denial of Service), or brute-force encryption keys.

2.3.3 Classification of Malware

The classification of malwares can be done on the basis of three factors: susceptibility, charge, and mechanism of propagation. Based on the above factors, the malwares are classified into three generations. The description of the three generations according to him is as follows.

The malwares anticipated in the first generation includes those malwares that pursue those replicating and propagation properties of virus which are generated by the actions performed by humans like emails or the sharing of the file over the Internet or among computers. The second generation inculcates those malwares that share the properties of worms. The second-generation malwares don't need human actions arbitration for their replication. They are comprised of some characteristics and features of virus and Trojans and are hybrid in nature. The third-generation malwares are specific to organizations or are geographically situated. The main function or working of the third-generation malwares is attacking the technologies and products which are mainly related to security engaging the vectors which continuously give multiple attacks. Another theory explains the classification of malwares into viruses, worms, Trojans, spyware, rootkits, botnets, and adware. Subsequently, they defined the aforementioned terms further. A computer program which keeps on replicating itself and continuously infects different files of the system. This type of computer program is known as Virus. Then, computer software which is capable of replicating itself and can be shared with other computers using the Internet or any other network. These types of computer software's are known as worms. When a software program hijacks or steals the password of the user to attain the system control and personal information via imitating the behavior like an authentic program is known as Trojan. On a computer system when a software gets installed without any prior knowledge or concern of the user for the purpose of collecting complete confidential and personal information of the user. These types of software are known as Spywares. When the software controls the infected machines by attaining access of administrator of the system are known as Rootkits. The name was given to this form root under UNIX. Botnet is autonomous software which is controlled remotely. Botnet is zombie program that can be controlled for any network. When the malicious software or application gets installed in the computer then the automatic download of advertisements or display of advertisements takes place. These types of software which supports advertising are known as adware. The Polymorphic Malwares work as a malware variant. The polymorphic viruses are those viruses which keep their original code intact but give a different look each time whenever being replicated. Their malicious code is encrypted, and module is decrypted in the polymorphic malware. The method implemented in these polymorphic malwares is polymorphic code. The functioning of this malware is that the code is mutated using the polymorphic generator, and the original algorithm is kept integral. The implementation process includes the encryption of malware keeping the encryptor or the decryptor inside the code. Specific designed mutation engines are incorporated in polymorphic malwares. The charge of the polymorphic virus is constantly being encrypted using a different decryptor. The mutation engines generate a new decrypted routine by simply switching the instruction order. The body of the virus is encrypted and the functionality of the polymorphic virus is that it is performed by using the variable routine decryption front-end. Hence, as the capability of the mutation engine is that it can generate many different types of the decryption routes, the scanning of polymorphic malwares is not possible as they are encrypted. It is also entailed the details about Metamorphic Malwares. These are malwares whose body changes from one instance to another. They can be called as the body polymorphic. Different types of obfuscation techniques are being used for transforming and reprogramming the code within themselves. The technique used by them is similar to the original code. The mutation of these malicious code takes place through the network they spread making the detection ineffective which was signature based. The working in short of the metamorphic malware is that first the base version is recovered then, different charge is inculcated in that similar base version to avoid detection. Some techniques included in metamorphism are assembling, permutation, expansion, disassembly-DE permutation/shrinking, and other transformations.

Malwares are classified in many ways. Sometimes they are classified on the basis of behavior, their target platform, or their attack directive. In this section, we are going to classify malware randomly by mixing all the categories. The different classes and terms related to malware are as follows:

# Virus	# Worm	# Logic Bomb	# Trojan Horse	# Backdoor
# Spyware	# Exploits	#Downloaders	# Auto rooter	# Kit(Virus generator)
# Spammer	# Flooders	# Keyloggers	# Rootkit	# Zombie or bot

Each of the above-mentioned classes causes a massive amount of damage to the system or software. The details of the given malware classes are as follows.

2.3.3.1 Virus

Virus is a category of malware that, when executed, tries to replicate itself into other executable code, and when it succeeds, the code is said to be infected. When the infected code is executed, the virus also executes. A computer virus is a kind of bad software code (*"malware"*) that, when runs, multiplies by reproducing itself (copying its own program code) or *tainting* other computer programs by editing them. Such types of computer programs can easily corrupt data files, or the "boot" sector of the hard disk.

2.3.3.2 Worm

A worm is a computer program that can run without any support, i.e., it runs independently and can propagate a complete working version of itself onto other hosts on a network. A computer worm may also be thought of as an independent vindictive computer program that creates copies of itself in order to spread to other machines. Most of the time, it uses a distributed environment to spread itself, depending on vulnerabilities or weaknesses on the target computer to access it. Unlike a computer virus, it does not require to attach itself to an existing program.

2.3.3.3 Logic Bomb

It is a program inserted into a system or software by an intruder. It remains in the dormant state until a predefined condition is met. On meeting the condition, an unauthorized action is performed. Software that is intrinsically vindictive, such as viruses and worms, mostly consist of logic bombs that run a certain consignment at a predecided time or when some other criteria are fulfilled. This method can be used by a virus or worm to attain impulse and spread before being caught. Viruses that attack their host systems on particular dates only, such as on Friday, the 13th, or April Fools' Day, are frequently called time bombs.

2.3.3.4 Trojan Horse

It is a computer program that appears harmless, but it is actually a harmful program. It has a hidden and potentially malicious function which evades the security process, sometimes by exploiting legitimate authorizations of a system entity that invokes the Trojan horse program. Trojans are most of the times propagated by some form of social engineering, for example where a user is lured into running an e-mail attachment disguised to be harmless, (e.g., a routine form to be filled in), or by drive-by download. Although their consignment can be anything, many new forms act as a backdoor, communicating with a controller which can then have illegitimate access to the smitten computer system. This corruption allows an attacker to access system owner's personal details such as banking credentials, passwords, or personal identification details.

2.3.3.5 Backdoor

A backdoor virus is a software program that makes entry into a computer system without being notices and caught and executes in the background to open ports. It allows third parties to control the computer surreptitiously. These harmful backdoor programs can pass themselves off as legitimate ones. It is a type of program that bypasses a normal security check; it may allow the unauthorized access to the crucial information.

2.3.3.6 Mobile Code

It is a software that may be a script, macro, or any other type of portable instruction that can be moved unaltered to different types of platforms and get executed with similar semantics. Mobile code is any software program, application, or data content that is able to perform movement while existing in an email, document, or website. Mobile code uses distributed environment or storage media, such as a Universal Serial Bus (USB) thumb drive, to execute local program execution from another machine. The term is often used in a malicious context, mobile code creates varying degrees of computer and system damage. Mobile code, also known as executable content, remote code, and active capsules, is usually downloaded via the body of an HTML email or email attachment.

2.3.3.7 Exploits

These are the kind of codes which are specific to a particular type of vulnerability or a set of vulnerabilities. Exploits attack on the system on finding certain type of weakness. An **exploit** is a part of software program, a piece of data, or a serial arrangement of commands that takes benefit of an error or weakness in order to cause unintentional or unanticipated demeanor to exist in a computer software, hardware, or anything electronic. Such behavior mostly includes acting like gaining control of a computer system, allowing privilege rise, or a denial-of-service (DoS) or related distributed denial of services (DDoS) attack.

2.3.3.8 Downloaders

It is a kind of program which if gets executed on a machine disrupt installs other program or items on a machine. Normally downloaders are sent through emails. On opening the email, the user is lured to download a program which in turn downloads other malicious items. Downloaders are harmful programs with the intention to seditious download and install malware on a victim's machine. Once executed, a downloader communicates with its command-and-control (C&C) server(s) through C&C channels. After receiving download guidelines, it then directs at least one download channel to load malware through the network.

2.3.3.9 Auto Rooter

Auto rooters are the harmful program or software that act as tools that are used to break into new machines lying at different locations through network. The phrase "autorooter" is based on a security jargon for successfully breaking and obtaining privileged access to a computer system. The act, called "rooting" a machine, takes on form or shape from the name of the administrative account on a UNIX box - "root". The word "auto" stems from the fact that these devices necessarily package, or automate, the breaking process from beginning to end. Autorooters can be designed to scan a network for weak machines in terms of security or attack everything they encounter. Once a computer system is successfully captured or compromised, or rooted, some type of harmful code can be installed and configured: data might be caught using a software component known as sniffer, web pages defaced, or servers installed. Some autorooters are destroyed after sending the results back to the cracker, while others may install bots that wait for further directions from the attacker.

2.3.3.10 Kit (Virus Generator)

These are the set of programs or software which act as tools and have capability to generate new viruses on their own. These work through an automated system. It is a program that creates a virus or worm on its own with any role of the user. They make it possible for those people who have very little knowledge of viruses or even computers to develop viruses. As early viruses were almost entirely coded in assembly language, it was nearly impossible for anyone to create a virus or worm without having good experience with computers.

2.3.3.11 Spammer

These are the software programs used to send large volumes of unwanted emails which fill the mailbox of person under attack. These mails are sometimes called junk mails or spam mails. These are sometimes a list of individuals and organizations noteworthy for engaging in bulk electronic spamming using the spamming software program, either on their own behalf or on behalf of others. It is not a list of all spammers, only those whose actions have attracted substantial independent attention.

2.3.3.12 Flooders

These are the types of malware form or software programs that are used to attack the networked computers with a massive amount of data traffic to carry out a DOS (Denial of Service) attack.

2.3.3.13 Keyloggers

These are the programs which capture keystrokes and log them. These are the types of information stealers which record keypresses and stores them locally for later retrieval or pass them to a server lying at remote location that the attacker has access to. Keystroke logging, mostly referred to as keylogging or keyboard capturing, is the process of recording the keys pressed on a keyboard, usually secretly, so that the person typing on the keyboard is ignorant of the fact that their events are being recorded. Keylogging may also be used for studying human–computer communication. Large number of keylogging techniques exist, they range from hardware and software-based methodology to auditory investigation.

2.3.3.14 Rootkit

A rootkit is a set of tools that enable root- or administrator-level access on a computer system by a hacker or cracker. A rootkit is an anthology of computer software, usually malevolent, developed to allow access to a computer system or areas of its software that would not otherwise be allowed, for example, to a nonpermitted user, and often hides its existence or the presence of other software. The term *rootkit* is joining of "root" (the conventional name of the advantaged account on Unix-like operating systems) and the word "kit" (which refers to the software tools that employ the component). The term "rootkit" has harmful implications through its connection with malware.

2.3.3.15 Zombie or Bot

Zombie is a program stored or activated on a compromised machine used to launch different types of attacks on other machines.

"Bot" is the short form of the word "robot", which is another form of malware and is a kind of machine-driven task that interacts with other distributed services. An exemplary use of bots is to collect information (such as web crawlers) or communicate on its own with instant messaging (IM), Internet Relay Chat (IRC), or other web based interactive tools. A typical bot software allows an operator to remotely control each machine and group them together to form what is commonly referred to as a bot army or botnet. Attackers use these zombies or bots as anonymous proxies to conceal their actual identities and magnify their attacks.

A botnet is a magnanimous pool of compromised computer systems across the Internet. Attackers can use a botnet to set up broad-based, remote-control, flood-type attacks against their targets. Presently the bots found in the wild are a mix of previous threats. This means they may transmit like worms, conceal from detection like many viruses, attack like many stand-alone components, and have a coordinated command and control system. Botnets have also been known to make good use of back doors left opened by worms and viruses, which permits them entry to controlled networks to access networked components. Bots try to conceal themselves as much as they can and taint networks in such a way that bypasses immediate notice.

2.3.3.16 Spyware

Spyware is a software program that collects information without the victim's knowledge and transmits it to another system. It is software that aims to collect information about an individual or a company without their awareness and that may send such information to another entity without the owner's permission, or that claim control over a computer without the consumer's consent. Whenever spyware is used for harmful reasons, its presence is normally hidden from the user and can be intricate to detect. Some spyware, such as keyloggers, may be sent by the owner of a shared, commercial, or public computer deliberately in order to monitor users.

2.3.3.17 Adware

It is a kind of badware that displays pop-up commercial ads, or it redirects the browsers to other business websites. The term adware is frequently used to describe a form of malevolent software which presents unwanted ads to the user of a computer. The advertisements produced by adware are sometimes in the form of a pop-ups or sometimes in a Window that cannot be closed. Adware, or advertising-supported software, is any software package that automatically deliver commercials in order to produce monetary gain for its developer. The advertisements may be in the user interface of the software program or on a screen shown to the user during the installation procedure.

2.3.3.18 Ransomware

It is a kind of malicious software program that takes control of data files and keep them as hostage and asks for the ransom amount from the owner in lieu of making such files are held by the ransomware, the user or owner of such files is unable to access them. Ransomware is a computer malware that installs secretly on a one's computer, executes an attack by encrypting all the document files that badly affects it, and demands a ransom payment to decrypt it or not publish it. Simple ransomware programs may freeze the system in such a way which is not difficult for an experienced person to overturn, and display a message asking for a payment to unlock the system. Highly developed and superior malware encrypts the victim's computer's useful files, making them unapproachable, and insists a ransom amount to decrypt them or unlock them. The ransomware may also encode the computer's Master File Table (MFT) or the entire contents hard drive. Thus, ransomware is a kind of denial-of-access attack that avoids computer users from accessing files since it is difficult to decrypt the files without the decryption key. Ransomware attacks are normally carried out using a Trojan that has a consignment concealed as a genuine file.

2.3.3.19 Hacker's Useful Components and Other Harmful Programs

Hacker useful components and other harmful programs include:

- Components such as constructors that can be used to create viruses, worms, and Trojans.
- Libraries of programs specially designed and developed to be used in developing malicious software.
- Hacker-created malicious utilities that encrypt infected files to hide them from antivirus software.
- Programs that intentionally supply wrong information to users about their actions in the system.
- Other harmful programs that are deliberately designed to directly or indirectly damage local or networked machines.

2.4 Terminology for the Cyber Attackers

1. **Black Hat:** Sometimes it is also referred to as crackers not a hacker. Black hat community hacks the system or network for their personal benefits. They compromise the entire network or system to capture information. This is unauthorized access of network. They steal, destroy, and prevent the authorize user from accessing the system.

2. **White Hat:** White hat people are also referred to as a genuine hacker who solves all the computer- or network-related issues ethically. This expertise of the organization sorts out issues by evaluating the security mechanism of the organization. White hat people prevent network from outside attacks.

3. **Grey Hat:** Grey hat people are the expertise who have enough expertise on different languages through which they can easily trace out the vulnerabilities and inform to the administrator to resolve all the issues. However, they later start initiation for their own personal gain.

4. **Blue Hat:** Blue hat people are basically a security professional whose work is outside of an organization. These security professional's main work is to find out the vulnerabilities and to detect the bugs through penetrating testing and they also perform cyber-attacks without any harm to others.

5. **Red Hat:** Red hat people continuously monitor the hackers and their activities. They follow on empathy not in sympathy. They use wrong path to do good work

by penetrating cyber-attacks when they find black hat people. They launch distributed denial of services attacks, malwares on black hat hackers by infecting their system.

2.5 Types of Attacks

There are a number of attacks that are caused by cyber attackers. Distributed Denial of Services (DDoS), spam, and personal information thieving are the most common among them.

2.5.1 Distributed Denial of Service Attack

Distributed Denial of Service (DDoS) attacks are the most common attacks caused by a botnet, and it usually makes a large quantity of financial loss. The concept of distributed denial of services is to paralyze the operation of certain services that belongs to an organization.

In a DDOS attack, the botnet consumes (exploits) the bandwidth and thereby disables the network services of the victim for an instance a botherder may connect to the IRC channel of the target and then send him millions of service requests from the botnet. The targets get compromised on IRC network in such type of attacks. As per records, the Transmission Control Protocol (TCP) flooding, Synchronize (SYN) flooding and User Datagram Protocol (UDP) flooding attacks are the most commonly implemented. To prevent a DDOS attack, a number of infected systems must be controlled along with disabling the remote control mechanism. However, a part from these measures, even more, advance and efficient techniques are required for avoiding such attacks. By exploring the hidden bots in honey pots that also presented a new approach for preventing DDoS attacks.

In the computation resource consumption, SYN flood is most common and easy to implement. SYN flood happened when the attacker used the vulnerability of TCP protocol. In TCP protocol, the three-way handshake is needed to ensure the integrity of data which is transmitted. The process of three-way handshake is that the user has to send a request to the server with an SYN packet, which is used to inform the server that a user needs to connect to it. Then, the server will send an SYN/ACK packet back, which means the connection is approval. Finally, the user has to send an ACK packet to the server, and it means the start of the connection. Via three-way handshake in TCP protocol, data transmits more safely. SYN flood happened when the attacker sent a large number of SYN packet to the server to request a connection. With overmuch SYN packet, the server cannot handle too much request. If a legal user has to connect to the victim, the server will have too much request to deal with the legal user, and it will be out of connection because it is full of SYN packet. In the bandwidth consumption, the most common attacks are UDP flood, Internet Control Message Protocol (ICMP) flood and Hypertext Transfer Protocol (HTTP) flood. It is similar to computation resource consumption, which paralyzes the victim by sending a large number of packets. But there is still some difference between them because of the transmission protocol. UDP protocol (User Datagram Protocol) is not rigorous as TCP protocol that needs three-way handshake to ensure the establishment of the connection. Compared with TCP protocol, the header is much simpler, which only has the port of source and destination, length, checksum, and data. Although the reliability of UDP protocol is not as high as TCP, it can transmit data in a massive and quick way. Thus, the selection of protocol is important to enhance the security or efficiency of the network. Because UDP protocol is connectionless, which means that it does not check whether the data is received correctly, some attackers use the vulnerability of UDP protocol to launch Distributed Denial of Service attack (DDoS), which is called UDP flood. The attack model of UDP flood is also covered in identification chapter that is shown as SYN flood, UDP flood attacks the victim by sending a large number of packets to a random host that the port is open for certain services.

If the number of members that belong to the botnet is larger, the scale of UDP flood will be larger. The characteristic of UDP flood, the bandwidth of the victim, is huge due to the massive transmission of the packet. After the bots receive the command from the botmaster, the bots send the packet with high capacity to paralyze the bandwidth that the victim owns. If the victim encounters with UDP flood, the change of network traffic is very obvious and that makes the victim unable to connect to the Internet. ICMP flood is also a commonly distributed denial of service attack that belongs to bandwidth consumption. The purpose of the ICMP flood is to saturate the network by sending numeric ICMP packets. ICMP protocol (Internet Control Message Protocol) is used to reply the connection status between two hosts. Round-trip delay time is calculated by the number of successfulreply and the time between them. It can check whether the destination host exists or not and compute the transmission time between source and destination host. Through "echo request" and "echo rely on" sending by ICMP protocol, the reply time can check the connection status between two hosts. ICMP flood is similar to UDP flood, and it launches an attack by sending numeric ICMP flood that makes the victim cannot afford to process it. If the victim receives too much ICMP flood, the bandwidth will be paralyzed. The effect is the same as UDP flood, which intercepts the connection ability of the victim.

2.5.2 Spam

Spam is also a serious problem that still exists in the current network environment. Internet security industry is concerned with the growing number of spams. As per their observation near about 70%–90% of the times the botnets are the main cause behind this spam. The report further reveals that when bots open socks v4/v5 proxy (TCP/IP RFC 1928) on compromised malicious or infected bots, the infected machines can be utilized for spreading spams. Some bots by using their special functions are capable of gathering electronic mail addresses. This characteristic of the bots is utilized by the botherder for spreading a huge number of spams. To overcome the concerns caused by spams with the help of botnets, the research and scientist have to come up with the trinity. Trinity is a proposed distributed content–independent spam classification system that is expected to resolve the spanning problems. Bots responsible for spamming spread mass emails within a fraction of a second; therefore, sending a message from such infected addresses may further lead to the spread of more spams. As the Trinity is still under trial, its effectiveness cannot be completely trusted upon.

Xie et al. have propounded AutoREFramework (a spam signature generation framework) for studying the aggregate (average) behaviors of bots that are responsible for spam generation. It further aims at investigating the potential benefits from their detection in future. Their study further reveled various features of spamming botnet such as

1. Spammer's letters contain some random and legitimate URL so that the detection can be prevented.
2. Botnet IP addresses are distributed over many autonomous devices with a small number of machines (system) in every autonomous system.
3. The target victims with the same email address may get the spam with different contents.

The fruitful utilization of these features for detecting the attacks and preventing the spams is the matter of investigation shortly.

Due to the development of a cyber attacks, spam has become harder to solve because of its scale. Spam is also called junk mail, which attracts the click and links to the malicious websites. These kinds of websites will make the victim infect with the botnet by downloading malicious software. Mail spam has some properties like the content with a malicious link or some attractive software. Mail spam usually sends by batch, i.e., spam sends numeric emails to the users in a way that is designed previously. Through the control with the command, the bots will send emails to the receiver at certain time. The content usually has some links that attract users to click. The terminology of spam includes spammer, spam receiver, and spam filtering service. The spammer is the unit that launches spam attack, which wants to gain some profit from it. The spam receiver is the victim who receives a larger number of spam mails. If the spam receiver cannot resist the attraction of the content in spam mail, some losses will happen, like personal information thieving and infecting with the botnet. Spam filtering service is used to filter spam mails in some rules, and it is installed in client or mail server. By filtering mails with a spam filtering service, spam mails cannot send to the end user easily. Some researchers and reports suggest that the mails from a sender who is not in the friend list should not be opened. According to the current network environment, if the sender is infected with a botnet, which means the botherder can totally control it, the mail from the infected sender is not safe. Due to the behavioral model of spam from a botnet, the spam mail is sent by a command from botherder, and it makes the scale of spam grow quickly. Once the receiver clicks the links or downloads the file in it, it is possible that the user will post some private data to the server which bot masterly owns. If the receiver downloads the malicious software from the spam mail, it is possible that the infection happens. The receiver will become a member of the botnet and wait for the command from the bot master.

2.5.3 Personal Information Thieving

Generally, some of the bots makes the security networks lunatic and there by compromised through commands and control of victim's system. The botherder with the help of such malicious code can retrieve the useful and sensitive information from the infected machines such as user password, banking details, etc. The list of incidents also indicates that botnet has become a major cause of concern for the corporate and industry as well. As the bots are capable in bypassing the security systems, and ability to infect the host, the bot master thieves the sensitive and significant financial and strategical information. The infected systems are beyond the security scan and, therefore, are difficult to be caught. Inner attackers can be prevented with the key login. Such bots monitor the activity of the system and report to the botherder who in return sends command to these bots. So that the personal information can be thieved from the infected machine. In this condition, key login can prevent such thieving of personal data.

Besides Distributed Denial of Service (DDoS) and mail spam, one of the serious troubles from cyber attackers is personal information thieving. Personal information is valuable, like name, email, address, account password, etc. This personal information is stored in the memory, and it is easy to be gotten by the botherder. As mentioned above in the behavioral model of a botnet, some malicious software is injected into the victim's computer and the bot master will control the victim via the control and command server. The purpose of personal information thieving is just information gathering and gets financial profit from selling personal information. The personal information is thieved by two ways: uploading and recording. In uploading, the infected user uploads some insensitive data to the bot master. Some information stores in a cookie when the user saves their data intentionally or otherwise. Such file that stored in the memory usually has some insensitive data, like account and password. If the file that stores sensitive data is usurped, it is possible that the data inside can be extracted by information techniques. Besides uploading, recording is also a method to thieve personal information. Through the injected malicious software, it can record the input character when the infected user enters some sensitive data, like account, password, email, or address. By recording illicitly by the software, the input data is gotten by the bot master, and among them, "Spyeye" is one of a famous malicious software that thieves personal information. It is hard to be detected and monitor the victim to record the data from it. Some famous websites, like Google, Yahoo, eBay, and Twitter, have stolen personal information by Spyeye. It monitors the victim by forcing them downloading a configuration file and records the input illegally. If thieving of personal information occurs in the bank, it will be very severe because the stolen data is extremely sensitive. With more personal information that thieved from a botnet, the bot master can have more financial benefit by selling to certain organizations.

2.5.4 Click Fraud

Click fraud is a new term coined in the encyclopedia of a botnet. This is a very interesting form of the attack in which a bot creates a fake impression of being an advertisement sometimes manually or automatically. The user clicks on such advertisement and gets into the loop. Online advertisement business is the worst hit by the click fraud. It basically aims at increasing the revenue by having maximum number of clicks on the content. But now people in adtech industry are gradually taking cognizance of it and are looking for the ways to overcome the issue. According to Andrew Goode, Chief Operating Officer (COO), Project Sun block, a click fraud creates a false impression in the minds of the advertisers that their content is the most hit one. It also gives a fake hike to the advertisement as the content seems to be hit a huge number of times.

Click fraud can be operated in two ways: manually and automatically. In the click fraud done manually, the bot master manually hits the site or the ad, whereas in the case of automatic click fraud, a software or malicious code is utilized which keeps hitting the advertisement without any manual support. The objective of both is to inflate the economic value of the ad by increasing the number of hits. In the case of manually operated click fraud, it is difficult to trace the difference between the actual people and the fraud software that is hitting the ads. Many companies employ workers to hit their ads and click the link manually to inflate their value. Niall Hogan, Integral Ad science (IAS), managing director U.K. has beautifully explained how the attacks are utilized for making click fraud. He states that it is a process where a malware is downloaded to the user's system without their knowledge. From the moment the bit is installed, it starts functioning according to the commands given by the bot masters and builds a lucrative cookie profile. It further generates the fake impression on a site and in this way by inflating the traffic network the revenue is generated through automated click fraud.

The activity of utilizing bots to one lac, for click fraud, is known as "click farm" as the single machine with a single bot is not that hazardous, but in practice it is observed that thousands of bots operate together for generating fake impression and now this is more dangerous. However, James Collier, Ad Truth, general manager, EMEA has come with a solution; according to him, telltale signs can be utilized for identifying the fraud click. According to him, the environment with very low or very high conversations must be subjected to investigation. High rates of conversion can be single for click fraud, which can be detected by training the user who shows a pattern of the frequent visit and continuous hitting on the same site.

Bot attackers utilize botnets for installing advertisement add-ons and browser helper objects (BHOs), and by providing a maximum hit to an ad or link, its economic value can be increased. Such bots are capable of generating a higher click through (CTR). Similar to Google's Ad Sense program, the botnet helps to get higher CTR by clicking the link artificially.

2.5.5 Identity Theft

Identify fraud, also known as identity theft, is one of the fastest growing cybercrimes on the Internet. An identity theft takes place when a fraudulent person with the unethical means accesses to the personal information about an individual with the intention of utilizing it for fraudulent practices. This information may include name, address, educational testimonials, and address details. This is one of the most dangerous threats in the cyber world as the personal information of an individual may be utilized for creating a fake identity card or fake passport for a terrorist attack. The user or the victim is unaware about his identity information being stolen, and the kind of fraud for it is utilized.

Generally, the botnet is utilized for committing identity theft. Phishing mail is a classic example of such id theft. It infects the server and network creates a malicious Uniform Resource Locator (URL) and encourages the user to submit his personal information using that URL. Huge spams are sent to the users' mail address with the help of botnet. There is another way of fetching the personal data of user, i.e., creating a fake website. Identity fraud is the serious cause of concern for all as the stolen confidential information about an individual can be utilized for several criminal offenses like for doing a financial fraud by opening a bank account and obtaining loan and other facilities on that account or it can be utilized for criminal offenses by making fake passport, fake driving license, fake identity card, etc. on the victim's name.

Questions

Q.1. What do you understand by distributed denial of services?

Q.2. What do you understand by attack intention? What are the motives behind cyber attacks? Explain in detail.

Q.3. Define the term hacker. Critically evaluate the statement "hacking is the curse for the society" and write your opinion.

Q.4. Explain the difference between the hacker and the cracker?

Q.5. Explain the term cyber stalking with a suitable example?

Q.6. How can we prevent society from child pornography?

Q.7. What do you understand by malware? Explain the types of malware.

Q.8. Exaplin the term data diddling. What do you understand by counterfeiting?

Q.9. Write the evolution phases of malware.

Q.10. Explain the difference between virus and worm.

Q.11. What do you understand by identity theft? Illustrate click fraud with suitable examples.

Bibliography

P. Bacher, T. Holz, M. Kotter, and G. Wicherski, "Know Your Enemy: Tracking Botnets," http://www.honeynet.org/papers/bots, 2005.

S. M. Bellovin, "Security Problems in the TCP/IP Protocol Suite," *ACM SIGCOMM Computer Communication Review*, vol. 19, no. 2, pp. 32–48, 1989.

A. Bijalwan and S. Harvinder, "Investigation of UDP Bot Flooding Attack," *Indian Journal of Science and Technology*, vol. 9, no. 21, pp. 1–4, 2016.

A. Bijalwan and E. S. Pilli, "Crime Psychology Using Network Forensics," *Computer Engineering & Information Technology*, vol. 2014, pp. 1–4, 2015.

D. Dagon, G. Gu, C. P. Lee, and W. Lee, A Taxonomy of Botnet Structures, *Twenty-Third Annual Computer Security Applications Conference, 2007. ACSAC 2007* (pp. 325–339), IEEE, 2007.

T. Dubendorfer and B. Plattner, "Analysis of Internet Relay Chat Usage by DDoS Zombies," PhD thesis, Department of Information Technology and Electrical Engineering, Swiss Federal Institute of Technology Zurich (ETH), 2004.

E. Filiol, M. Helenius, and S. Zanero, "Open Problems in Virology," *Journal of Computer Virology*, vol. 1, no. 3–4, pp. 55–66, 2006.

F. C. Freiling, T. Holz, and G. Wicherski, Botnet Tracking: Exploring a Root-Cause Methodology to Prevent Distributed Denial-of-Service Attacks, *European Symposium on Research in Computer Security* (pp. 319–335), Springer, 2005.

S. Gadhiya and K. Bhavsar, "Techniques for Malware Analysis," *International Journal of Advanced Research in Computer Science and Software Engineering*, vol. 3, no. 4, pp. 1–5, 2013.

S. H. C. Haris, R. B. Ahmad, M. Ghani, and G. M. Waleed, TCP SYN Flood Detection Based on Payload Analysis, *Research and Development (SCOReD), 2010 IEEE Student Conference on* (pp. 149–153), IEEE, 2010.

Y. Ilsun and K. Yim, Malware Obfuscation Techniques: A Brief Survey, *International Conference on Broadband, Wireless Computing, Communication and Applications*, 2010.

S. Kramer, J. C. Bradfield, "A General Definition of Malware," *Journal of Computer Virology*, vol. 6, pp. 105–114, 2010.

Y. Kugisaki, Y. Kasahara, Y. Hori, and K. Sakurai, "Bot Detection Based on Traffic Analysis," pp. 303–306, 2007.

F. Lau, S. H. Rubin, M. H. Smith, and L. Trajkovi, Distributed Denial of Service Attacks, *IEEE International Conference on Systems, Man, and Cybernetics* (vol. 3, pp. 2275–2280), IEEE, 2000.

C.-Y. Liu, C.-H. Peng, and I.-C. Lin, "A Survey of Botnet Architecture and Batnet Detection Techniques," *International Journal of Network Security*, vol. 16, no. 2, pp. 81–89, 2014.

K. Pappas, *Back to Basics to Fight Botnets*: Nelson Publishing, 2008.

C. P. Pfleeger, S. L. Pfleeger, " Analyzing computer security: A threat/vulnerability/countermeasure approach", Prentice Hall, 2012.

M. Prince, "The DDoS That Almost Broke the Internet," *CloudFlare blog*, March, vol. 27, 2013.

S. Robin, "An introduction to malware," Spring 2012. Retrieved on April 10, 2013 http://orbit.dtu. dk/fedora/objects/orbit:82364/datastreams/file_4918204/content.

F. Sullivan, *Enterprises Harness Social Networking for Increased Agility and Responsiveness*, Finds Frost & Sullivan [Pressemitteilung] [Online], 2014.

A. H. Sung, J. Xu, P. Chavez, and S. Mukkamala, Static Analyzer of Vicious Executables (SAVE), *Proceedings of the 20th Annual Computer Security Applications Conference (ACSAC"04)*, IEEE, 2004.

Y. Xie, F. Yu, K. Achan, R. Panigrahy, G. Hulten, and I. Osipkov, "Spamming Botnets: Signatures and Characteristics," *ACM*, vol. 38, pp. 171–182, 2008.

V. Yegneswaran, P. Barford, and J. Ullrich, "Internet Intrusions: Global Characteristics and Prevalence," *ACM SIGMETRICS Performance Evaluation Review*, vol. 31, no. 1, pp. 138–147, 2003.

3

Network Forensics Process Model

LEARNING OBJECTIVES

This chapter reveals the in-depth knowledge of network forensic process model. After reading this chapter, you would

- Have basic knowledge of process model.
- Understand the recent trends in network forensics.
- Understand the life cycle of network forensics.
- Have knowledge of the generic process model of network forensics.
- Have knowledge of various framework designs in the field of network forensics.

3.1 Introduction

Ranum first coined the term network forensics. Further, many researchers defined network forensics. Network forensics can be defined as "the reconstruction of network event to provide definitive insight into action and behavior of users, applications as well as devices". However, network forensics is about utilizing the scientific method and tools for collecting, identifying, collaborating, examining, analyzing, and generating the document using digital information from live network sessions.

Network forensics involves capturing (fetching) the network traffic and retrieving the clues in reconnaissance from multiple devices, systems, processes, and other resources. The information given by network forensics is utilized to strengthen the security tools by understanding the modus operandi of the attacks. The available observations can be utilized in the future also to prevent a potential threat to network security.

Network forensics can be said to be both a proactive and a reactive approach. It not only ensures network security but also facilitates law enforcement. The prime objective of network forensics is to measure the level of intrusions, to investigate them, and to provide information to recover from an intrusion so as to strengthen system security and retrievable evidence presentation.

Dr. ES Pilli in 2009 defined the concept of network forensics as "it deals with data found across a network connection mostly ingress and egress traffic from one host to another". He further defined network forensics as it goes beyond network security as it not only detects the attack but records the evidence as well. There are certain attacks that do not breach network security policies but may be legally prosecutable. These crimes can be handled only by network forensics. Forensic systems act as a deterrent, as attackers become cautious. They spend more time and energy to cover the tracks in order to avoid prosecution. This makes the attack costly and reduces the rate of network crime, thereby enhancing security.

Network forensics is also defined as

> use of scientifically proven technique to collect, fuse, identify, examine, correlate, analyze, and document digital evidence from multiple actively processing and transmitting digital sources for the purpose of uncovering facts related to the planned intent or measured success of unauthorized activities meant to disrupt, corrupt, and or compromise system components as well as providing information to assist in response to or recovering from these activities.

The researcher also designed Netstore to store a very large amount of network flow data and analyzed them. Netstore is useful in such cases where the suspects host's all activities keepwatch. For this purpose, there is a requirement of fast access to a large amount of data for forensic analysis. It has an efficient compression method for the network flow data. Network forensic systems are also classified into two categories: catch-it-as-you-can tools and stop-look-and-listen tools. Catch-it-as-you-can tools are utilized for capturing all the packets, which pass through a specific traffic point and write them to the storage. This method demands a huge amount of storage as the analysis is done in the batch mode. In stop-look-and-listen tools, each packet is analyzed in a minimal required way, and only important parts are stored in the memory for the future reference. For this approach, a faster processor is required. In both the tools, a large amount of storage is required, and in both the cases, the tools keep updating themself by erasing the old data so that space can be made for new information.

The network forensic tools can be either host-based tools or network-wide tools. Host-based network forensic tools are attached to a single host in the network. These tools capture all the packets passing through the host and analyze them. Analyzing their behavior at a particular point at the host, it looks for the malicious activity, and if any activity is detected, it also tries to prevent them and thereby maintains the security of the network; TCPdump, wireshark, and Snort are the examples of host-based network forensic tools.

In the case of network-wide forensics, the tools can be utilized for multipoint surveillance on the network by installing tools at different points on the network. This tool facilitates a comprehensive view of the network activity. Niksun and Net detectors are the widely used network-wide forensic tools.

3.2 Recent Trend in Network Forensics

Changing the technology paves the necessary requirements of niche expertise of various fields that may think over it. It is abstruse to find out the source of a problem and how to mitigate it if we do not have the knowledge of core technologies. These mavens opt out the findings through certain methodologies. There are certain recent trends in the wide scope of network forensics as follows.

3.2.1 Malware Forensics

Malware forensics is the analysis of malware. It is directly associated with the malicious activity caused by Distributed Denial of Services, phishing, spam, etc., and the forensic investigation is needed to get rid of this problem. For this purpose, malware analysis and its behavior are needed.

3.2.2 Botnet Forensics

Botnet forensics is the real-time analysis of the network traffic. It can be done through continuous monitoring of the network by using significant resources. It is the process of detecting the intruders as they break into the sensitive networks by focusing on the analysis and monitoring of the anomalous network traffic. Botnet forensics analyzes the network traffic, identifies the logs, and then collects packets and data that it stores, which move throughout the network, further stores it for some period, and also locates the suspicious systems. It captures the digital evidence during an investigation before any specific event takes place.

3.2.3 Cloud Forensics

Cloud forensics is a cross branch of digital forensics and the cloud computing. It can also be referred to as a subset of network forensics that deals with the forensic investigation on cloud. Cloud forensics is the field of crime investigation that belongs specifically to networks, servers, applications, storages, and services. It is a technological practice to process past cloud events through identification, detection, analysis, examination, and reporting. The experts investigate in cloud environment in which they have to deal with many issues compared to the computer and the network investigation. Virtualization environment allows all evidence that resides everywhere in the world. The experts investigate it through various cloud forensic techniques.

3.2.4 Grid Forensics

The next-generation power system is generally referred to as smart grid. These smart grids can enhance the efficiency and the reliability of the future power system with the advancement of communication technologies. It is a combination of cyber and physical security, and hence, there is an extensive need to observe any kind of attacks. Once the attack is launched on smart grid system, the expert has to set postmortem analysis of a power system to protect the grid against any possible future attacks. This field not only ensures to protect the grid from similar attacks, but it also avoids failures of the grid in the future. Here, the clues can be traced from the smart meter and through the frequency of power grid.

3.3 Life Cycle of Network Forensics

Life cycle of network forensics is a kind of methodology for embedding forensic readiness in information systems, based on the NIST Information Systems Development Life

Cycle (ISDLC), which was devised to incorporate security across the life cycle of systems development. If information assurance is redefined to include digital forensics, then a methodology that develops secure systems should also be a vehicle for delivering forensic capability, as depicted in Figure 3.1. Design of such a system should take into consideration the necessary legal requirements for compliance with evidence collection and storage standards for courtroom admissibility and affect each phase of the life cycle. The phases of network forensics' life cycle segregated into five phases as follows:

1. **Initiation Phase:** Additional steps to the preliminary risk assessment would include determination of what assets on the network would warrant digital forensic protection. In other words, what assets of the organization justify the pursuit of legal redress if deliberately compromised? In preliminary conversations with practitioners, such a selective approach would limit the initial cost and administrative burden associated with forensic readiness.

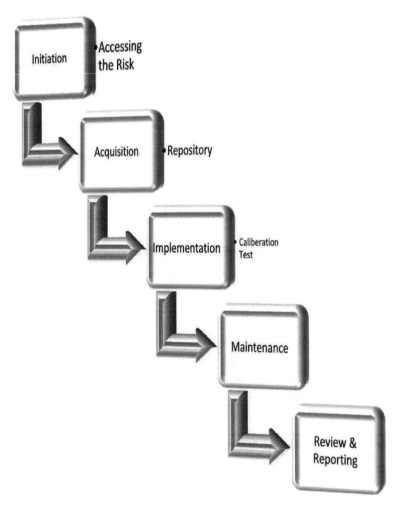

FIGURE 3.1
Network forensics life cycle.

2. **Acquisition/Development Phase:** System requirements would be generated that would include assurance that any device or procedure collecting forensic data on the system will do so in a manner compliant with courtroom standards. Analysts in this phase might find previous research that is useful to determine what existing forensic procedures/tools/technologies could be embedded, building on prior research.

3. **Implementation Phase:** Calibration tests are recommended to verify the performance of devices used to collect evidence and to document the performance of the network itself. This would be accomplished by the first base lining of the network, or network segment, being made forensically ready. Network base lining is "the systematic analysis" of a network, point to point, for dataflow, communication sequencing, and performance statistics. This would be followed by calibration/verification of the performance of network devices involved in collecting evidence in order to understand how they behave across a range of characteristics. Calibration is the "determination of the accuracy of an instrument, usually by measurement of its variation from a standard" and is useful in establishing foundation evidence that tools used for forensic evidence gathering function as intended.

4. **Operation/Maintenance Phase:** Audits would be performed at regular intervals, as the network grows and changes, to confirm results of previous baseline and verification/calibration tests. Documentation would be generated and maintained as evidence that the network and forensic devices continue to function properly, recording any adjustments that were necessary.

5. **Review and Reporting Phase:** Chain of custody procedures would be incorporated into this phase to ensure preservation of the value of potential evidence residing in a retired system.

3.4 Network Forensics Process Model

Network forensics is the process of investigating the attack that describes how an incident happened and the involvement of the parties in this process. The network forensics investigation of the digital evidence has been employed as the postincident response for an activity, but it is definitely not an incident that complies with the organization's terms and policies. Therefore, there are various frameworks and techniques proposed in order to investigate the digital evidence. Figure 3.2 describes the generic process model in which the attack intention and types can be easily analyzed according to their malicious intent.

3.4.1 Authorization

In this stage, background is set toward the higher ground tasks. Various network security tools such as intrusion detection system or intrusion prevention system, firewalls, and the packet analyzers are deployed at a number of points on the network, and also, they require taking the access of the sensitive data on the network. Trained staff is required in order to handle these tools and ensure to collect the quality evidence to facilitate the acknowledgment of network security attacks. Required legal warrants and authorization

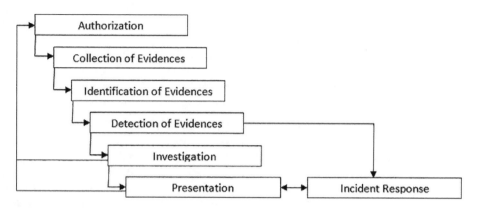

FIGURE 3.2
Generic process model for network forensic investigation.

must be obtained in order to ensure that the privacy of an individual and the organization is not violated.

3.4.2 Collection of Evidence

Various tools including software and hardware are deployed to capture logs as much as possible. The various sensors are also installed to reconnoiter the activities. Network evidences are collected by the various NFATs employed such as TCPdump, Wireshark, TCPflow, Snort, SiLK, PADS, and bro. As the incoming traffic changes very rapidly and also it is not possible to retrieve exactly the same traces at the same time, it is critical to analyze at that point or stage. The network must be monitored, and the integrity of the captured traces must be maintained as well to identify the future attacks. Sometimes the large amount of memory space requires keeping the logs intact. Logs are more in quantity, so the system must be able to handle it in a proper manner.

3.4.3 Identification of Evidence

Data collected in the previous stage is identified by the network forensics specialist for further investigation. This stage also makes sure to preserve the copy of the network data so as to facilitate legal requirements, and as soon as the process is repeated on the original data, the results obtained after investigation are proved to be the same. Without modifying original data, a copy of the data is analyzed and also a hash of data is preserved.

3.4.4 Detection of Crime

In case of eccentricity, alerts have been generated by the deployed security tools like TCPdump, wireshark, PADS, bro, snort, etc. These tools help to detect the security breach and the privacy violation. These eccentricities are further analyzed for the various parameters in order to persuade the presence and nature of the attack. To determine the attack or for further analysis, a quick validation process has been carried out. This process decides whether to continue or ignore the alert as false alarm. If the analysis goes on, then it performs two actions: collection of the clues and incident response of the clues. Network traffic is classified through SVM for multiclass classification.

3.4.5 Investigation

The data received in the previous stage may consist of the reluctant data or contradictory data. Therefore, in this stage, an examination is made, and a mythological search is conducted so that no crucial information is lost. The data collected are classified and clustered into the groups to reduce the stored volume of data into manageable portions. The highest possible evidence and the data containing the least information are identified to remove the redundancy. After examination, these evidences are analyzed to identify network intrusions. Data mining and soft computing techniques are used to search the data and correlate the attack patterns. To understand the nature and the workability of the attackers, the attack patterns are then put together. The attacks are further reconstructed and replayed. Few important parameters related to network connection establishment are operating system fingerprinting, DNS queries, packet fragmentation, and protocol. Validation of the suspicious activity is the final outcome of this phase. The information obtained from the previous stage is used to check who, where, when, how, and why of the incident as it helps in the source traceback, attribution to a source, and reconstruction of the attack scenario. The result of the previous phase further observes to see the way from where the attack emanates. It is observed from any intermediate systems and through communication pathways. The data for incident response and prosecution of the attacker are the final outcome of this phase. Attackers hide themselves using two simplest approaches: stepping-stone attack and the IP spoofing. Similar anomaly-based approaches are used to detect these attacks. The approach of the investigation depends on the type of the attack.

3.4.6 Presentation

In this phase, observations are presented in the process model in a required format. It provides the explanation of the various procedures to reach at the conclusion of the investigation process. The conclusions are drawn from the visualizations so that they can be easily understood. Here, the system documentation is also being done to meet the legal requirements. A detailed review of the incident is done, and countermeasures are recommended to prevent the similar incidents in the future. The entire case documentation is done for the future investigations and network security.

3.4.7 Incident Response

For detecting the security attack, the response is initiated depending upon the information to be collected for validating the incident. This response is predicated on the nature of the attack identified. It is governed by the organizational policy and legal and business constraints. For preventing the future attacks and to get rid of the attacks, an action plan is performed. The decision is also taken at the same time to proceed for investigation and trace collection. This phase is applicable where the attack is still in progress and investigation is already being initiated.

This is an anatomy of network forensics which works both in real-time and postattack scenarios. The real-time network traffic is shown in the first three phases. The authorization phase ensures that all observing tools are well in place, and the collection phase captures the network traces ensuring integrity of the data. The detection phase helps in the discovery of the attacks. Suitable incident response hinge upon the nature of the attacks finally. The last two phases are the same for both real-time and postattack scenarios.

Investigation and presentation phases exhibit the postattack investigation. The input to this phase are various sources and identified attacks. Attack patterns are classified using various data mining, soft computing, or statistical approaches in the analysis phase. The traceback technique, attribution, and final presentation phase results in the accomplishment of the attacker in the investigation phase.

3.5 Detection and Investigative Network Forensics Frameworks

In this section, we discuss about the various frameworks designed and built in the field of network forensics. Herein, first we discuss about the process model that is designed for botnet and its activities. Subsequently, detection and investigative frameworks including detection-based, bot Gad-based, system architecture-based, AAFID-based, P2P-based, soft computing-based, honeypot-based, attack graph-based, and network monitoring-based frameworks are also described.

The previous research has shown the botnet revelation process model in which the main source of revelation is an internet as depicted in Figure 3.3. The traffic is filtered through different tools. A classifier classifies this filtered network traffic into different categories which are further given for monitoring the network traffic. When all infection clues are recognized, they will further be sent to the data store. Figure 3.3 shows the designed generic architecture for effectively detecting the bots by monitoring the network traffic over the Internet.

The term catholic model came itself as the catholic nature of this model for the network forensics. This model is shown in seven different phases. These seven phases are traffic collector, traffic filtration, bot detection, packet analyzer, evidence collector, data extraction, and report. These phases explains the entire process of botnet forensics in which how systems get infected and become a bot, the process of an attack on system and find out the involvement of sources or the networks (Figure 3.4).

The flow diagram for botnet investigation is also provided in Figure 3.5. The proposed framework is based on the approach of passively monitoring network traffic. This framework is focused on the normal traffic flow which passes through bot detector. If the bot detects, the bot analyzer categorizes the bot, takes appropriate action as per the category of bot, and makes the system secure.

Framework provides the generic functionality to the software through which the complex programming can be written in an easy way and the target can be achieved. Complex work can be achieved by framework. Framework makes it easier to work with complex technologies in the field of network forensics alongside umpteen authors providing many detection frameworks.

3.5.1 Detection-Based Framework

Architecture view refers to the new broad detection framework shown in Figure 3.6 that exhibits the P2P- and IRC-based botnets and that are hinge upon passive tracking network traffic. It can group traffic as IDS approach. P2P part of this framework depends on the definition of botnet, and the IRC part of this framework depends on evaluating delay time (Td). This is a time frame between sending IRC and NICK commands.

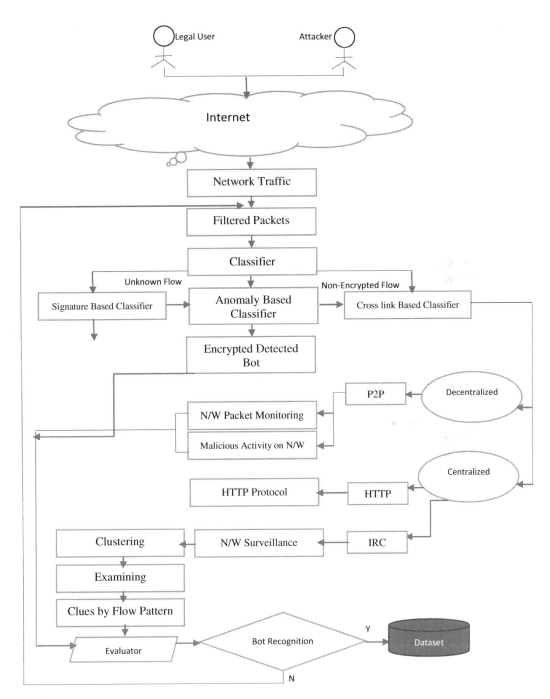

FIGURE 3.3
Botnet revelation process model.

Refining is used with the aim to slow down the traffic workload, and that makes the performance of the system efficient. Architecture view of detection framework shows the three stages of refining: In C1, it filters only those packet whose targets (only receiving IP addresses) are recognized server and unlikely host Command and control server. In C2, it

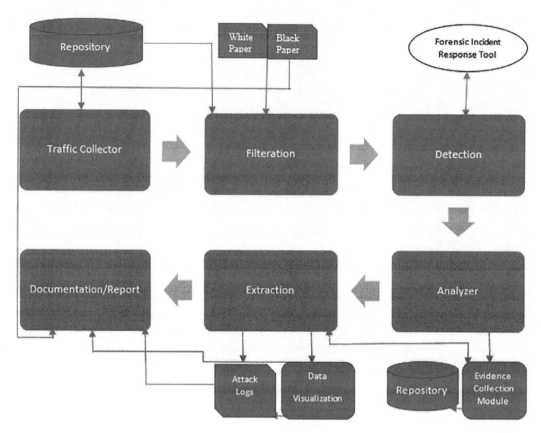

FIGURE 3.4
Network forensics catholic process model.

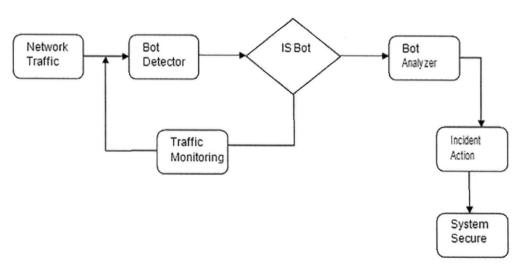

FIGURE 3.5
Botnet flow diagram.

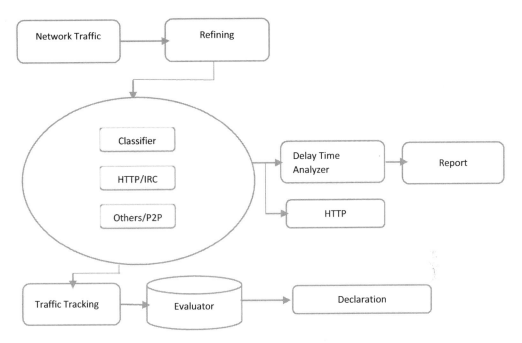

FIGURE 3.6
Architecture view of detection framework.

filters traffics that are maintained from outside host toward inside hosts. In C3, it refines handshaking processes (connection establishments), i.e., the processes by which two devices can interact with each other, i.e., to maintain a connection for communication, each device must send a SYN and receive a corresponding acknowledgment ACK for it from the ones that are not completely established. Next phase application analyzer divides IRC and HTTP traffic from all the other traffic and after that sends that traffic for tracking, clustering, and HTTP components. This IRC traffic analysis is done for the content of the packets, i.e., matching is done of the traffic packets with the user-defined string. For instance, HTTP traffic can be separated and forwarded to classified part. For this inspection, the first few bytes of http request and those that have some different patterns or string are then separated and sent to centralized part in the next step. Now, for P2P communication, it is difficult to get P2P traffic due to the large size of P2P protocol and excessive use of random number. Payload-based classification approaches bind the P2P traffic while detection of the P2P traffic by the transport layer, but for identifying P2P traffics, the author used three level patterns, the social level, the functional level, and the application level. The third-phase delay and time analyzer analyze the traffic to identify flow, and these flows mainly belong to the botnet communication. The next phase is traffic tracking to detect a group of hosts that have the same type of features (behavior and communication). Through analyzing features of flow and similarities from network traffic, traffic tracking can detect the botnet, and for this purpose, it can be used as an open-source tool that is Audit Record Generation and Utilization System (ARGUS) for tracking flows and recording information. The flow record can be analyzed with sender IP (SIP) address, receiver IP (RIP) address, sender port (SPORT), receiver port (RPORT), duration, protocol (Pr), number of packets (*np*), and number of bytes (*nb*) transferred bidirectionally. The last part of this framework is an analyzer for the detection of botnet, which mainly used the result of the previous part that is traffic tracking that is used in getting common host.

3.5.2 BOT GAD-Based Framework

BotGad is a framework mechanism given by H. Choi that detects botnet; this detection or mechanism does not need all network traffic content or known signatures, but for detecting botnet, it only requires a small amount of DNS traffic. BotGad extracts multiple DNS traces from separate areas either small ISP network or large ISP networks. even if, the botnet perform any encrypted interaction, BotGad can still detect botnets easily. Figure 3.7 shows that there are five main parts of a BotGad framework: data collector, data mapper, correlated domain extractor, matrix generator, and similarity evaluator.

The data accumulator uses sensors for receiving and aggregating DNS traffics. Second, the data mapper takes hash map data structure like mentioning each item that is stored at a particular index; this index is called hash, parses the DNS traffic, and inserts DNS information into the hash map data. Third, for calculating a similarity score matrix generator, a matrix is generated. Fourth, the associate domain extractor uses hash maps to categorized domain sets using the DNS-based features. Fifth, hypothetical test is used to make a decision in the similarity evaluator and used to detect botnet domains to calculate the similarity score of generated matrixes.

There was one more detection framework prototype that analyzes through real traffic collection taken from the University of Minho by Mendonça et al. This framework was implemented as a nfsen plugin that was developed in Perl with a supporting database. This framework mentioned the Netflow and traffic characterization value, traffic attributes heuristics, communication fingerprints, and botnet detection process and used anomaly-based detection process.

There is one another framework named the Universal Peer-to-Peer Network Investigation Framework (UP2PNIF). This framework is used for the newly discovered P2P network, and this is done significantly faster with a very few labor investigations by finding common areas in the functionalities of the network. The framework can intelligently find the best methods that are dependent on the investigation resulting mainly by the evidence gathering process. This framework helps the investigator to look and find evidences from any of the P2P networks. The architecture exploits the common attributes of these networks mentioned below in system architecture.

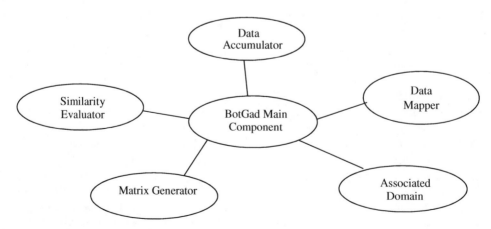

FIGURE 3.7
Main components of BotGad.

3.5.3 System Architecture-Based Framework

The software framework of UP2PNIF mainly comprises four main parts as shown in Figure 3.8. This framework is mainly designed especially for the forensic laboratory in a cloud environment. It is used in "on-the-fly" scenario. This scenario uses and stores evidences from all the network. Evidences that was collected from the above scenario can be stored either in the cloud or in the remote hard drive. And after evidences collection, the data are used to analyze the cluster and classify the traffic. Then, a botnet crawler was implemented in which the methodology that improves the botnet size estimation was described.

Packet gathering module keeps track of network traffic either in a particular system or in a group of systems. Packet sniffing which is a form of wiretap applied to computer instead of phone network was conducted by a libpcap. Packet pattern database module preserves all the patterns of various known patterns which include common hostnames, commands, updated method, IP addresses, peer discovery methods, and update frequency. In packet resolution module, analysis is done of the collected traffic, and the pattern can be identified through the frequency, content/pattern, and destination IP addresses. In emulation module, a number of investigations can be done through a client application that depends on specific network investigations like network registrations which concentrates on attempting to register the entire network population with bandwidth, computational power, and another investigation like Network Usage and Network Anatomy/Modeling which concentrated on finding out what the network is being used for and to distinguish the network's design and the structure and client software.

3.5.4 Fast Flux-Based Framework

Koo et al. used a concept called fast-flux technique and designed a framework with the use of this concept to detect malicious domains using FFSN in domains obtained from the Malware Domain index. The system design they have made is shown in Figure 3.9. Fast flux is a DNS technique used by botnet to hide phishing and malware broadcasting sites behind an ever-changing network of compromised hosts acting as proxies. To investigate the actual application in the cybercrime and to analyze the distributions of infected nodes can be obtained from the malware domain list that further identifies the FFSN domains.

Data stored in malware domain index was obtained from the Internet. Central sever determines whether the source data were FFSN domains which was the main program and analyzes whether the source data were FFSN after integrating and processing the DNS lookup information. Then the results were analyzed and then stored separately in the fast-flux black list and authorized user database.

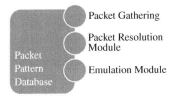

Packet Gathering

Packet Resolution Module

Emulation Module

Packet Pattern Database

FIGURE 3.8
UP2PNIF system.

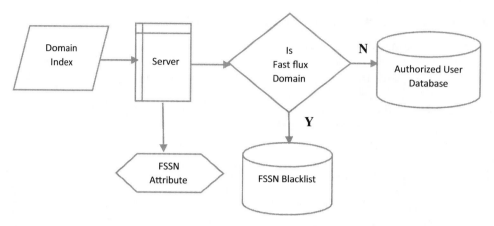

FIGURE 3.9
System design.

3.5.5 Mac OS-Based Framework

Franco et al. describe a framework known as Neofelis which works on Mac OS X operating system for high-interaction honeypots, through which a system administrator can create a high-interaction honeypot that is feasible to several different scenarios. Honeypot is a system on the Internet that is deliberately set up to allure and trap users who try to attempt and penetrate other user's systems, and there are two different types of honeypots, i.e., low interaction and high interaction. In high interaction, the available tools to deploy this were ARGOS and honeypotX, which are closer to the Neofelis architecture. Mac OS X is the operating system which had the highest growth in terms of the number of users in the past years and is used as the base platform for Neofelis. Figure 3.10 depicts the general framework of Neofelis, and the three main components involved in the Neofelis are firewall, honeypot, and the back-office.

The firewall is used to filter the accesses made from the honeypot to the outside, not allowing any communication through ports that are not associated or related to those used by the available services. In this way, it is possible to prevent communications, e.g., through

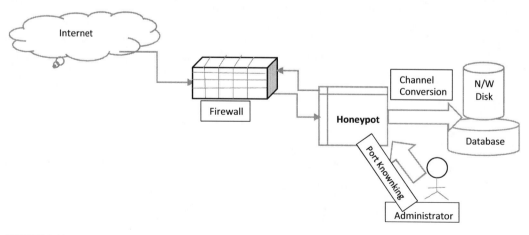

FIGURE 3.10
Neofelis internal architecture.

Internet Relay Chat (IRC) (normally used to botnet control) or the execution of Denial of Service (DOS) attacks from the honeypot to external systems. The back-office will provide support for the honeypot administration process, storing in a persistent way all captured data. Convert channel was used between the back office and honeypot, and these techniques are used to prevent the attacker from easily detecting and/or subverting the data exchanged in the network during the data collection process. This framework allows to create honeypot that can be applied to any network service. In this chapter, the author uses a configuration with two different scenarios: a brute-force7 attack against a SSH server and HTTP server exploitation.

3.5.6 Open Flow-Based or AAFID Framework

Another framework that has the advantages of Open Flow network programming APIs is called AAFID (Autonomous Agent for Intrusion Detection). This design is built to monitor and control plane over distributed programmable virtual switches to considerably ameliorate the attack revelation scenario and for mitigating the attack from the network. Intrusion detection system is a system or software application that looks for network or system activities for malicious activities, and this is the approach for detecting doubtful traffic through different ways. IDS helps in securing the networks. An AAFID structure allows gathering data from different sources and therefore can combine features of regular host-based and network-based IDSs. It catches the suspicious traffic without any impact on the consumer purposes and can improve detection probability. AAFID makes use of the incident graph design to help execute incident detection. The actual suggested alternative investigates how we can use switch-based application program methods to refine detection precision and beat unwilling recipient exploitation stages of collaborative problems.

3.5.7 P2P-Based Framework

Koo et al. used a system framework estimating the size of P2P botnets. P2P is decentralized communication model in which each party has the same capabilities and either party can initiate a communication session. Therefore, in P2P botnets, all bots connect and communicate with each other to remove the need for centralized sever, and therefore, Botmaster can command the bots only. Figure 3.11 shows the overall system architecture.

The above framework mainly contains three modules: the peer list gathering module, the peer list inquiry module, and the size calculation module. In this framework, research collects peer lists and stores the data of all the bots which were in the P2P botnet, and more data were collected by the researchers of the neighboring nodes and CRM (Capturing-Recapturing method) used to estimate the overall size of the P2P botnet. The Jolly-Seber model is usually used for open capture-recapture models. This method consists of two or more rounds of random sampling.

Balasooriya et al. designed a next-generation security framework that detects botnet on a computer network. This framework is useful for the researchers who want a new model to detect the botnet. This proposed framework was based on passively tracking network traffics. The concept used in this framework was that so many bots perform similar communication patterns and malicious activities within the same botnet. Figure 3.12 shows the architecture of the proposed next-generation security framework to detect botnet on computer networks. It consists of six main components: filtering, traffic classifier, HTTP-based bot detector, IRC-based bot detector, SMTP traffic analyzer, and peer-to-peer bot detector.

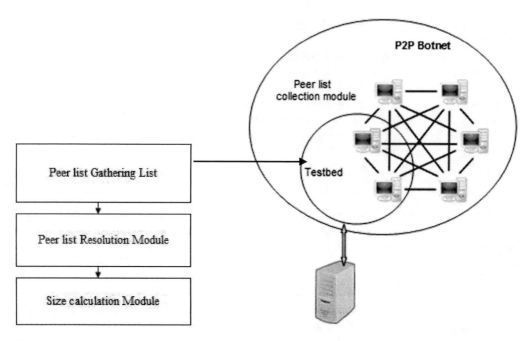

FIGURE 3.11
System module framework.

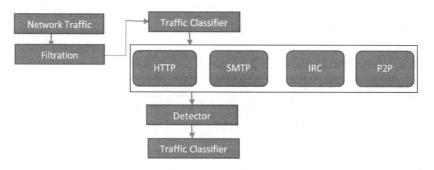

FIGURE 3.12
Next-generation security framework.

Porous et al. showed a framework in which correlated systems with skeptical evidence were traced, and tracing chains were maintained to coordinate among correlated systems with abnormal evidence. In this framework, they described different detection, tracing, and immunization strategies. This framework is known as contact tracing framework through which contact tracing for P2P botnet detection and control is done. In P2P botnet, contact is defined as maintaining a connection between any two peers. Skeptical evidence defined as at a rate higher than a preset threshold. There are five possible states.

Normal state exists when there is no infectious evidence in a peer, connected state exists when skeptical or a feasible state were contacted with a peer, skeptical state exists when a peer has infectious evidence, feasible state exists if there is confirmation of infection in peer and if it is on an established contact tracing chain then declared as feasible, and immunized state exists when a probable peer has been cleaned and patched changes. In Figure 3.13,

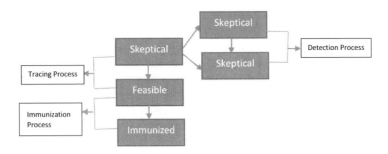

FIGURE 3.13
Peer state transition.

there are three processes: detection process, tracing process, and immunization process. Detection process detects infectious evidence of a peer, tracing process is to keep the contact history of suspicious peers and establish contact, tracing chains are to confirm peer infections, and immunization process is to clean and patch the infected peers.

Asghari et al. describe a conceptual framework with factors, actors, and incentives that effect botnet activity at the ISP level in Figure 3.14.

The distributed surveillance intrusion and detection framework used a new-version microphone for an operating system such as Windows and Mac that reveals the threat and permits the attacker to trace back. It is used for the complete set of controlled attack that is referred as roving bugnet. It is used for observing remote distributed controlled system. Bugnet contains compromised system or devices called bugbot. It is designed as a preliminary mitigation framework that is compatible with most of the Window's platform.

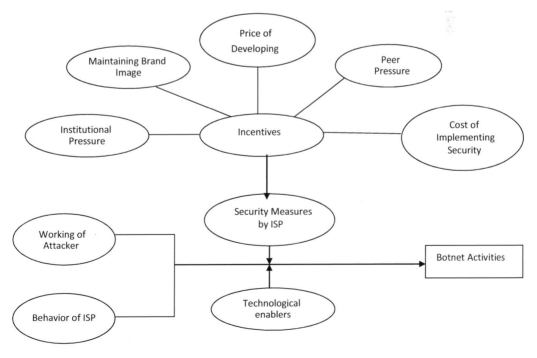

FIGURE 3.14
Conceptual framework of factors affecting botnet activities.

In botnet, financial framework is based on the Dorothy framework and blacklist-based IP reputation system. This framework exhibits botnet network mapping. This architecture promotes and increases the involvement of low enforcement authorities and financial institution after sharing intelligence information. The developed detection framework is based on a common pattern and the characteristics of malicious hosts. In the present time, this framework focuses on P2P-based botnets. But it also has the potential to deal with centralized botnets adding new components to it. This framework aims at detecting the group of the infected host that is engrossed in malicious activities and after identification looks for other host replicating the same behaviore and communication.

The novel information fusion model effectively discards the irrelevant information from sensors so that it improves the detection accuracy. Propagation, infection, communication, and attack are the four stages of botnet activity cycle. However, botnet is capable of performing multiple activities in a single stage of its activity cycle, for instance, spreading spam, mailing, etc. Botnet activities have a wider area coverage. It covers personal host LAN and strongest pillars of the network. The Botmaster always attempts to keep his malicious activities under wraps. These activities are not revealed as more secretly and in a hidden manner. Botnets infect the network and affect the traffic the more time it gets to corrupt the security system and update itself. This specialty of botnets of attacking hide-hit-update-hide poses a big challenge for the botnet detection. However, it is an established fact that the botnet activities can be traced by recording their activities over a wider range utilized for this purpose such as different types of antivirus software available in the market, by applying various botnet detection tools and techniques, or simply by monitoring packet and their communication behavior and so on.

The classification of the Network Forensics Framework (NFF) is based on an exhaustive literature survey. By implementing the architectural framework of network forensics, we derive such classification which narrows down the scope and allows a comprehensive study of the area. NFFs are classified mainly into five categories: traceback NFFs, soft computing network-based framework, honeypot-based framework, attack graph-based framework, and formal method-based frameworks. A full operational perspective of each NFF and the structural aspect and its implementation objectives are presented here in this section.

3.5.8 Distributed Device-Based Frameworks

It is a famous framework that presents the local area network and Internet. It is distributed in nature because the servers and the clients are at different physical locations. These logs must be collected and analyzed. General architecture for the distributed framework is presented in Figure 3.15.

3.5.9 Soft Computing-Based Frameworks

There are two main functions of this framework. The first component is to capture and analyze the data, whereas the other component is to classify the data. For an effective and automated analysis system, a Network Forensic-Based Fuzzy Logic and Expert System is used. Four important functions of this system are the fuzzification, acquisition, preprocessing, and knowledge base. The construction of knowledge base and the fuzzy inference engine mutually exchange the information. A general architecture of the fuzzy logic-based frameworks is presented in Figure 3.16.

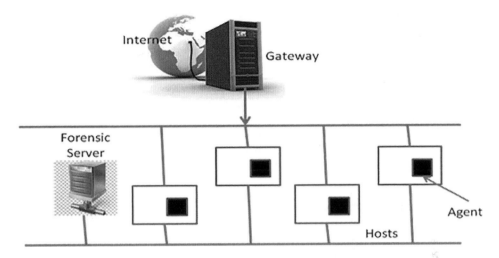

FIGURE 3.15
General architecture for distributed framework.

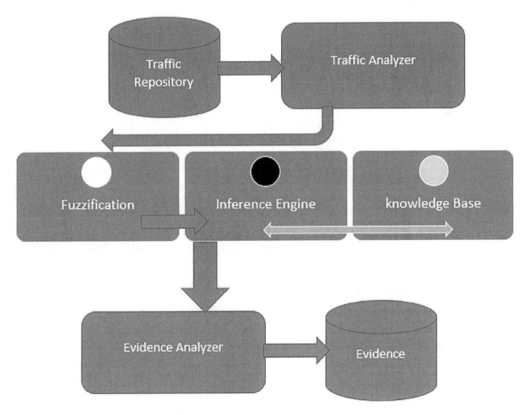

FIGURE 3.16
Fuzzy logic-based framework.

3.5.10 Honeypot-Based Frameworks

Honeypot frameworks are used to analyze the attack process methodology of the attacker and improve defense mechanisms. By using various tools, this model integrates results of the data logged into a single system to reduce human intervention by exploiting computational intelligence. The tool used to integrate data logs is referred to as Automated Network Forensic tool. For collecting the data, open-source forensics tools are used, and an isolated network of virtual machines is built into a honeynet. At one stage, some tools characterize information produced and at other stages it is then transformed using other tools. Identification and automation are done for the time-consuming and error-prone processes and data sets are first partitioned and then tested.

3.5.11 Attack Graph-Based Frameworks

Wang and Daniels implemented a graph-based approach toward network forensics analysis in 2008. This model facilitates automated reasoning and evidence presentation. This framework consists of six important modules, namely, evidence collection, preprocessing, attack, asset knowledge, evidence graph, and attack reasoning module. Attacks are analyzed combining with the results from both levels.

3.5.12 Formal Method-Based Frameworks

In 2008, Rekhis developed a system for Digital Forensics in Networking (DigForNet) which is fruitful for analyzing the security incidents and explaining the number of ways considered by the attackers. Further, DigForNet has taken formal reasoning tools (I-TLA and I-TLC). It is also compatible for intrusion response teams to reexamine and reconsider all the attack scenarios. Identification of attack scenarios is also possible through Investigation-based Temporal Logic of Actions (I-TLA). Investigation-based Temporal Logic Model Checker (I-TLC) executes attack scenarios and also can easily show progress of the attack. These generated scenarios are used to identify the risk that can compromise the system and entities originating from the attacks and to confirm the investigation of different steps that have been taken. These hypothetical steps can handle all these unknown attacks.

3.5.13 Formal Method-Based Frameworks

Aggregation framework is developed to improve from the limitation of already-present tools instead of developing new tools for finding out the clues of forensic investigation.

3.5.14 Network Monitoring Framework

Anchit Bijalwan et al. propounded a correlation network monitoring framework to understand the functioning of vulnerable network system. For understanding network attack, we will have to build and design network lab as shown in Figure 3.17, to deploy the network monitoring system. Effective network monitoring system needs continuous, comprehensive, concrete, and convenient work for achieving the desired output or the target.

> **Continuous**: To escape from the detection, network vulnerability changes its location very rapidly in the network. So we will have to keep continuously reconnaissance the network log and update the changes.

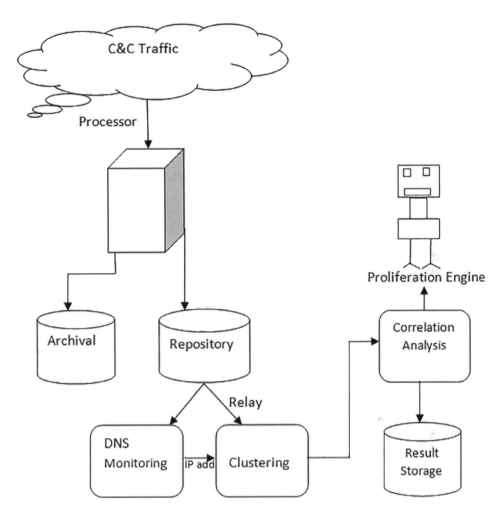

FIGURE 3.17
Network monitoring framework.

Comprise: The system should understand the propagation of the network vulnerability especially botnet and the technique used for propagation in the network.

Concrete: System requires providing concrete information as early as possible because vulnerability (botnet) constantly changes its place. So information of specific kind of botnet and its value also degrades quickly.

Convenient: The system should get this information within a time so that the value cannot change.

However, it is a requirement of individuals to have domain knowledge and its analysis. The system will collect information about various aspects of vulnerability including its flooding, i.e., denial of services, communication infrastructure, propagation technique, identities of compromise host, and details of activities then participated in.

Questions

Q.1. What are the recent trends in network forensics? Explain in brief.

Q.2. Write down the network forensic process model.

Q.3. What do you understand by frameworks? Explain all detection-based frameworks.

Q.4. Explain network monitoring framework in detail.

Q.5. Explain fuzzy logic-based framework in detail.

Q.6. What do you understand by process model? What are the differences between process model and the frameworks?

References

A. A. Ahmed, "Investigation Approach for Network Attack *Intention Recognition*," *International Journal of Digital Crime and Forensics*, vol. 9, no. 1, pp. 22, 2017.

H. Asghari, *Botnet Mitigation and the Role of ISPs: DelftUniversity of Technology*, 2010.

K. Bailey, Chief Information Security Officer University of Washington, and J. Winn, Director of the Shidler Center for Law Commerce and Technology, University of Washington, Personal interviews. Seattle, WA March 31, 2006.

A. Balasooriya and S. Fernando, "Next Generation Security Framework to Detect Botnets on Computer Networks," *International Journal of Engineering and Technology*, vol. 5, no. 2, p. 257, 2013.

A. Bijalwan and E. S. Pilli, Understanding Botnet on Internet, *Computational Intelligence and Computing Research (ICCIC), 2014 IEEE International Conference on* (pp. 1–5), 2014.

A. Bijalwan, S. Sando, and M. Lemma, "An Anatomy for Recognizing Network Attack Intention," *International Journal of Recent Technology & Engineering*, vol. 8, no. 3, pp. 803–816, 2019.

B. Carrier and E. H. Spafford, "Getting Physical with the Digital Investigation Process," *International Journal of Digital Evidence, vol. 2*, no. 2, pp. 1–20, 2003.

H. Choi, H. Lee, and H. Kim, Botnet Detection by Monitoring Group Activities in DNS Traffic, *7th IEEE International Conference on Computer and Information Technology, 2007. CIT 2007, Aizu-Wakamatsu, Fukushima* (pp. 715–720), IEEE, 2007.

B. E. Endicott-Popovsky, B. Chee and D. Frincke, Role of Calibration as Part of Establishing Foundation for Expert Testimony, *Proceedings 3rd Annual IFIP WG 11.9 Conference*, January 29–31, Orlando, FL, 2007.

J. M. Franco and F. N. Rente, Neofelis, High-Interaction Honeypot Framework for Mac OS X, *2nd. OWASP Ibero-American Web Application Security Conference IBWAS 2010 Lisboa, Portugal* (pp. 25–33), 2010.

S. Garfinkel and G. Spafford, *Web Security, Privacy & Commerce*: O'Reilly Media, Inc., 2002.

G. Gu, R. Perdisci, J. Zhang, and W. Lee, "BotMiner: clustering analysis of network traffic for protocol-and structure-independent botnet detection," *USENIX security symposium 2008*, pp. 139–154.

V. Jacobsen, C. Leres, and S. McCanne, "Tcpdump/libpcap," http://www.tcpdump.org/2005.

B. B. Kang, E. Chan-Tin, C. P. Lee, J. Tyra, H. J. Kang, C. Nunnery, Z. Wadler, G. Sinclair, N. Hopper, and D. Dagon, Towards Complete Node Enumeration in a Peer-to-Peer Botnet, *4th International Symposium on Information, Computer, and Communications Security Sydney, NSW, Australia* (pp. 23–34), ACM, 2009.

T. Karagiannis, K. Papagiannaki, and M. Faloutsos, "BLINC: Multilevel Traffic Classification in the Dark," *ACM SIGCOMM Computer Communication Review*, vol. 35, no. 4, pp. 229–240, 2005.

P. Kaur, P. Chaudhary, A. Bijalwan, and A, Awasthi, Network Traffic Classification Using Multiclass Classifier, *Advances in Computing and Data Sciences* (pp. 208–217), 2018.

T. M. Koo, H.-C. Chang, and C.-C. Chuang, "Detecting and Analyzing Fast-Flux Service networks," *Advances in Information Sciences & Service Sciences*, vol. 4, no. 10, 2012.

T. M. Koo, H.-C. Chang, and W.-C. Liao, "Estimating the Size of P2P Botnets," *International Journal of Advancements in Computing Technology*, vol. 4, no. 12, pp. 286–295, 2012.

L. Mendonca and H. Santos, Botnets: A Heuristic-Based Detection Framework, *Proceedings of the Fifth International Conference on Security of Information and Networks Jaipur*, India (pp. 33–40), ACM, 2012.

G. L. Palmer, "Forensic Analysis in the Digital World," *International Journal of Digital Evidence*, vol. 1, no. 1, pp. 1–6, 2002.

E. S. Pilli, R. C. Joshi, and R. Niyogi, "Network Forensic Frameworks: Survey and Research Challenges," *Digital Investigation*, vol. 7, no. 1, pp. 14–27, 2010.

P. Porras, H. SaÃ⁻di, and V. Yegneswaran, A Foray into Confickerâ€™s Logic and Rendezvous Points, *USENIX Workshop on Large-Scale Exploits and Emergent Threats*, 2009.

R. Rowlinson, "Ten Steps to Forensic Readiness," *International Journal of Digital Evidence*, vol. 2, no. 3, pp. 1–28, Winter 2004.

W. B. Saunders Harcourt Health Sciences. "Definition: Calibration," Retrieved from the World Wide Web July 31, 2006. http://www.mercksource.com/pp/us/cns/cns_hl_dorlands.jspzQ.

M. Scanlon and M. Kechadi, Universal Peer-to-Peer Network Investigation Framework, *Eighth International Conference on Availability, Reliability and Security* (ARES) (pp. 694–700), IEEE, 2013.

P. Sharma, S. Tiwari, A. Bijalwan, and E. Pilli, "Botnet Detection Framework," *International Journal of Computer Applications*, vol. 93, no. 19, pp. 29–34, 2014.

M. Simon, Chief Technology Officer, Conjungi Corporation, *Personal interviews*. Conjungi: Seattle, WA, Summer, 2005.

S. Sitaraman and S. Venkatesan, "Computer and Network Forensics," *Digital Crime and Forensic Science in Cyberspace*, vol. 3, pp. 55–74, 2006.

Y. Tang and T. Daniels, A Simple Framework for Distributed Forensics, *Proceedings of the 25th IEEE International Conference on Distributed Computing Systems Workshops, June 2005, Columbus, Ohio*, 2005.

A. Yaar, A. Perrig, and D. Song, Pi: *A Path Identification Mechanism to Defend Against Ddos Attacks*: IEEE, 2003.

H. R. Zeidanloo, F. Hosseinpour, and F. F. Etemad, "New Approach for Detection of IRC and P2P Botnets," *International Journal of Computer and Electrical Engineering*, vol. 2, no. 6, pp. 1793–8163, 2010.

4

Classification of Network Forensics

LEARNING OBJECTIVES

This chapter reveals the in-depth knowledge of network forensics and its classification. After reading this chapter, you would

- Have basic knowledge of network forensics and its classification.
- Understand the types of network forensics classification.
- Understand about payload and its classification.
- Have knowledge of signature-based classification.
- Have knowledge of the meaning of ensemble and ensemble-based classification.

4.1 Introduction

Intrusion detection systems play an important role to filter out all the known malicious content inside the network and watch in nook and corner of the organization where it installs. Intrusion detection is a tool that monitors known malicious activities and potential malicious activities in the ingress network. It provides in-depth defense for securing the computer network. It is first introduced during the 80s; however, over a period of time with the advancement of intrusion detection systems, attackers too were equipped with advanced techniques to evade it. It happens due to the most widely used commercial IDs. It gives an alarm when it detects suspicious activities. Generally, IDS detects the vulnerabilities through two approaches that are as follows:

1. Signature-based or misuse detection
2. Anomaly-based or hybrid detection.

4.1.1 Signature-Based or Misuse Detection

Misuse-based detection came into existence with known attack signature. It is a predefined set of attack signatures. It can monitor when known attack pattern reflects some malicious behavior that can easily be evaded by novel attacks. It is difficult to retain all signatures as there are a continuously increasing number of vulnerabilities. Misuse detection can be obtained through the previous description of known malicious activities. It is framed

DOI: 10.1201/9781003045908-5

in one set of rules that are often known as attack signatures. If such activities match the attack signature, then it can be abbreviated as malicious. Generally, ingress packets are to check with the specific pattern which is already predefined by a set of attack signatures. All normal and malicious behaviors are used to monitor by comparing them with the previous observed behaviors. The previous observed behaviors give an idea to the administrator for quickly identifying all the current attacks. They can find which kind of attack currently the system is facing. There will not be any alarm raised, if monitored data do not get the log file of previous attack signature.

Comparatively, anomaly-based intrusion detection system is the most promising method to detect the vulnerabilities and its variations; however, it produces high false positive rates. Many researchers worked on to reduce the high rate of its false positive.

It is a stand-alone system that observes all network links in real time for extracting the attacker's traffic transit. Network intrusion detection system can be bifurcated into two ways. The system in the first way is to rely on audit information collected by the host in the network where they try to protect all information of egress and ingress traffic. The ways are those that observe passively all the stand-alone network traffic through packet filtration tools. It may also be possible to detect attack by watching the demilitarized zone (DMZ) links passively.

There are few important aspects before executing the experiments to watch intruder's activities as follows.

4.1.1.1 Monitoring

When an outside host connects to the network, we can't assume the possible threats through it. The large-volume and high-speed monitoring can be done by continuously watching the demilitarized zone cover a single link. This link is FDDI ring that captured the traffic up to 100 Mbps, and the volume of traffic is around 20 GB/day.

4.1.1.2 Capturing (Avoidance of Packets Drop)

The system has to capture all the packets so that the experts find out all possible threats. Sometimes if it is unable to consume all ingress packets, there should be a filter that can create a buffer for later consumption. There is a chance of getting some clues on the drop packets for the investigations. It might also be possible that these drop packets contain the source of identification of the attacks. So avoidance of getting packet drops is further more important for forensics investigation.

4.1.1.3 Notification

Early notification reduces the delay incurred before the attack detection. If the detection of attack is generated through the real time, the expert can apply all the traceback techniques to find out the attacker's identity and location to minimize the damages incurred by them. They may focus on prevention through break-in and inspect all network activities at bang on dot so that possibility of threats can be overcome or weed out before more damages.

4.1.1.4 Software Initiation

To implement high-speed and large-volume traffic requires a sound design and an efficient mechanism to classify it. Software mechanism plays an important role in dealing with such kind of circumstances. Sound software system provides the simplicity and flexibility to analyze differently these kinds of scenarios.

4.1.1.5 Multiperspective Environment

The nature of attack can differ at a time. It is quite obvious that one technique cannot produce exactly the intention of the attackers. The setup of the system should be as per the multiperspective environment so that new types of the attack can also be discovered.

4.1.2 Anomaly-Based or Hybrid Detection

Network-based attacks are increasing day by day with the technological advancement. There is an annual report of joint computer security institute and FBI during 2005 that many respondent companies faced a financial loss of around 130 million $. Anomaly detection can be detected through normal activities. It is a description of benign activities. Herein, the gap between the description of new network activity and the normal activities can be referred to as a kind of malicious activity. It gives more false positives than misuse detection, but it detects zero-day attacks which is not possible with the signature-based detection. Anomaly-based detection system is a statistical network system that can easily extract the attack variants alongside novel attack without a priori knowledge. The complex computation makes existing anomaly detection system more inefficient for the real-time detection. Sometimes, it gets quite convoluted with heavy consumption of system resources. It is indispensable of feature reduction to create an effective anomaly-based detection system. However, many feature-based reduction techniques can cumbersome such as SVM, principle component analysis (PCA), correlation-based feature selection (CFS), independent component analysis (ICA), PCA-ICA, generalized discriminant analysis (GDA), and linear discriminant analysis (LDA) to reduce the header features of packets.

Like intrusion detection system, the firewall retards all known vulnerabilities from coming inside the network. These kinds of systems are specifically designed to detect all known attacks by identifying their signature of attacks. However, such system requires frequent rule-based updates, which is not enough to detect unknown attacks. Irrespective of anomaly detection system, a subset of intrusion detection system enables them to find out known as well as unknown "zero-day" attacks.

4.1.3 Comparative Difference between Signature- and Anomaly-Based Detection

Traditionally, intrusion detection systems can be classified into two ways:

Signature-Based Detection
This identifies the patterns of traffic or application data to find out the malicious activity. The main advantage of signature-based detection is to trace all known attacks. Known attack can be detected with a low false positive rate. The disadvantage is that it requires a signature to define all possible threats that can be utilized by an attacker.

Anomaly-Based Detection
The anomaly detection is also called hybrid compound detection. It generally combines techniques from two approaches. The main advantage of anomaly detection is that it can detect unknown attacks too with the "'zero-day" attacks.

The system of anomaly detection framed normal operation of system as well as network, and it further classifies the deviation from them. Here, the normal activities are customized for every system and network, and all the applications make it more stringent from the attack. The attackers are unable to lurk and launch their malicious intentions though they can evade it. However, there is a disadvantage also in this kind of detection system that it generates a high percentage of false alarm. Due to this, it is difficult to determine which specific event shows the alarm.

4.2 Detection and Prevention System

Before understanding the basics of network forensics, we should have a knowledge of detection and prevention system. Whenever we set up the network equipment within an organization, we take care of all precautionary steps so that the intruder cannot evade the network boundaries. Somehow, if he would be lucky to have it, all sorts of prevention mechanism make it the way out.

4.2.1 Detection System

The detection system should have the characteristics of detecting actions and events that attempt to compromise confidentiality, integrity, and availability of assets and the resources. It is capable of detecting all kinds of malicious attacks in the network. It detects all network traffics of host-based attacks, vulnerable services, unauthorized logins, application-related data-driven attacks, all sensitive files, and different characteristics of malware. They can be further analyzed through different machine learning algorithms with pattern recognition algorithm. It is applied to monitor round the clock. These threats can also be classified as follows:

Internal penetration

External penetration

Misfeasance.

This can be used for monitoring purpose to detect the vulnerability with ease for further analyzing purpose.

The main general features of detection system are as follows:

1. These detection systems are designed to monitor and alert passive vulnerabilities inside of an organization.
2. The detection system can be real time or out of band.
3. It can easily understand what to look for.
4. It is generally misuse- or signature-based detection.
5. However, anomaly-based system can catch oddities in transactions.

Generally, we can bifurcate the detection systems into three categories as follows (Figure 4.1):

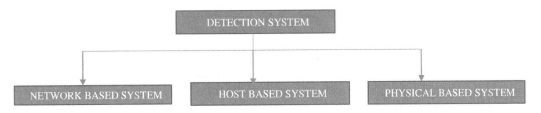

FIGURE 4.1
Categories of detection system.

I. Network-based detection system

II. Host-based detection system

III. Physical-based detection system.

I. Network-Based Detection System

Network-based detection system weeds out all the attack packets at initial level. It detects and stops all the vulnerability from entering the organization. These network-based detection systems can be a set of hardware and software. It may be built through the multilayer firewall or software-level firewall or may be through bastion host. This kind of detection system is typically built for an organization that may not be able to purchase dedicated firewall. The most common software for detecting the vulnerability inside of a network is "SNORT". It is a kind of packet sniffer.

II. Host-Based Detection System

Host-based detection system works the possibility of vulnerability on system and system-related things. It is typically designed to look at the entire systems. It monitors every aspect of the system. It generally installs as an application. These kinds of software generally monitor security events, system behavior, and normal communication. The common software for the host-based detection system are AIDE, OSSEC, Tripwire, etc.

III. Physical-Based Detection

Physical-based detections are those detection systems that are designed specifically for the monitoring purpose. These all are external peripheral devices to record the events. This is a simple security guard to watch every moment of the organization. It can be installed in department store gate. This physical-based detection system can be a security camera and alarm that is designed to monitor and alert the events. It can further be used as a deterrent.

4.2.2 Prevention System

The prevention systems are systems that detect all the actions and events that attempt to compromise confidentiality, integrity, or availability of the assets and resources for further taking actions based on it. Intrusion prevention system always watches and protects the system from any kind of threat. These prevention systems are designed to monitor, alert, and act as a gatekeeper for the systems. They work in active mode and understand what to look for. Prevention-based system works in real time and inline and typically follows both signature- and heuristic-based approach. Sometimes it can be difficult to set up due to the mass traffic flow. If prevention system faces failure, traffic stops flowing immediately.

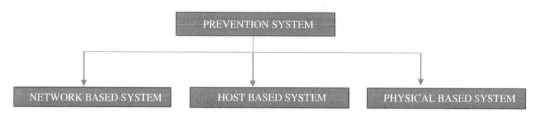

FIGURE 4.2
Categories of prevention system.

This prevention system can also be bifurcated into the same group as for the detection system. Its types are as follows (Figure 4.2):

I. Network-based prevention system
II. Host-based prevention system
III. Physical-based prevention system.

I. Network-Based Prevention System
    Like network-based detection system, prevention system is also a set of both hardware and software. It can also be built into bastion host, as application layer or multilayer firewall. Generally, the organization has a large network use intrusion prevention system to protect from all threats. In such kind of system, prevention must be in line to be most effective and rarely other software can send TCP resets out of band. It is mostly performed by hardware.

II. Host-Based Prevention System
    Host-based prevention system is designed to look at the entirety of a system. It monitors many aspects of a system. It typically lives as an application. In this kind of system, software can monitor nearly every aspect of the system. To prevent the host system from any infection, the prevention system uses sandbox or virtualized software.

III. Physical-Based Prevention System
    Physical-based prevention system stops someone from doing harm physically like electric fences.

4.3 Types of Network Forensics Classification

Network forensics classification facilitates the identification of various applications and protocols involved in the network. There are different operations that can be performed on the traffic after identification or classification of traffic like monitoring, discovery, control, and optimization aiming at network improvement. These identification classifications can be classified into two sections:

1. Payload-based network forensics identification
2. Statistical-based network forensics identification.

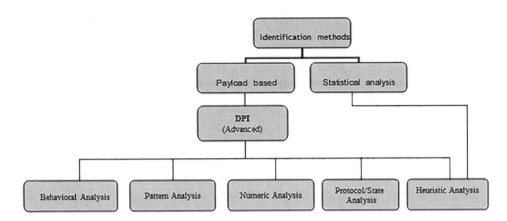

FIGURE 4.3
Network forensics classification.

Figure 4.3 shows that traffic classification is divided in two parts, i.e., payload-based and statistical analyses, but generally, the broad classification is as follows.

4.3.1 Payload-Based Identification

Payload is actual data meant to carry alongside header during transmitting information from the sender to the receiver side. It is an intended message which is packed while sender transmits the data through communication channel. When the user deliberately sends the malicious data to the vulnerable user, the payload carries this sort of malware contents that later perform undesirous actions on the intended system or network. The payload bundles in some type of frames such as point-to-point frames, Ethernet frames, fiber channel frames, etc. Generally, malware forwards its payload on a computer by sending infected files. It further gets infected by opening and running the infected programs (Figure 4.4).

The payload field can be of a fixed length or variable length size. The frame is set to a fixed size on a fixed size payload. The length of fixed size payload acts as delimiter of the frame; hence, fixed size frame does not require any end flag. In variable length payload, a pattern is used as a delimiter to determine the size of the frame. Alternatively, a length field is kept that contains the frame size (Figure 4.5).

In payload-based traffic classification, packets are classified in the field of the payload. Payload uses classification techniques like deep packet inspection (DPI) for verification and classification of traffic. For understanding and verifying various applications, deep packet inspection utilizes the signature analysis. In most of the applications, unique pattern of signatures exists. There are different signature analysis methods as follows: pattern analysis, protocol analysis, heuristics analysis, numerical analysis, and behavioral analysis.

Header	Payload	Flag

FIGURE 4.4
Payload structure-I.

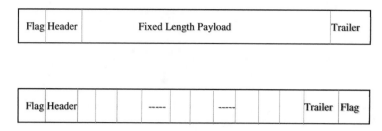

FIGURE 4.5
Payload structure-II.

In pattern analysis, applications have some pattern in the payload of the packets, which can be used to identify the protocols. These patterns may be presented in any position in the packet, and only after this, the classification is possible. Numerical analysis includes the numerical characteristics of the packet, for example, payload size, the number of response packets, etc. Behavioral analysis and heuristic analysis go simultaneously, and several antiviruses utilize both techniques for identifying viruses and infections. In protocol analysis, protocols are a set of rules of a particular action. For example, a typical FTP GET request from a client is followed by a valid response from the server. Such protocol conformance can be used to classify such applications.

4.3.1.1 Deep Packet Inspection

Packet analysis is a basic traceback technique in network forensics. As we know, a network packet contains the metadata. Network packet streams reconstruct the files that transfer through network. This process is also known as network carving. Packet capture exports supporting files using packet analyzer or network carver. It further helps to find the clues during network data transfer. It yields the first traceback technique through packet analysis. It happens through intensive examination of IP header using extracting the parameter from upper layer 4 and layer 7.

The inspection of all the packets that traverse through network is generally known as deep packet inspection. Sometimes, deep packet inspection is called packet sniffing. It is a kind of data processing that involves rerouting, logging, and blocking of contaminated packet from the network. It filters the malicious packets. Deep packet inspection set some inspection points through which the packet header of a data is to be evaluated. In case of some anomaly observed, it blocks it and reroutes it, logging it from the inspection point. Sometimes, deep packet inspection is required to inspect the packet payload that cannot be traced properly through packet filtering conventional methodology.

Deep packet inspection works in the application layer of open system interconnection. All the packet headers are evaluated through the checkpoints of DPI. Here, there is a set of rules managed by various levels of internet service providers (ISP) or through network administrators. DPI weeds out all nefarious content in real time. The DPI analyzes deeply all the content of the packet, and it ensures the arrival source of the packets. It also finds out that the packets come from either the service side or the application side. It also works with functionality of the firewall to filter out or redirect the network traffic from an IP address or through any online service.

DPI works for both intrusion detection system and intrusion prevention system or sometimes works for intrusion detection or intrusion prevention where firewall, IDS, and IPS are not capable of finding out the attacks. There is an overall advantage of all these systems firewall, IDS, and IPS that they can easily identify the specific attacks. DPI completely hinges upon policies and rules defined by the user and their network administrator that restrict all prohibit applications inside of network. DPI also allows internet service providers (ISPs) to prevent distributed denial of services (DDoS) attacks on all the exploitation of Internet of Things (IoT) and its related devices through blocking all malicious requests.

Primarily, firewall and intrusion detection system (IDS)-based techniques are utilized for detecting the attack purpose, but due to their inability to recognize specific attacks, deep packet inspection mechanism comes into picture to get rid of these issues. This methodology can be used as part of IDS and IPS. The technique generally used for a deep packet inspection is signature matching in which all the known attack patterns inside the database are analyzed with the new arrived packets. Another technique is anomaly-based detection in which unknown packet traverse from the appropriate algorithm "default deny". This security approach bifurcates the corrupt and intact packets, and then it allows travel inside of the network. Intrusion prevention system generally opt the deep packet inspection technique. This technique blocks all the identified attacks in real time. This technique gives comprehensive protection from all vulnerabilities.

DPI also helps to prioritize the messages to speed up the important mail over the least important mail. Buffer attack can also be prevented by the DPI. There is an option to slow down the data rate on peer-to-peer channel through DPI. The application area of DPI can be utilized by mobile service operator, network administrator, and various levels of service providers. It helps to the different level of service provider to weed out unwanted traffic as well as content, e.g., few ISPs get the pornography sites blocked through dpi, political sites, religious sites, and many more as per their requirement. However, the disadvantage of DPI is when the load of the processor increases, the performance of computer automatically decreases, but it increases the firewall's complexity.

There is a privacy concern with the deep packet inspection that it monitors and detects the content of both sender and receiver. The confidentiality can be breached when the user details are permeated into the companies for publicizing their product. Deep packet inspection can be classified into five phases. However, heuristic analysis is also a part of statistical identification-based network forensics.

I. Behavioral analysis

II. Pattern analysis

III. Numeric analysis

IV. Protocol/state analysis

V. Heuristic analysis.

The details of all these analyses are as follows (Figure 4.6).

I. Behavioral Analysis

It is a must to read the behavior of packets when they arrive in boundary of any network. When there is a term related to deeper inspection, it categorizes this terminology into three ways, i.e., the analysis of dynamic port, the behavior analysis, and the signature reconnaissance application. The description of all these three ways is as follows:

Analysis of Dynamic Port

TCP and UDP ports are easily available for all known applications, and they do not have any requirement of deep packet inspection engine (DPI). DPI

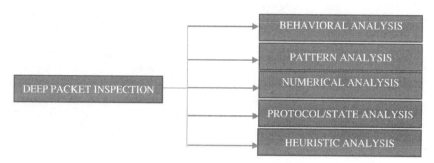

FIGURE 4.6
Deep packet inspection classification.

engine is crucial to inspect all the applications in real time. When such application randomly negotiates to continue a session and new ports do not have any prior knowledge about the conversation of known applications, DPI can monitor all the established conversations. Subsequently, it can authenticate the genuine applications too.

Signature Reconnaissance Application

Recent applications can easily evade the firewall by manipulating their basic nature through known fixed ports like http port 80. These applications work like a normal web surfing. DPI generally exchanges the reassemble multiple packets at first stage, and then it looks toward for the signature. It is a kind of tedious string of bits that refers to the features of an application that matches with the set of signatures in database. The DPI thoroughly inspects it for further decisions.

Behavior Analysis

Behavior analysis is a way of behavior, function, or operation to find out information. If any protocol is unable to find out the vulnerability during data flow, then it is must use behavioral analysis to implement it. This analysis is basically based on the user behavior. The analysis also relies on the special terminal like spam mails. It finds other alternate sources to get information about the packets. In case of completely relying on the signature of the application, deep packet inspection monitors other parameters of the application too. Sometimes it might be possible that the application is too scrambled, or it might also be possible that it is too compressed. During that time, it is abstruse to get information or search a port from signature-based analysis. It is a must to find an alternate solution to that. The other parameters like order of the packet or the length of packet define complete in and out of the packets.

II. Pattern Analysis

Pattern analysis for deep packet inspection relies on the pattern and its behavior. The pattern analysis depends upon misuse as well as the hybrid nature of the detection. As described earlier, the misuse detection is possible when known attack pattern reflects some malicious behavior that can easily be evaded by novel attacks. It is difficult to retain all signatures as there is a continuously increasing number of vulnerabilities. It obtains through the previous description of known malicious activities. It is framed in one set of rules which is often known as attack signatures. If such activities match with the attack signature, then it can be considered as malicious. Generally, ingress packets are to check with the specific pattern which is already predefined by a set of attack signatures. All normal and malicious behaviors are to monitor and then compared with the previous observed behavior. The previous observed behavior gives an idea to the administrator for quickly identifying all the current attacks. They can find which kind of attack the system is facing currently. There will not be raised any alarm, if monitored data do not get the log file of previous attack signature.

III. Protocol/Static and Stateful Analysis

Static analysis filters the traffic by matching with their prescribed rules based on address port, source, destination IP, etc. Every packet has to be checked against filtering rules irrespective of packet being part of traffic or it is a standalone. Static analysis is also known as stateless filtering. This analysis was used in earlier days.

Stateful inspection is also known as dynamic analysis. A firewall makes all connections in its "state table" which is a legitimate all-connection list in a table. If something is not related to that, it is discarded. The stateful analysis checks all connections related to arrival packets and their characteristics. The advantage of stateful analysis is that instead of checking all packets individually, it keeps tracks open. It compares ingress traffic through the firewall. A stateful connection inspection observes TCP flags and TCP sequence number, and all that makes it stringent in security. Spoofed packets cannot barge-in into legitimate traffic connection and clandestinely cross the firewall. Generally, interaction with application is allowed by the stateful at a certain level, whereas the higher version of deep inspection allows firewall to see the actual data that pass through its premises. Earlier, only they used to keep track of connection information.

4.3.2 Statistical-Based Identification

Statistical analysis is a science that discovers the facts and uncovers all the desired patterns on collected data. It is a powerful tool that can evaluate the pattern in real time. In many complicated areas, the statistical analysis helps to find out the solution and provide appropriate results.

4.3.2.1 Heuristic Analysis

Heuristic analysis can be categorized inside of statistical network forensics identification. As the name suggests, it is a problem-solving method through either deep packet inspection or statistical methodology. It totally hinges upon features of empirical pattern of the applications. Heuristic analysis can be used for protocol or application. This analysis is based on the best classification methodology for obtaining the high accuracy rate.

Heuristic analysis inspects several packets before initiating any transaction. It initiates when the application clarifies all the processes with three known ports. Hence, heuristic analysis controls the quality of services for any transaction. It also focuses on access control, so the network traffic pattern can create security issues, and it also provides more visibility toward data traffic distribution.

The analysis of the real-time traffic shows the following observations:

I. Binary pattern in IP payload

II. Connectivity patterns

III. IP flow metrics pattern.

The type of protocol can be determined by the signature in data bit stream which is inside of IP payload. The characteristics of some parameter activities such as protocol within certain changes and port ranges and their scanning can be identified through connectivity patterns. The characteristics of traffic such as average packet size, average bit rate, etc. can be observed through IP flow metrics pattern.

4.4 Network Forensics Analysis Classification

This section gives a general classification of the analysis of network forensics. This classification is based on signature, decision tree, and ensemble. The details of these classification can be obtained through sections as follows.

4.4.1 Signature-Based Classification

The signature-based analysis is based on prior characteristics of virus that may enter through input files. It is a different sequence of bytes that basically do not often exist in normal files. These signatures can be traced by forensics experts through network analysis. The main objective of the signature-based classifier is to detect and investigate the nature and feature of a bit string in operating the given payload. There are so many applications that use initial protocol, e.g., in tcp protocol, three-way handshaking is used. This classifier is utilized on Fred-eZone, a free network service provider (Wi-Fi) operated by the city of Fredericton in which work load of Wi-Fi network over a day was 500G in bytes, and there were 1058k different IP addresses of source found. If we saw destination IP addresses, then there were about 1228k different IP addresses found only in a day, and about 30783k and 994M flows and packets were there. But these flows were bi-directional. Now, with the application of payload signature classification, nearly 249,000 flows could be identified within an hour. Whereas 215,000 flows could not be detected and the classification result of an hour on Fred-eZone shows 249 K flows, 102 K source IP and 202 K destination IP were found, but this result shows only known application. Shafi et al. also focus on the analysis of theoretical bounds for learning signatures using existing theory defining a framework for online extraction of signatures using a supervised classifier system presented that allowed identification and retrieval of signatures adaptively as soon as they are discovered.

4.4.2 Decision Tree-Based Classification

The structure of decision tree-based classification looks like a tree. In this, by splitting the dataset into smaller subsets, the decision tree also developed simultaneously, and the outcome is presented in the form of a tree which has decision nodes and leaf nodes. It is a better method of classifying the unknown traffic. It can be further utilized for classification of traffic by initiating from roots of the tree and moving upto complete classification till the leaf node that defines a simple and efficient model for classification of the unknown application into different categories.

A decision tree is a very simple and widely used classification technique. In decision tree classification, a tree-like classifier is built based on some already classified data samples.

In decision tree classifier, all nonleaf nodes represent attributes and leaf nodes represent the class labels. For any particular data set, a lot of decision trees are possible. But the main point of focus is splitting criteria, i.e., how to get more informative attributes at the upper part of the tree. So a lot of techniques are applied to fulfill this criterion like Gini index, information gain, entropy, etc. Examples of decision tree-based algorithms are Id3, C4.5, etc.

4.4.3 Ensemble-Based Classification

The Botnet traffic can be identified using the machine learning technique. It can be obtained through segregation of whole traffic into IRC and non-IRC traffic. After segregation, it can further differentiate the IRC traffic and real traffic and subsequently compare this analysis with J48, naïve Bayes, and Bayesian network classifiers. Beigi et al. focus on statistical network flow features rather than packet content and found that it is unable to differentiate between Botnet IRC traffic and benign traffic. The researcher shows the loophole on previous methods such as principal component analysis (PCA), correlation feature selection (CFS), minimum redundancy maximum relevance (mRMR), and improper evaluation of features set on testbed datasets. He built a dataset which incorporates different varieties of Botnet of different protocols in realistic environment. Saad et al. further proposed a new approach (detecting P2P bot before launch the attack) to characterize and detect through network traffic behavior. Using the machine learning technique, it extracted and analyzed the set of C&C traffic behavior and its characteristics. This research differentiated among five machine learning techniques, i.e., super vector machine (SVM), artificial neural network (ANN), nearest neighbor classifier (NNC), Gaussian-based classifier (GBC) and Naïve Bayes classifier (NBC). Rokach et al. divided ensemble model into dependent and independent method. In dependent method, the most well-versed model instance is boosting which is known as resampling and combining. It is used to improve the performance of week classification on distributed training data. Through iterative process, AdaBoost is a well-known ensemble algorithm to improve simple boosting algorithms. In an independent method, Bagging and Wagging are well known.

Ensemble method is used to improve the quality and robustness of supervised and unsupervised learning algorithm. Initially authors used the bagging method for ensemble learning. A meta-algorithm of model averaging was built for classification initially. It used the multiple training set by utilizing bootstrap, it is used in many versions of training set. It is an ensembled meta-algorithm of machine learning which is made for improving the accuracy of machine learning algorithm for both regression and classification. Each version of data set is utilized for training of different models. Through averaging, voting output of the model can combined with other that create a single output in case of regression and classification.

Ensemble classifier is a methodology to lift several other classifiers. Ensemble classifiers combine different classifiers in order to obtain the output for improving the accuracy. For this purpose, we can select any different pairs of individual classifiers and combine them for the improvement of the algorithm. Generally, there are two ways to generate ensemble classifiers: data-independent and data-dependent. So, it is possible to use-data dependent as implicit-dependent and explicit-dependent too.

Ensemble classifier is a combination of different classifiers run either serially or in parallel in order to improve the accuracy of classification. The strengths of various techniques are combined to perform better classification and improve the performance metrics like accuracy, specificity, and sensitivity. We used the term "lift" to mean the increase or improvement in the accuracy of classification after combining the single classifier. Ensemble-based classifier performs better than the single classifier by combining multiple classifiers. We have used three mechanisms to perform ensemble classification – Bagging, AdaBoost, and Soft-Voting. We selected various combinations of the classification techniques, i.e., k-nearest neighbor (KNN) and decision tree (DT) along with the ensemble mechanisms together. The various methods of ensemble-based mechanism and the various classifiers are combined as shown in Figure 4.7. These combinations can be modified as we may add more classification algorithms and ensemble mechanisms.

Dependent algorithm: dependent ensemble-based classifier is a framework where the output of one classifier is used as the input of the next classifier. It can generate the knowledge from the first iteration used as a guide in the next iteration. The main two approaches of dependent framework are incremental batch learning and model guided instance selection. To build the next classifier, the incremental batch learning method used current trained set with classification of previous classifier. The classifier used for the last iteration

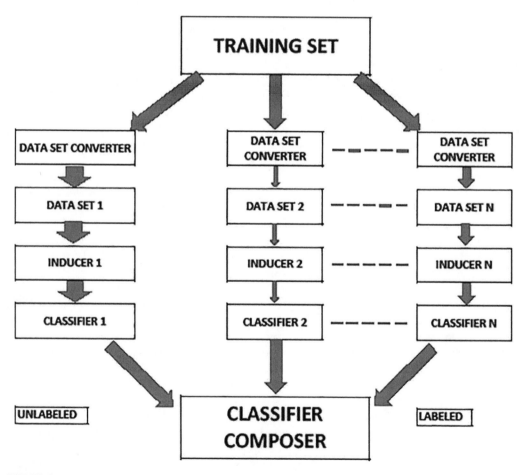

FIGURE 4.7
Ensemble of classifier.

is set as a final classifier. In such model-guided instance selection framework, the classifier who made the last iteration checks the misclassified set, and then it is again used after manipulating the training set for improving the results.

Independent methods transformed all original datasets into many datasets from which classifiers are trained. In this type of classification, the dataset is made through the original training set. It may be separated from each other or overlapping. This combining method is used to produce output of the final classification. Some examples of independent methods are bagging, random forest, and cross validated committees, etc.

4.4.3.1 Voting

There are some simple and real statics which can apply for making decision by majority vote that is actually already taken or implied potentially which deserve to understood further.

There are two main methods: combination method and weighting methods. There are other two methods for joining the output of individual classifiers: weighting methods and meta-learning methods. If individual classifiers perform the same task and obtain some success, weighting method is utilized successfully. Meta-learning methods are well suited when some classifiers classify correctly in regular interval or misclassify some instances.

4.4.3.2 Adaptive Boosting

Adaptive boosting (ADABoost) was first introduced in 1996 by Freund and Schapive. This is a well-known ensemble algorithm that improves the simple boosting algorithm through iterative process.

The main reason of this algorithm is to focus more on the pattern in the training set because the accuracy of boosting algorithm to detect bot is less than adaptive boosting. This algorithm is used with weak learner in which the detection concept is hard to classify. Weightage depends upon the complexity. More weight is assigned to that pattern in which detection is difficult. Initially, we can provide same weight to all patterns in the training set. So in iteration process, the weight of easily classified instances get decreased, and in case of misclassified instances, weights are increased. Weight measures overall accuracy. Weak learner is forced to focus on difficult instances of the training set after performing more iteration and making additional classifier.

AdaBoost is a powerful classifier that works effectively both in basic and complex recognition problems. It combines all weak and inaccurate classifiers and makes one ensemble classifier. AdaBoost classifier trains by classification of data structure.

4.4.3.3 Bagging

Bagging is also known as bootstrap aggregating. It is a well-known and independent method. The main aim of this ensemble method is to increase the accuracy by joining various learned classifiers' output into single prediction. All classifiers are trained on instance sample taken with replacement from the training set. Here, sample size is always the same as the original training set. Some instances have been represented many times. Figure 4.7 describes the flow diagram of ensemble-based classifier.

4.5 Implementation and Results

The implementation and the results of the classifier that is mentioned in the above section can be obtained through some formula as follows:

- **Accuracy:** Accuracy exhibits the description of systematic errors and the statistical bias. The ISO defines the term trueness for the accuracy. The accuracy of a classifier on a given test set is the percentage of test set tuples that are correctly classified by the classifier.

$$Accuracy/Recognition\ Rate = TP + TN\ /\ P + N \qquad (4.1)$$

- **Precision:** Precision is the fraction of retrieved documents that are relevant to the query. The precision and recall measures are also widely used in classification. Precision can be thought of as a measure of exactness (i.e., what percentage of tuples labeled as positive are actually such), whereas recall is a measure of completeness (what percentage of positive tuples are labeled as such).

$$Precision = TP/TP + FP \qquad (4.2)$$

- **Recall:** Recall in information retrieval is the fraction of the documents that are relevant to the query that are successfully retrieved. In binary classification, recall is called sensitivity. So, it can be looked at as the probability that a relevant document is retrieved by the query.

$$Recall = TP\ /\ TP + FN = TP\ /\ P \qquad (4.3)$$

- **F_1:** F_1 score (also F-score or F-measure) is a measure of a test's accuracy. It considers both the precision p and the recall r of the test to compute the score. F1 score is the harmonic mean of precision and recall.

$$F_1 = 2 \times ((p \times r)\ /\ (p + r)) \qquad (4.4)$$

In above equations, P is positive tuples (tuples of the main class of interest), N-negative tuples (all other tuples).

True positives: True positive means the classifier correctly labeled the positive tuples. True positive is denoted by TP.

True negatives: True negative means the classifier correctly labeled the negative tuples. True negative is denoted by TN.

False positives: False positive means the negative tuples incorrectly labeled as positive. False positive is denoted by FP.

False negatives: False negative means the positive tuples that were mislabeled as negative. False negative is denoted by FN.

Confusion Matrix: The confusion matrix is an important tool for analyzing how well your classifier can recognize tuples of different classes. TP and TN exhibit when the classifier is accepting right things. On the other hand, FP and FN exhibit when the classifier is accepting wrong things. Table 4.1 presents confusion matrix shown with totals for positive and negative tuples.

Questions

Q.1. What do you understand by intrusion detection system? Explain the types of detection system.

Q.2. Define signature-based detection system.

Q.3. What do you understand by anomaly? Explain the anomaly-based detection system in brief.

Q.4. Explain the difference between misuse and hybrid-based detection systems.

Q.5. What do you understand by intrusion prevention system? What are the tools available for prevention system?

Q.6. Explain the details for the classification of network forensics.

Q.7. Explain the important aspects before executing the experiments to watch intruder's activities.

Q.8. Explain the heuristic analysis for statistical-based identification.

Q.9. What do you understand by deep packet inspection (DPI)? Why is it so important in the field of network forensics?

Q.10. Explain the state and stateful analysis in detail.

Q.11. Explain the ensemble-based classification. What is the benefit of ensemble classification over others?

References

E. B. Beigi, H. H. Jazi, N. Stakhanova, and A. A. Ghorbani, Towards Effective Feature Selection in Machine Learning-Based Botnet Detection Approaches, *IEEE Conference on Communications and Network Security (CNS), 2014 San Francisco, CA* (pp. 247–255), IEEE, 2014.

L. Bernaille and R. Teixeira, "Early recognition of encrypted applications," in *International Conference on Passive and Active Network Measurement, LNCS, Springer*, 2007, pp. 165–175.

L. Bernaille, R. Teixeira, I. Akodkenou, A. Soule, and K. Salamatian, "Traffic Classification on the Fly," *ACM SIGCOMM Computer Communication Review, vol. 36, no. 2*, pp. 23–26, 2006.

A. Bijalwan, "Botnet Forensic Analysis Using Machine Learning Approach," *Security and Communication Networks*, vol. 2020, 2020. doi:10.1155/2020/9302318.

A. Bijalwan, N. Chand, E. S. Pilli, and C. R. Krishna, "Botnet Analysis Using Ensemble Classifier," *Perspectives in Science*, vol. 8, pp. 502–504, 2016.

J. Erman, A. Mahanti, M. Arlitt, I. Cohen, and C. Williamson, "Offline/Realtime Traffic Classification Using Semi-Supervised Learning," *Performance Evaluation*, vol. 64, no. 9, pp. 1194–1213, 2007.

C. Livadas, R. Walsh, D. Lapsley, and W. T. Strayer, Usilng Machine Learning Technliques to Identify Botnet *Traffic, 31st IEEE Conference on Local Computer Networks, Proceedings 2006 Tampa, FL* (pp. 967–974), IEEE, 2006.

W. Lu, M. Tavallaee, G. Rammidi, and A. A. Ghorbani, BotCop: An Online Botnet Traffic Classifier, *Seventh Annual Communication Networks and Services Research Conference, CNSR '09* (pp. 70–77), IEEE, 2009.

A. W. Moore and K. Papagiannaki, "Toward the accurate identification of network applications," in *Passive and Active Network Measurement*, Springer, 2005, pp. 41–54.

L. Rokach, "Ensemble-Based Classifiers," *Artificial Intelligence Review*, vol. 33, no. 1–2, pp. 1–39, 2010.

S. Saad, I. Traore, A. Ghorbani, B. Sayed, D. Zhao, W. Lu, J. Felix, and P. Hakimian, Detecting P2P Botnets Through Network Behavior Analysis and Machine Learning, *Ninth Annual International Conference on Privacy, Security and Trust (PST), Montreal, QC* (pp. 174–180), IEEE, 2011.

L. Salgarelli, F. Gringoli, and T. Karagiannis, "Comparing Traffic Classifiers," *ACM SIGCOMM Computer Communication Review*, vol. 37, no. 3, pp. 65–68, 2007.

S. Sen and J. Wang, "Analyzing Peer-to-Peer Traffic Across Large Networks," *IEEE/ACM Transactions on Networking (ToN)*, vol. 12, no. 2, pp. 219–232, 2004.

K. Shafi and H. A. Abbass, "Analysis of online signature based learning classifier systems for noisy environments: a feedback control theoretic approach," in Simulated Evolution and Learning, Springer, 2014, pp. 395–406.

Part B

Network Forensics Acquisition

5

Network Forensics Tools

LEARNING OBJECTIVES

This chapter focuses on imparting in-depth knowledge about various tools applied for network forensics. After reading this chapter, you would

- Have knowledge about network forensic analysis.
- Have knowledge about classification of tools.
- Understand the various tools that are applied for the network forensics.
- Understand Windows- and UNIX-based analyses.
- Have knowledge about various tools such as IP tracing, monitoring, analysis, and traceroute tools.

5.1 Introduction

Network forensic analysis tools aid the network security issues as these tools are efficient enough for analyzing and correlating the network traffic and data from different security tools, and this feature of network forensic tools is desirous for the users and security administrators as it provides required multilevel security to the network in the dynamic world of network forensics. The network forensic analysis tools are gaining a tremendous positive response. Information security magazine has defined network forensic analysis tools (NFATs) as a product that captures and retains all the network traffic and facilitates its user with the features like replaying, isolating, and analyzing a network attack or stealthy behavior, which further enables the users to strengthen their security system.

Some of the functions of network forensic analysis tools (NFAT) are as follows:

- Recording network traffic and analysis
- Anomaly detection
- Hardware determination and different protocols
- Incident recovery
- Prediction of future attack targets
- IP protection
- Assessment of risk

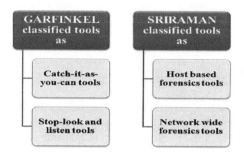

FIGURE 5.1
Classification of tools.

- Exploit attempt detection
- Aggregation of data from various resources inclusive of firewalls, IDSs, and sniffers
- Detection of employee misuse and abuse of networks and resources by employees
- Network performance

There are three main properties of NFATs:

- **Evidence Gathering:** It observes and monitors the network traffic closely. By listening and monitoring network traffic activity, it collects the proof (evidence).
- **No Alteration**: Since NFATs are un-intrusive, they do not allow the alteration of data. So, the data on the networks remain unaltered.
- **Replaying Function**: This feature facilitates the users or administrators with the proofs of a security attack or breach, wherein the proof on the machine remains unaltered.

In a broad sense, the network forensics analysis tool facilitates close monitoring of network traffic, managing the incoming and outgoing data flow, and a superior way of recording all the activities and events. This in turn helps the network security breach-proof. Generally, the investigators utilize the combination of multiple tools as single tools is not efficient enough to solve the purpose. For example, if the focus is on analyzing the network traffic, the investigators are familiar with the nature of network traffic and will according apply the utilizers based on Unix-like Ngrep, TCP Dump, or Omnipeek/Etherpeek with more advance and complex security issues. The tools such as Wireshark, NetMiner, Driftnet, etc. are utilized. There are some other tools also such as NetWitness, which provide efficient analysis options for network monitoring. It also provides a protection cover against malicious insider activity and abuse (Figure 5.1).

5.2 Visual Tracing Tools

Visual tracing tools are the tools that provide mapped graphical representation of traceroute. These visual tracing tools generally make a traceroute from the server to the requested IP addresses. The tools under visual tracing mechanism are as follows.

5.2.1 NeoTracePro

NeoTracePro is a reliable, efficient, accurate, and fast route-tracing tool with extremely full of useful functionalities. It can easily trace the paths on the web and forward its information back to the source system. As the basic advantage of visual tracing tool, NeoTracePro also traces the data in map form, diagram, along with table and by providing the list of servers. The status of induced server can also be traced by NeoTracePro. This tool shows how the packet travels from one computer to another by reflecting all nodes from source to recipient system within a network. It helps to check all the information on the network. It is a fascinated tool that allows us to geographically trace an IP address (Figure 5.2).

5.2.2 VisualRoute

VisualRoute is another tool for tracing an IP address or host name geographically. It helps to find out network-related issues like loss or latency of packets, bottleneck, etc. This tool contains umpteen other subinformation such as custom maps, network scanning, trace route history, remote access server, port probing, response time graphing, reverse tracing, continuous trace routing and save traceroute as text, image, and html, etc. This tool also has a java version (Figure 5.3).

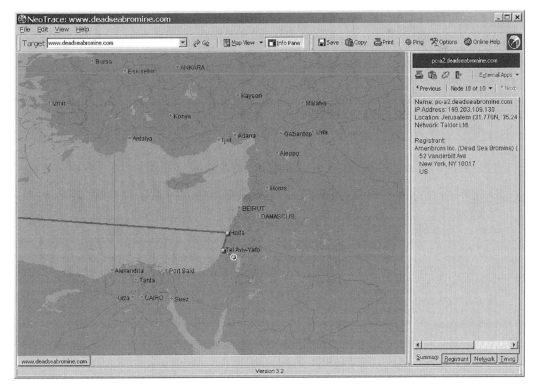

FIGURE 5.2
Image from NeoTracePro tool.

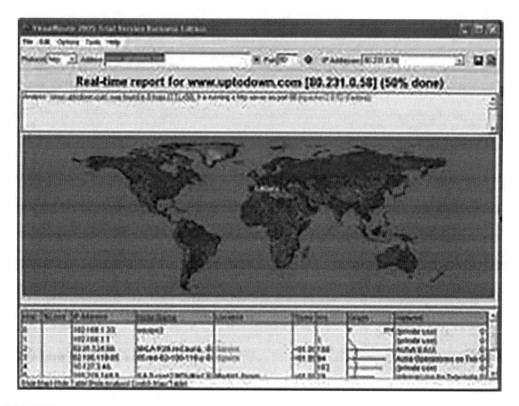

FIGURE 5.3
Image pic from VisualRoute tool.

5.2.3 Sam Spade

Sam Spade is a window software tool for tracking the sources of spam emails. It was authored by Steve Alkins in 1997. Sam Spade is named after a fictional character. This tool generally focuses on data gathering. It allows the user to collect all information through different techniques on particular host name or IP addresses. These tools include whois, finger, ping, and nslookup, although these already have different windows operating systems (Figure 5.4).

5.2.4 eMailTrackerPro

eMailTrackerPro is a software based on Window operating system only. Visualware has created this software to identify the sender of email messages, trace them, and report spammers. eMailTrackerPro allows mails to be searched to the emanates system instead of tracking IP addresses.

5.3 Traceroute Tools

Traceroute tools are required when someone has an ardent need of knowing that how many hops are necessary on a network and refers sequentially each hop that displays information like hop#, roundtrip time, best time in ms, IP address, TTL, and country.

FIGURE 5.4
Image from Sam spade tool.

Generally, traceroute tool is a network tool that refers to the route taken by packets across an IP network. These tools help us to identify the problems and determine the reason of poor connection by the server.

It helps us to know how all systems are connected with each other. It also shows how the receiver system connects and elucidates the information about how ISP connects with the network. There are many different types of traceroute tools available on the network as follows.

5.3.1 Text-Based Traceroute

Text-based traceroute tool belongs to both Window- and UNIX-based operating systems. These kinds of tools help to show the path from source to the recipient system. This is completely based on text-based normal pages. It is a commonly available, effective, and commonly used tool. The main disadvantage of this kind of tool is not having an advanced option to show.

5.3.2 3D-Based Traceroute

Earlier, it was abstruse to find out the reason of slow connection and internal mechanism; for example, if we used to interact to the website, we were unable to surf properly, pages had not been opened and most of the time it hadn't taken load to open the pages. 3D-based traceroute tools are the solution to find out behind-the-scene mechanism and spill the bean. It can monitor the internet connection and find the trouble component.

It is bundled with one packet tracer and generates the 3D chart. This chart reflects the location and the route of the packet through computing the distance, average, the latency, minimum time, maximum time, the time by standard deviation of the round trip, etc. It displays the direction from source node to the recipient. This tool also reflects the longitude, latitude, and altitude where recipient system location as well as the router's position resides.

5.3.3 Visual Traceroute

Visual traceroute tool provides the exact direction from the location of source system to the location of recipient system through mapping. It provides the exact view of system's geographic location. Visual traceroute displays the organization name alongside system's IP address.

5.4 Monitoring Tools

Network sniffing or monitoring tools are a combination of hardware and software. It is made for capturing and intercepting packets from the network. Data packet can be captured through sniffer tools. It can easily decode the packet for further analyzing purposes. The analysis tool extracts the feature for further forensic investigations. Sniffing and analyzing tools both work for monitoring, capturing, and identifying the exploitation. Subsequently, these monitoring tools detect the vulnerabilities, isolate them, and further analyze and find out the real source of attacks for forensics. Some packet sniffing tools are as follows.

5.4.1 Packet Sniffer Tool

Packet sniffer is the software and hardware tools that monitor the network traffic for classification, identification, and analyzing the packets on the network. The packet sniffer tool is basically based on application program interfaces such as packet capture (pcap) and library packet capture (libpcap). Pcap is used for Unix operating system, whereas libcap is used in window-based operating system. Packet sniffer tool captures the packets from the network traffic and copies them into a file. The intercepted data traffic can be traced through wired or wireless network. Unlike systems generally designed to ignore the network traffic, it is always ready to trace the log. Whenever the packet sniffing software get to install, network interface card (NIC) multifariously sets the command like tool can be trace and process all network activities into the system.

Packet sniffing tool helps the user by enhancing the network capacity, monitoring network activities, enhancing the security, managing the bandwidth, etc. The common packet sniffing software for monitoring purpose are as follows.

5.4.1.1 Wireshark

It is an open-source packet analyzer, which is extensively used as a tool for analyzing the network traffic. In the past, it was famous as Ethereal. It captures and displays the packets in human-readable format by utilizing real time. It is powerful software utilized for troubleshooting network issues for free of cost. It can capture the packets on only those networks that are supported by Pcap, snoop, and network sniffer. Microsoft network monitors are an exception to this. It can capture the packets on these networks as well. It analyzes each packet. It stores captured data into multiple files which can be useful for a

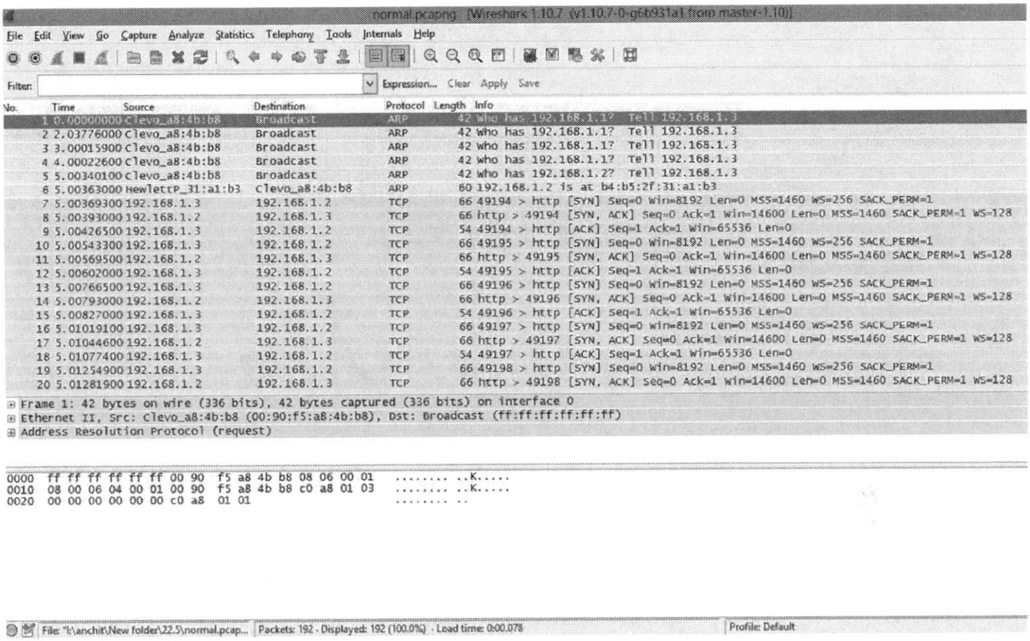

FIGURE 5.5
Wireshark contains normal packets.

longer period of time. It has various functions like stop capture, capture filters, and spam which enable the user to obtain the specific results (outcome) from the given network issues (Figure 5.5).

Wireshark is a cross-platform application. It uses the Qt widget toolkit in its current versions, which implements its user interface and also uses pcap to capture packets; it can run on Microsoft Windows, MacOS, Linux, Solaris, BSD, and some other UNIX-like operating systems. There is one more terminal-based (CUI) version called TShark. Wireshark and the other different programs distributed along with it such as TShark, WShark, etc. are the free software liberated under the conditions of the GNU General Public License. Wireshark is a program or package which acts as a tool for data capturing. It understands the makeup of various networking protocols. It can analyze syntactically and show the fields, along with their significance as specified by various other networking protocols. Wireshark uses the specialized program pcap to capture packets, so it can only capture data packets on the types of networks that are supported by pcap. In the area of computer network management, pcap stands for packet capture, and it consists of an Application Programming Interface (API) for capturing network data traffic. The computers having UNIX operating system implement pcap in the libpcap library; Windows uses a port that belongs to libpcap called WinPcap.

5.4.1.2 Argus

It is an open-source tool and network monitoring application used for network forensics written in Perl language. It shows services of network's status along with server's status. It sends alert when there is any problem. It monitors the results from extracting using graphs and monitors the results from SQL queries. It analyzes the log SQL queries. It also analyzes

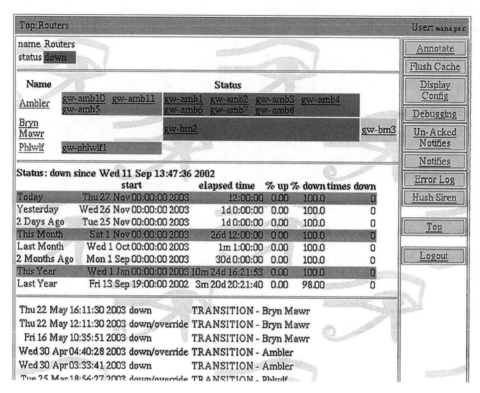

FIGURE 5.6
Argus monitoring software.

the log and provides rate limit multiple notifications to prevent paging floods through graphics. The main advantage of this tool is that it observes umpteen network services such as SNMP, FTP, SMTP, ICMP, HTTP, NTP, WHOIS and many others on common platform. It supports both IPV4 and IPV6 services (Figure 5.6).

5.4.1.3 TCP Dump

TCP Dump is a tool for monitoring the network and debugging protocol and used for the acquisition of data. It is a network packet analyzer which supports the network forensic analysis. This tool works on command line. After capturing the logs, it retains network traffic in different output formats. It filters and collects data. It is able to read packets from network card, interface card, or an old-saved packet life. The communication of other users or systems (computers) can be intercepted and displayed by using TCP Dump (Figure 5.7).

5.4.1.4 OmniPeek

OmniPeek is also one of the best sniffing tools developed by Savvius Company. This tool also supports an application program interface (API). It is also a packet analyzer for protocol analysis, generating the statistics, network visualization, and network troubleshooting. It provides the visibility in real time through network analyzer (Figure 5.8).

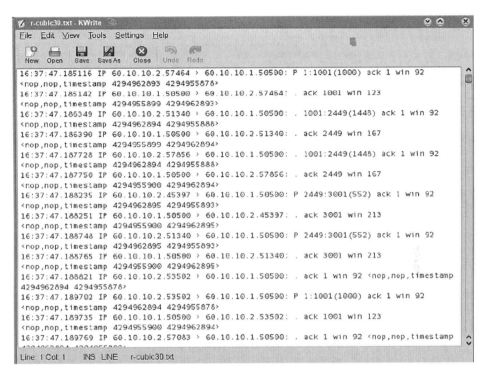

FIGURE 5.7
TCP Dump tool.

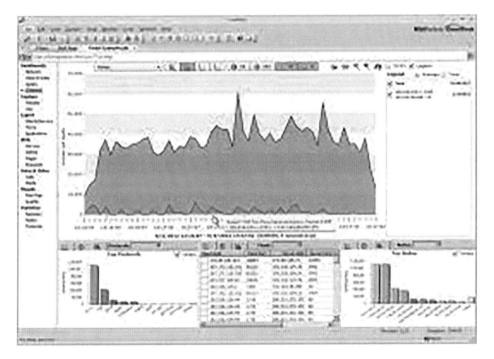

FIGURE 5.8
OmniPeek tool.

5.4.2 Intrusion Detection System (IDS)

Intrusion detection systems are used to detect intrusions, i.e., malicious attacks or abnormal behavior in a system. Unauthorized access to the network and the computer system can be detected by the intrusion detection system. It is a software tool that responds by giving an alert. Data are collected from two main sources which are traffic passing through the network and the hosts connected to the network. IDSs are divided into two categories that is analyze network traffic and those that analyze information available on hosts such as operating system audit trails. The common tools for intrusion detection are as follows.

5.4.2.1 Zeek

Zeek is formerly named Bro. It is first developed by Vern Paxson in 1994. It was named in the reference of fictional character big brother from the novel "nineteen eighty-four". This is an open-source software used for detecting the network vulnerabilities in real time. It is a stand-alone system used for monitoring the passive abnormalities. The advantage of bro system is that it monitors real-time network vulnerability and real-time notification and defines the exact policies, extensibility and the mechanism. It can monitor the DNS, FTP, SNMP, and HTTP traffic.

All the IP network packets are firstly forwarded for the analysis purposes. Pcap captures IP packets and sends it to event engine for accepting or spurning it. Neutral events can be obtained by the analysis of all the ingress record and live and capture traffics by an event engine. It alerts when any contaminated packet triggers. It executes when the zeek tool processes it. This kind of events happens when zeek finds the new transmission control protocol (TCP) connection or any hypertext transfer protocol (HTTP) request. Zeek uses common ports to detect the abnormal packets. The policy script interpreter receives all the accepted packets from the event engine (Figure 5.9).

5.4.2.2 SNORT

It is an extensively used tool for network intrusion detection, prevention, and network forensic analysis. The role of Snort tool is protocol analysis, content searching, and content

FIGURE 5.9
Zeek tool.

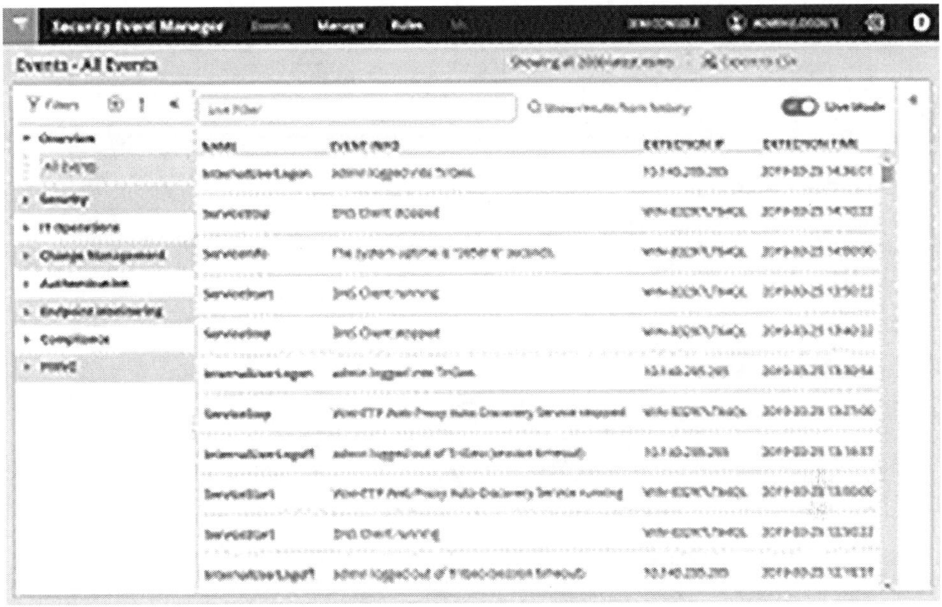

FIGURE 5.10
Snort tool.

matching. This tool can be used for intrusion detection and intrusion prevention, and it is first created by Martin Roesch in 1998. SNORT is an open-source software for the analysis of network traffic in real time. It has an ability to search the content and match the abnormal behavior by an analysis of protocol on the network.

Snort can also detect different events such as fingerprinting, stealth port scans, and attacks. It also has an ability to update the signature and reports in real time. Snort is fully based on libpcap and works for TCP/IP packet sniffer. Snort can detect various attacking methodologies for a buffer flow attack, denial of services (DoS), CGI attacks, and stealth port scans. It detects all precarious payloads with all fishy anomalies. When any abnormal activities reflect on the network, snort tool sends alert to the syslog in real time (Figure 5.10).

5.4.3 Finger

Finger system provides the complete information related to the user whether it ordinary or suspicious. This system can traced the recipient user's address efficiently.

5.4.3.1 Nmap

Nmap is an open-source tool that is used as a security scanner in computer network. The full form of Nmap is network mapper. It specifically sends crafted packets to the target host and analyzes the response. Host discovery, port scanning, version detection, and performing audits are the features of this tool. It checks the system security and identifies the network. It is widely used by the network as well as system administrator. Nmap generates customized packets which is forwarded toward the aim for understanding the response packet. The collection of these packets is further compared with knowledge repository. Knowledge repository basically contains operating system information related to the interpretation of IP stacks for the internet RFC's recommendation (Figure 5.11).

FIGURE 5.11
Network mapper tool.

5.4.3.2 POF

Passive operating system fingerprinting termed as POF is a strong operating system fingerprinting technique that sniffs the packets silently. POF is originally referred to as P0F where zero is in mid. It is created by both Michael Zalewski and Bill Strarns. Unlike Nmap, it is a passive fingerprinting tool for scanning the packets. POF is simple, efficient, invisible, and smother of all the incursion. It is useful for mapping the vulnerabilities to the system, and it can improve the diagnosis for the forensics (Figure 5.12).

POF works as a sniffer, but there is no generation of packets, whereas Nmap is an active fingerprinting tool. This tool has advantages of not to tamper any legitimate traffic with no engagement of intrusion detection system to scan illegitimate traffic. It observes the traffic without generating the packets and then forwards it to the aim. It is having POF-specific operating system fingerprints in knowledgebase. These fingerprints have been included in regular basis as and when it finds some new type of fingerprint. In both endpoints, POF provides high scalability and the fastest identification comparison of Nmap.

5.4.4 Pattern-Based Monitoring Tool

Pattern analysis application tools have some pattern in the payload of the packets, which can be used to identify the protocols.

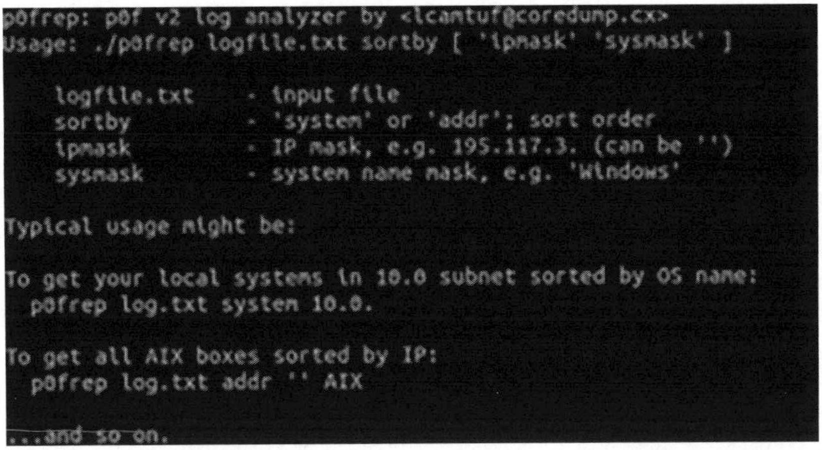

FIGURE 5.12
Passive traffic analysis OS fingerprinting tool.

5.4.4.1 NGREP

Ngrep is a low-level network traffic debugging tool in UNIX. It facilitates specifying hexadecimal expression or is extended to match against data payload of packets. It is useful for identifying and analyzing anomalous network communications, and it debugs the plaintext protocol interactions. It also stores, reads, and reprocesses pcap dumps files at the time of finding a specific data pattern. The advantage of this tool is that it works with HTTP basic authentication and FTP authentication, and it can be utilized for more mundane plain text credential collection. It supports a wide range of protocols such as TCP, UDP, ICMP, IGMP, and PPP (Figure 5.13).

5.4.4.2 TCPXTRACT

TCPxtract is a pattern-based tool that extracts the files on the network that relies on file signature. It is also referred to as one of the data-recovering techniques. It focuses on carving, i.e., file type header and footers. It finds the intercepted file which transmits over the network. It works like a data file system's carver, and it searches the byte sequence to determine the first position and the end position of a file.

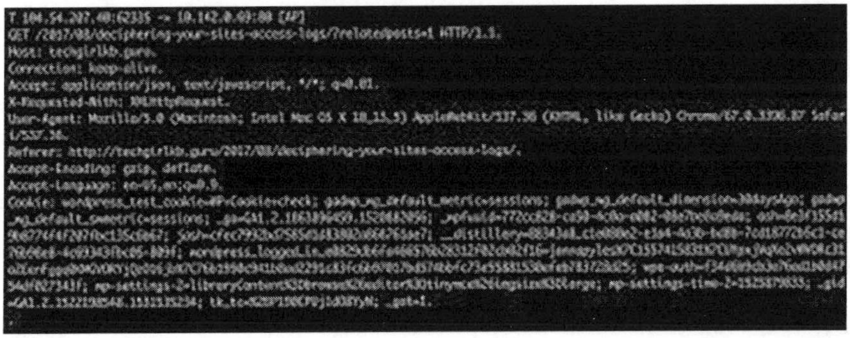

FIGURE 5.13
NGrep tool.

5.4.5 Statistics-Based Monitoring System

Statistics-based monitoring system provides results when the final upshot is proven statistically accurate.

5.4.5.1 NetFlow

It is a software package used to collect, send, process, and generate reports from NetFlow data from Cisco and Juniper routers. This tool is used for deployment. It analyzes the log and filters and collects the data.

5.4.5.2 TCPstat

It is a network security and monitoring tool that captures data transmitted as part of TCP connections. It processes "tcpdump" packet flows also. It allows the analysis of the network traffic and can also reconstruct thousands of TCP connections at a time and saves the results in ordinary files, making it easy to analyze data.

5.5 Analysis Tools

Network forensic analysis tools (NFATs) provide an extended view of the data collected and also allow inspecting the traffic from the protocol stack. NFATs also allow the best possible analysis of security violations. It was determined that the firewalls and intrusion detection systems (IDSs) are the well-developed tools for the network security. But NFATs mutually stimulate with firewalls and IDSs in two ways. They retain a long-term record of the network traffic and allow the quick analysis of the inconvenient spots that are identified by these two tools. While accessing NFATs, it determines what traffic is of the interest and also analyzes that traffic very quickly and efficiently. NFAT performs the three tasks very well: capturing the network traffic, analyzing the network traffic according to the user's needs, and system user discovering the convenient and provocative things about the analyzed traffic.

NFAT must maintain the complete record of the network traffic. For further analysis, a successful NFAT must be able to capture and store the traffic from the fully sopped network. NFAT actually captures the traffic, but under some circumstances, NFAT uses the filter and might be able to eliminate the irrelevant traffic, mitigating the storage and the performance concerns at any cost. Greater the NFAT discarding the traffic, longer will be the interval in which it can extract the traffic, and smaller will be the scope of the possible post hoc analysis. NFAT user interface must simplify the traffic and the content examination. This interface lets the operator precisely specify the traffic which is of interest and avoids viewing the traffic. Generally, network monitoring tools support the criteria for specifying the traffic such as IP addresses, end point media access control (MAC), TCP, or UDP port numbers. NFAT systems can enhance this by granting the selection procedure according to the user or file names, specific content types, and so on. NFAT user interface must specify the selection criteria easy and definite.

Network forensic analysis tools support the concepts of security in deepness as they can analyze the network traffic and correlate data from other security tools. This is required by the security administrators as they need to have multiple levels of security. According to the Information Security Magazine, NFAT can be defined as follows: NFAT products capture and retain all network traffic and provide the tools for forensic analysis. NFAT user can replay, isolate, and analyze an attack or suspicious behavior and then boost the network security accordingly. NFATs in general help the security administrators to monitor the security firewalls, obtaining information about rogue servers, to manage the data flow going in and coming out of the network and offer a better way to record all the events. These analysis tools can be bifurcated into open-source tool and proprietary-based tools. These tools are following.

5.5.1 Open-Source Tool

Open-source tools are those that perform a specific task. Open-source tools are available everywhere without any charges. The source codes of open-source tool are published openly. It is further distributed and can be modified as per the user requirement. The advantages of such kind of software are that it is user intrinsic like modification, free download, accessible, and transferable for another user project.

5.5.1.1 NetworkMiner

It is a network forensic analysis tool. This tool is used as a passive network sniffer/packet capturing tool in order to detect operating systems, sessions, hostnames, open ports, etc. without putting any traffic on the network. This tool can be used in different platforms. Pcap files can also be parsed and further analyzed by the NetworkMiner tool when the user is offline too. This analysis can also regenerate the transmitted file. The main purpose of this tool is to gather evidence for the forensic investigation. It collects the data from network traffic, and it is not a very heavy tool so it does not take more storage. This tool is very much helpful for incident response, law enforcement, and forensics. NetworkMiner contains multiple functions such as live sniffing, parsing pcap files, extracting files from FTP, TFTP, HTTP, SMTP, POP, OS fingerprinting, and command line scripting support.

5.5.1.2 PyFlag

It is a network forensic analysis tool and a web-based and log analysis GUI framework. This tool is written in python. It parses and extracts pcap files and breaks this in low-level protocols like TCP or UDP, IP, and Ethernet. The TCP stream reassembler collects TCP packets into stream, and then it performs the retransmission with reordering of the packet. It will work along with the bifurcation mechanism with the higher-level protocol such as HTTP, IRC, and others. It checks the data recursively. It can search the files and build an index and contains the hash databases. The messages from JavaScript pages can easily be extracted by this tool that supports also to interact with Yahoo mail, Hotmail, Gmail, and others. The advantage is that this tool can handle the images coming in different formats.

5.5.2 Proprietary Tools

Proprietary-based tools are the software that completely depends upon the owner of the organization or the creator of the specific tool. The creator of the software or the governing body of the organization prepares all the rules and regulations for their user. They have a right to grant charge-free licenses. Proprietary tools are those that are not commercially available. The creator or owner of a software has a right to operate, maintain, and modify their previous existing application tool.

5.5.2.1 NetIntercept

It is a network monitoring and analyzing tool. It is placed in firewall. It is the combination of hardware and software with complete system, placed into the firewall boarder. It has the ability to store large data logs. NetIntercept can not only decrypt SSH-2 sessions and accept only secure remote administration into the device but also permits other tools to inspect and analyze its log files. Main advantages are capturing the network traffic, analysis of the network traffic, and data discovery. This tool has also an advantage that there is no need to connect the system and no need to monitor and analyze the traffic from the console part of the system. When it is placed into the place, simply it has to connect and plugin to the network at the firewall. It simply captures the traffic from the network and store them on hard disk for further analysis instead of recording in real time. Whenever the tool records the traffic over the period of time, i.e., round a clock, weekly or monthly as per the requirement, and if the size as well as the average bandwidth as per the configuration of the NetIntercept gets shortened, it starts recording the oldest information.

5.5.2.2 SilentRunner

SilentRunner provides a three-dimensional network view to the user so that the user can observe and monitor. It monitors all the packets entering the network and dives graphical view, and it correlates the network traffic. It captures all evidence from the services of the events for analyzing the traffic. It alarms when any abnormality is found in the network.

Now there is a brief introduction about the NFATs in Table 5.1, and the classification is reflected in Figure 5.14.

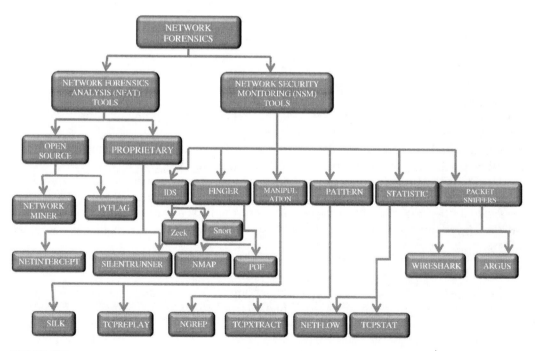

FIGURE 5.14
Network forensics tool classification.

The commercial NFATs available in the market are NetIntercept, NetDetector, Netflow, SilentRunner, EnCase, and VisualRoute. The open source/freeware NFATs are TCPDump/Libpcap/WinDump, Wireshark, Snort, Nmap, P0f, Tcpstat, Tcptrace, and Tcpflow. Various commands are also available which are inbuilt in many modern operating systems and are very useful for network forensics: Nslookup, Traceroute, Netstat, Nbstat, Whois, Ping, and Wget.

There are a number of network forensic analysis tools (NFATs) available in the market that are utilized for commercial purposes. They are listed in Table 5.1.

TABLE 5.1

Analysis Tools

Name of the Tool	Description	Features	Advantages
SilentRunner	Silent Runner provides three-dimensional network view to the user so that user can observe and monitor. It monitors all the packets entering the network and dives graphical view, and it correlates the network traffic.	It captures all evidence from the services of the events for analyzing the traffic	It alarms when any abnormality is found in the network.
NetIntercept	It is a network monitoring and analyzing tool. It is placed in firewall. It is the combination of hardware and software with complete system, placed into the firewall boarder. It has the ability to store large data logs.	NetIntercept can not only decrypt SSH-2 sessions and accept only secure remote administration into the device but also permits other tools to inspect and analyze its log files.	Main advantages are network traffic capture, analysis of the network traffic, and data discovery.
NetDetector	Net detector imports and exports the data in multiple (numerous) heterogenous formats. Primarily NetDetector is a passive capturing, analyzing, and reporting on network traffic. It is supported with an intuitive management console and also has full standard-based reporting tools.	GUI-popus, email or utilized by NetDetector as altering mechanism. NetDetector also enables the security administrator to run a complete forensics investigation by coupling with IDS	Many common network interfaces and internet protocols are supported by NetDetector.
TCPDump	TCPDump is a network packet analyzer which supports the network forensic analysis. This tool works on command line. After capturing the logs, it retains network traffic in different output formats.	It filters and collects data. It is able to read packets from network card, interface card, or an old, saved packet life.	The communication of other users or systems(computers) can be intercepted and displayed by using TCPDump
Ngrep	Ngrep is a low-level network traffic debugging in UNIX. It facilitates specifying hexadecimal expression or extended regularly to match against data payload of packets.	For identifying and analyzing anomalous network communications, it debugs the plaintext protocol interactions. It also stores, reads, and reprocesses pcap dump files at the time of finding a specific data pattern.	With HTTP basic authentication and FTP authentication, it can be utilized for more mundane plain text credential collection.

(Continued)

TABLE 5.1 (*Continued*)

Analysis Tools

Name of the Tool	Description	Features	Advantages
Wireshark	It is an open-source packet analyzer, which is extensively used as a tool for analyzing the network traffic. In the past, it was famous as Ethereal. It captures and displays the packets in human-readable format by utilizing real time. It is powerful software utilized for troubleshooting network issues for free of cost.	It can capture the packets on only those networks, which are supported by Pcap, snoop, and network sniffer. Microsoft network monitors are an exception to this. It can capture the packets on these networks as well.	It analyzes each packet. It stores captured data into multiple files which can be useful for a longer period of time. It has various functions like stop capture, capture filters, and Epan which enable the user to obtain the specific results (outcome) from the given network issues.
Driftnet	The images and audio stream in network traffic is captured by Driftnet. It is also known as a "graphical tcpdump" for UNIX.	Driftnet is used to capture MPEG audio stream from the network and play it through a player such as mpg123. Images may be saved by clicking on them.	-
Network Miner	This tool is used as a passive network sniffer/packet capturing tool in order to detect operating systems, sessions, hostnames, open ports, etc. without putting any traffic on the network. This tool can be used in different platforms.	The main purpose of this tools is to gather evidence for the forensic investigation. It collects the data from network traffic.	It is a network forensic analysis tool
Kismet	It is a packet sniffer intrusion detection system used for observing wireless suspicious activity.	It consists of wireless intrusion detection system.	This tool captures more packets. The sniffed packet's log is traced and stored in a compatible file.
NetStumbler	It facilitates detection of wireless LANs using the various WLAN standards and analyzes the network traffic for the windows.	It is used to verify configurations and search locations in a Wireless LAN	This tool finds out the unauthorized access point.
NetSleuth	This tool is used for network analysis. It analyzes pcap files and fingerprint. This tool is developed for forensic investigation.	Silent port scanning features provide the analysis of pcap file of the attack which is not detected in the network. it monitors the whole network	There is no requirement for the hardware or reconfiguration of networks.
Xplico	This forensic analysis tool is also used for data extraction from traffic. It can rebuild the stored contents with a packet sniffer.	It has the ability to process huge amounts of data and also manages pcap files of many Gbyte and Tbyte.	It can support the decoding of audio codec's and MSTRA.

(Continued)

TABLE 5.1 (*Continued*)

Analysis Tools

Name of the Tool	Description	Features	Advantages
PyFlag	It is a network forensic analysis tool and a web-based and log analysis GUI framework. This tool is written in python.	It parses and extracts pcap files and breaks this in low-level protocols. It checks the data recursively.	It can search the files and build an index and contains the hash databases.
DeepNines	It is a network security monitoring tool for providing real-time network defense for content and applications.	It filters and collects data. It extracts all applications.	-
Argus	It is a system and network monitoring application used for network forensics. It shows services of network's status along with server's status. It sends alert when there is any problem.	It extracts graphs. It monitors the results of SQL queries. It analyzes the log.	It provides rate limit multiple notifications to prevent paging floods.
Fenris	This tool is also used for debugging the code and network forensic analysis.	It filters and collects data.	It features a command line interface as well as a soft ICE-alike GUI and web frontend.
Flow-Tools	It is a software package used to collect, send, and process and generate reports from NetFlow data from Cisco and Juniper routers. This tool is used for deployment.	It analyzes the log and filters and collects the data.	-
EtherApe	It is a graphical monitor tool for storing the network traffic. After filtering the traffic, this tool can read packets from a file.	Live data can be captured	
Honeyd	It is open-source software that allows a user to run and set up multiple virtual hosts on a computer network.	Honeyd provides mechanism for monitoring the traffic and detecting the threats.	-
Snort	It is an extensively used tool for network intrusion detection, prevention, and network forensic analysis. The role of Snort tool is protocol analysis, content searching, and content matching.	It is used to detect the attacks including CGI, buffer overflows, stealth port scans, etc. It filters and collects data.	It generates real-time traffic analysis.
NetWitness	It shows the different network forensic threat analyses, the protection from data leakage, and compliance verification.	It provides the data stream and correlation features.	-
Solera	It provides network forensics classification analysis.	It captures high-speed data.	It improves the network security and optimizes network performance.

(Continued)

TABLE 5.1 (*Continued*)

Analysis Tools

Name of the Tool	Description	Features	Advantages
TCP Flow	It is a network security and monitoring tool that captures data transmitted as part of TCP connections. It processes "tcpdump" packet flows also.	It allows the analysis of the network traffic and also can reconstruct thousands of TCP connections at a time and saves the results in ordinary files and makes easy to analyze data.	-
NfDump	It collects and process Netflow data on the command line. Various tools fall under it which is working with Netflow format	It displays the Netflow data and creates the statistics of the flow IP addresses, ports, etc.	-
Nmap	It is a security scanner used in computer network. It specifically sends crafted packets to the target host and analyzes the response.	Host discovery, port scanning, and version detection are the features of this tool.	It checks the system security and identifies the network.

Questions

Q.1. What are the functions of network forensic analysis tool?

Q.2. "Catch it as you can" statement refers to what? Clarify.

Q.3. What do understand by open-source tools? Explain it with few examples.

Q.4. What do you understand by proprietary tools? Explain it with few examples.

Q.5. What do you understand by the statement, "stop, look, and listen"?

Q.6. Which tools come under "catch it as you can"? Explain with examples.

Q.7. Explain the tools under "stop, look, and listen"?

Q.8. How analysis tools work for the analysis of network forensics? Explain in detail.

Q.9. Explain statistics-based network monitoring system in detail.

Q.10. Explain all pattern-based forensic tools in detail.

Q.11. Explain the intrusion detection and prevention tools in detail.

References

A. Bijalwan and E. S. Pilli, "Crime Psychology Using Network Forensics," *Computer Engineering & Information Technology*, vol. 2014, pp. 1–4, 2015.

A. Bijalwan and E. S. Pilli, Understanding Botnet on Internet, *Computational Intelligence and Computing Research (ICCIC), 2014 IEEE International Conference on* (pp. 1–5), IEEE, 2014.

A. Bijalwan, S. Sando, and M. Lemma, "An Anatomy for Recognizing Network Attack Intention," *International Journal of Recent Technology & Engineering*, vol. 8, no. 3, pp. 803-816, 2019.

A. Bijalwan, V. K. Solanki, and E. S. Pilli, "Botnet Forensic: Issues, Challenges and Good Practices," *Network Protocols & Algorithms*, vol. 10, no. 2, pp. 28–51, 2018.

M. I. Cohen, "PyFlag-An advanced Network Forensic Framework," *Digital Investigation*, vol. 5, pp. S112–S120, 2008.

G. Costa and A. De Franceschi, "Xplico Internet Traffic Decoder-Network Forensics Analysis Tool," 2012. Available: http://www.xplico.org/, 21 Dec 2013.

S. Enterprises, "Netintercept: A network analysis and visibility tool," www.sandstorm.com.

C. P. Garrison, *Digital Forensics for Network, Internet, and Cloud Computing: A Forensic Evidence Guide for Moving Targets and Data*: Syngress, 2010.

R. Hunt, New Developments in Network Forensics-Tools and Techniques, *18th IEEE International Conference on Networks (ICON), Singapore (pp. 376–381)*, IEEE, 2012.

V. Jacobson, C. Leres, and S. McCanne, "TCPDUMP public repository," www.tcpdump.org, 2003.

J. Judge, M. Sogrin, and A. Troussov, "Galaxy: IBM Ontological Network Miner," *CSSW*, vol. 113, pp. 157–160, 2007.

U. Kuenapfel, H. Krumm, C. Kuhn, M. Huebner, and B. Neisius, "Endosurgery Simulation with Kismet, a Flexible Tool for Surgical Instrument Design, Operation Room Planning and VR Technology Based Abdominal Surgery Training, B. Groettrup," *Proc. Virtual Reality World95*, pp. 165–171, 1995.

G. F. Lyon, *Nmap Network Scanning: The Official Nmap Project Guide to Network Discovery and Security Scanning*: Insecure, 2009.

M. Milner, "Netstumbler v0. 4.0," San Diego, CA, Available at http://downloads.netstumbler.com/downloads/netstumbler v0.4.0release notes.pdf, Apr. 18, 2007, 10 pages.

A. Orebaugh, G. Ramirez, and J. Beale, *Wireshark & Ethereal Network Protocol Analyzer Toolkit*: Syngress, 2006.

J. Ritter, "ngrep," Network grep., J RITTER: http://ngrep.sourceforge.net/, 1999.

M. Roesch, Snort: Lightweight Intrusion Detection for Networks, in LISA (vol. 99, pp. 229–238), 1999.

M. J. Schoelles and W. D. Gray, "Argus: A Suite of Tools for Research in Complex Cognition," *Behavior Research Methods, Instruments, & Computers*, vol. 33, no. 2, pp. 130–140, 2001.

P. Venezia, "NetDetector Captures Intrusions," *InfoWorld*, vol. 25, no. 27, p. 32, 2003.

6

Network Forensics Techniques

LEARNING OBJECTIVES

This chapter discusses about all network forensics techniques. It also differentiates between conventional and advanced forensics techniques based on their advantages. After reading this chapter, you would

- Have knowledge about network forensics.
- Understand conventional network forensics techniques.
- Understand advanced network forensics techniques.

6.1 Introduction

Network forensics is a nascent science that generally works for three uses, i.e., monitoring the abnormalities on network, identifying the clues, and analyzing all evidences by law enforcement. It acts on two theories "stop, look, and listen" and "catch it as you can". Attackers have a tendency to delete all their evidence from their compromised network, but the network evidence can be preserved through continuous monitoring in real time, and subsequently efficient techniques help to investigate the crime for incident response. Crime response is convenient on the collected information which validates and assesses the event by organization strategy, authorized, and business constraint. It secures against future attacks and recovers from the existing damage, and preplanning is initiated. At the same time, the decision whether to continue the investigation and gather more information is also taken. A similar response is to be initiated after the investigation phase where the information obtained may require certain actions to control and reduce the attack.

The network forensics techniques find the vulnerabilities from the network by recording, capturing, and analyzing the events using different tools. The network forensics investigation of digital evidence is predominantly employed as a postincident response to an activity that cannot be defined definitely as to an incident or that does not comply with the organizational norms and policies. There are some existing techniques used to perform the network forensics techniques. These techniques help to identify, detect, and mitigate attack and are further used for incident response. This chapter describes related technologies that show their connection to network forensics and also their limitations. These techniques help us to detect, prevent, and mitigate the attacks from the network.

These network forensics techniques are classified as follows (Figure 6.1).

DOI: 10.1201/9781003045908-8

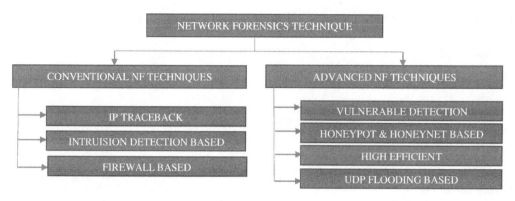

FIGURE 6.1
Network forensics techniques.

6.1.1 Conventional Network Forensics Technique

1. IP traceback Technique.
2. Intrusion detection-based techniques.
3. Firewall-based techniques.

6.1.2 Advanced Network Forensics Technique

1. Vulnerability detection techniques.
2. Honeypots and honeynet-based techniques.
3. Highly efficient techniques.
4. Random-UDP flooding technique.

These network forensics techniques are explained in detail in the following.

6.2 Conventional Network Forensics Technique

Conventional network forensics technique is almost utilized from the existence of the term network forensics. It is a method that has been adapted and utilized for a long time. Some of the conventional network forensics techniques are provided in Figure 6.2.

6.2.1 IP Traceback Technique

The IP traceback techniques allow a victim to identify the network paths traversed by the attack traffic without requiring interactive operational support from internet service provider. If the connection path between the attacker and the victim is given by $h_1, h_2, h_3, ...,$ h_n, then IP traceback problem is to find the hosts $h_1, h_2, ..., h_{n-1}$ given the IP address of the victim h_n. It is mainly used to deal with the masquerade attacks which can be produced at different layers. The IP traceback problem is considered very hard to resolve due to many reasons. The first reason is that an attack packet may be easily spoofed at different layers

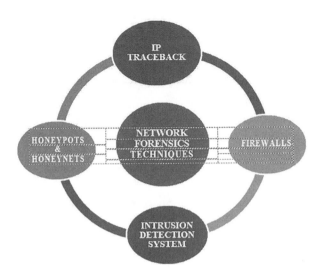

FIGURE 6.2
Main network forensics techniques.

of the TCP/IP protocol stack, which makes the identification of its original application difficult. In fact, an attack packet may be spoofed at the link layer by using a different MAC address than the original one, at the Internet layer by using a different source IP address, at the transport layer by using a different TCP/IP port, or at the application layer by using a different email address.

The second reason is that the attack flow may be generated by a remotely controlled host or may travel through a chain of compromised hosts, called stepping-stone, acting as a conduit for the attacker's communication. Another reason is that the security functions practiced in existing networks may also prevent the capability to follow the reverse path. For example, if the attacker lies behind a firewall, then most of the traceback packets are filtered at the firewall and one may not be able to exactly reach the attacker. Even with these difficulties, some IP traceback techniques have been proposed. Here we describe the major existing IP traceback techniques that have been designed to trace back to the origin of IP packets through the Internet.

IP traceback techniques are categorized as link state testing, input debugging, controlled flooding, ICMP traceback, packet marking, payload attribution, and Source Path Isolation Engine.

6.2.1.1 Link State Testing

This testing has to be used while the attack is in progress, and it consists of a traceback procedure from the router closest to the victim and thus determines the upstream link that is used to carry out the attack traffic. This technique is then recursively applied on the upstream routers until the source is reached.

6.2.1.2 Input Debugging

Debugging is the process of identifying the errors and further rectifying those identified errors from the network. The input debugging scheme as an IP traceback technique finds the source of attack signature. The nature of input debugging is based on the following characteristics:

Attack Signature: It can be defined as the common feature contained in all the attack packets.

Procedure: The victim recognizes that it is being attacked and communicates the attack signature to the upstream router which then employs filters that prevent the attack packets from being forwarded and then determines the port of entry. This is repeated recursively on the upstream routers until the originating site is reached or the trace leaves the boundary of the network provider or the ISP. Then, the ISP is requested to carry on this procedure.

Limitation: A considerable management overhead at the ISP level to communicate and coordinate the traceback across the domains limits the effectiveness of input debugging.

6.2.1.3 Controlled Flooding

In controlled flooding technique, the victim has to obtain the map of the Internet topology initially. The victim then selects hosts iteratively which could be coerced to flood each of the incoming links of the upstream router. The nature of controlled flooding is as follows:

Procedure: The victim forces the host to flood the links to upstream router. Since the router buffer is shared by all incoming links and the attacker also uses one of the links, due to flooding, the attacker packets would be dropped. The victim then analyzes the traffic of the attacker packets being received and then draws a conclusion about the path taken by the router. Once the router is reached, the same procedure is applied until the source is reached.

Limitations: An accurate topology map is needed for selecting the hosts, and it is indeed a complicated procedure to use flooding to detect distributed DOS attacks when multiple upstream links may be contributing to the attack.

6.2.1.4 ICMP Traceback

The internet control message protocol (ICMP) is a network layer protocol used for sending error messages. Network devices such as routers use this protocol for sending error messages that refer to the failure or success of the packets. Unlike transport protocols such as TCP and UDP that use exchanging data between systems, it is an error-reporting protocol to source internet protocol (IP). It indicates that packet delivery is unable to reach to the specific router or to the host. This protocol is not a transport protocol that forwards packet between systems. It does not use end-user application; however, it helps to troubleshoot an internet connection.

This technique also proposed an IP traceback by using a scheme called iTrace. This scheme is applicable for attacks that originate from a few sources and consists of flooding.

Procedure: Each router will sample one of the packets it is forwarding and copy the contents into an ICMP traceback message. This ICMP will have information about adjacent routers, and the message will be sent to the destination. The iTrace scheme uses HMAC and supports the use of X.509 digital certificates for authenticating and evaluating ICMP traceback messages.

Limitations: There are mainly two limitations. Firstly, ICMP traffic gets filtered compared to normal traffic. Secondly, all the routers in the attack must be enabled with iTrace, or else the destination would have to reconstruct several possible attack paths that have a sequence of participating routers.

6.2.1.5 Packet Marking Techniques

Generally, packet marking is a technique in which packet is to be marked when the router receives any packet; it generates a random number which is compared with the predefined value. The nature of packet marking technique is as follows:

Principle: The principle of this technique is that the path is sampled one node at a time. It is a probabilistic packet marking (PPM) technique that allows the traceback for an attack flow.

Procedure: The basic idea behind this technique is that during forwarding, routers probabilistically write partial path information into the packets, and there is a reserved field called marking which is large enough to hold a single router address in the packet header. For IPV4, the address is noted in the 32-bit field in the options portion of the IP header. The router writes its own address in the node field with a probability p. In such a case, the victim would receive at least one sample for every router in the attack path. The probability that a router marks a packet is p and is the same for all the routers. The probability of receiving a packet marked from a router d hops away and not marked by any other router is p (1–p) d.

6.2.1.6 Source Path Isolation Engine

Principle: The source path isolation engine (SPIE) is a hash-based technique that generates audit trials for traffic within a network. It creates hash digests of packets based on the packet header and a payload fragment. These are then stored in a bloom filter and used to trace the origin of any single packet delivered by the network in the recent past.

Architecture: The source path isolation engine is implemented independently within each autonomous system. It consists of three major architectural components

Data Generation Agent (DGA): It is in charge of computing the digests and storing them in the bloom filter.

SPIE Collection and Reducing Agent (SCAR): It generates the attack path within a region of AS by querying the DGAs in the region and based on the replies from the DGAs compiles the attack path.

SPIE Trackback Manager (STM): All the requests for the attack path are directed to the STM. It generates requests to the SCARs and then combines all the attack paths returned by the SCARs to form a complete attack path through the AS.

It is possible to trace an attack path for a single packet that traversed through various autonomous systems some of which might not have deployed SPIE.

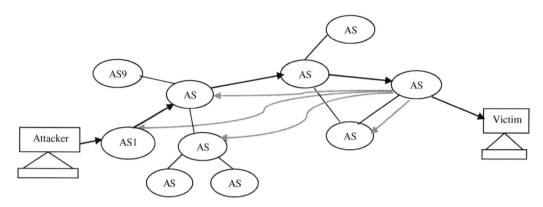

FIGURE 6.3
A network consisting of autonomous systems with and without SPIE.

In Figure 6.3, the attacker launches an attack from AS10 to AS1. When the victim reports about the attack packet to the STM in AS1, the STM queries its one-hop STMs in other ASes about the attacker. In this case, it queries STM in AS7, which then conducts an internal trace back and sends a negative reply upon which AS1 queries its two hop neighbors AS3 and AS4. These ASes' STMs then send a positive reply indicating the attack path in their AS. AS3 will redirect AS1 to AS10, and then upon query from AS1, the STM of AS10 conducts an internal traceback to identify the attacker in its system and reports the attack path. In this figure, curved arrow shows the positive reply message where the reverse arrow from AS1 to AS7 generates a negative reply messages.

6.2.1.7 Payload Attribution

In most of the cases, an investigator may not have any header information about a packet of interest but is aware of a part of the payload which he expects. The payload attribution requires the identification of sources, destinations, and the times of appearance on a network of all the packets that contained such payload. This problem is more complex because the size of the payload is usually very large, and information of the numerous substrings needs to be stored. The hierarchical bloom filter plays a key role in a payload attribution system. It has low-memory footprints and has a good processing speed at a low false positive rate. The implementation of HBF consists of breaking a string of length p into p/s blocks which are inserted into the HBF at level 0. At the next level, two subsequent blocks are combined and inserted into the HBF at level 1. In Figure 6.4, S0, S1, S2, and S3 carry offset 0, 1, 2, and 3, respectively.

6.2.2 Intrusion Detection System

Intrusion detection systems are used to detect intrusions, i.e., malicious attacks or abnormal behavior in a system. It responds by giving an alert. Data are collected from two main sources which are traffic passing through the network and the hosts connected to the network. Therefore, according to their deployment, IDSs are divided into two categories: those that analyze network traffic and those that analyze information available on hosts such as operating system audit trails. Intrusion detection systems are used to detect intrusions, i.e., malicious attacks or abnormal behavior in a system. Unauthorized access to the

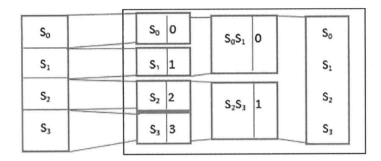

FIGURE 6.4
Payload attribution with string insertion.

network and the computer system can be detected by the intrusion detection system. It is a software tool that responds by giving an alert. The current trend in intrusion detection is to combine both host-based and network-based information to develop hybrid systems.

It is broadly classified as follows.

6.2.2.1 Knowledge- or Signature-Based IDS

In knowledge- or signature-based IDS, the incoming packets are compared with known patterns of attacks which are used to detect malicious threats, and if matches are found, then the alert is generated. The basic motivation is to measure how close a behavior is to some previously established standards of misuse or normal behavior. Depending on the level of a priori or domain knowledge, it is possible to design detectors for specific categories of attack (e.g., denial of service, user to root, remote to local).

6.2.2.2 Behavior- or Anomaly-Based IDS

In this method, the incoming traffic which does not match the normal or expected or behavior is alerted to be an intrusion. Intrusion detection systems can be implemented at network-level, host-level, or application-level IDS and work effectively in these levels. Intrusion detection systems assist by generating alerts, which can enable investigation process in network forensic systems. The basic functionality is just detection not investigation.

Sometimes, intrusion detection systems can give wrong alerts, i.e., false alarms, called as either false positives or false negatives. False positive refers to flagging of an alert, even though an attack has not occurred. False negative refers to inability to flag an alert, even though an attack has occurred. The anomaly detection first requires the IDS to define and characterize the correct and acceptable static form and dynamic behavior of the system, which is then used to detect abnormal changes or anomalous behaviors. An IDS is shown in Figure 6.5.

6.2.3 Firewalls

The firewall is a network security system that controls the incoming and outgoing network traffic based on a set of rules. It can be either hardware or software and acts as a barrier between the trusted network and other untrusted or less trusted networks like Internet.

It actually prevents the malicious attacks from entering the protocol unit by the rules that control the access in and out flow. Although the firewall detects some attacks and

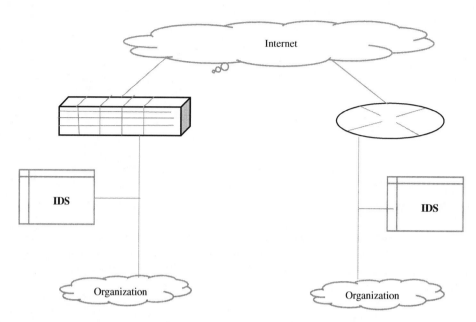

FIGURE 6.5
Intrusion detection system.

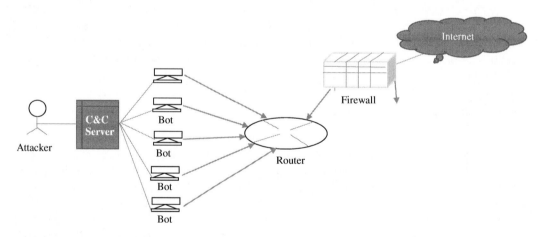

FIGURE 6.6
Structure of firewall.

viruses, it also has some limitations. The firewall becomes weaker and less effective as the attack model of the attacks changes day by day. The attacks occur as they are generated in the local network and firewall can just filter the packets from the WAN, as shown in Figure 6.6. The firewall is installed between the WAN and the LAN. The firewall can be divided into different categories as follows.

6.2.3.1 Network-Level Firewall

It is also called packet filters that operate at a relatively low level of the TCP/IP protocol stack, thus preventing packets to pass through the firewall unless they match the established rule set. It is of two types: stateful and stateless. The stateful firewalls maintain the information about the active session and use that state information to speed up the processing of the packets. The stateless firewall needs less memory and can be faster for simple filters that require less time to filter than to look up.

6.2.3.2 Application-Level Firewall

It works at the application level of the TCP/IP stack and may intercept all packets that travel to and from an application. They function by determining whether a process should accept any connection. They filter connections by examining the process ID of data packets against a rule set for the local process involved in the data transmission.

6.2.3.3 Proxy Firewall

Proxy server may act as a firewall by responding to input packets in a manner of an application while blocking other packets. It is a gateway from one network to another for a particular network application, in the sense that it functions as a proxy on behalf of the network user.

6.3 Advanced Network Forensics Techniques

Advanced network forensics techniques are utilized to find out the latest attacks propagated by an attacker. These techniques help to reduce the risk of attacks and involves in identifying, detecting, and mitigating the attacks and perform incident response on them. Some of the advanced network forensics techniques are as follows.

6.3.1 Vulnerability Detection Techniques

Vulnerability means weakness and severity level and refers to the exploitation range that is anything that can be exploited remotely. The weakness in the context of vulnerabilities can be any application, it can be a code level, or it could be a system based, or it could be system, or it could be something else. It can be explained as a lame security door lock which can be easily compromised by the thieves. A weak security system is a threat to the privacy and property of common men in the normal life. The other mean of weakness which gratuitously controlled and it could be a physically structure or someone forget to close a door and someone barge in and picked up the stuff from the house. Similarly, it is obvious that the weakness on any system, application and processes should be detected and further proceed for mitigation. Severity level is a classification of violation on system or network that depends upon level of seriousness. Generally, based on assessment, vulnerability can be categorized into active vulnerability, passive vulnerability, internal vulnerability, external vulnerability, network vulnerability, host vulnerability, wireless vulnerability, and application vulnerability.

The vulnerability detection technique can also be evaluated by the combination of data fusion, alert generation, and applying correlation mechanism to find out the vulnerabilities. These mechanisms are as follows.

6.3.1.1 Data Fusion, Alert Generation, and Correlation

The literal meaning of fusion means to join more than two things together to form one entity, and this entity refers directly to the data that define data fusion as to combine all segregated information at one place for getting meaningful, relevant, and more intuitive results. This process provides concreate, consistent, and accurate information by collecting all information from multiple data sources. However, the terms data fusion and information fusion are quite similar, but it is quite noticeable that the term data fusion is for the raw data, whereas the information fusion belongs to the processed data. Data fusion is defined by the joint directors of laboratories (JDL) workshop as "A multi-level process dealing with association, correlation, combination of data and information from single and multiple sources to achieve refined position, identify estimates and complete and timely assessments of situations, threats and their significance" (Castanedo 2013). The same term data fusion is also defined by Hall as "Data fusion techniques combine data from multiple sensors and related information from associated databases to achieve improved accuracy and more specific interference than could be achieved by the use of a single sensor alone."

Generally, data fusion technique is categorized into data association, state estimation, and the decision fusion technique. Data association is the technique which determines a set of measurements corresponding to each target. State estimation also refers to a tracking technique in which all the target observations cannot be relevant every time. The estimation problem finds the value of vector such as its velocity, size, and also position that can be fit with the observed data. Decision fusion is completely relied on knowledge of the perceived situation that can be taken by different sources in data fusion domain. It makes a high interference about the activities that are produced from the identified targets.

As the term correlation refers, this correlation technique shows a strong relationship among the variables that extract outcome through statistical methods. Correlation technique is able to analyze the suspicious network vulnerabilities. This technique helps to extract more valuable reconstruction of events. Correlation analysis can be done through various methodologies. Flow correlation technique is one among them to analyze the network that can be correlated to traffic flow over input and output links. Flow-based correlation method can be divided into frequency-based analysis and time domain-based analysis.

There are several techniques which are as follows.

6.3.1.2 Black-Box Testing

Black-box testing is used to refer the analysis of program execution from an external point of view. In short, it compares the software execution outcome with the expected result. In black-box testing, the current result is matched with the expected result on the basis of software requirement specification. There is umpteen ways to utilize black-box test for the network vulnerabilities such as error guessing, boundary value analysis, use case testing, state-transition testing, all pair testing, decision table testing, etc. It also checks the external factors responsible for the failure of the system and check the system as per the requirement.

In this type of testing, the various parameters such as performance issues, abruption of application failure, response time of the system, and system's interaction are to be checked. Black box testing is a method for software security in which the software controls, its defenses and design of an application tested. It takes the same approaches like an attacker applies on the network for intrusion purpose. It gives less false positive rate than other testing methodologies.

6.3.1.3 White-Box Testing

White-box analysis examines the code without executing it. Developers can do this in one of two ways: manually, during code inspections and reviews, and automatically, using automated analysis tools. There are various tools the tester uses for testing like WinRunnner and Quick Test Professional. The tester in white-box testing knows complete information about the system such as its IP addresses, installed software version, operating system, configuration, etc. The system tester has the capability to identify the vulnerabilities and validate it from the system and from the network. White-box testing makes the organization safe from the attacker as they do not have access to carry sensitive information.

White-box testing can also be utilized by umpteen ways like path testing, decision coverage, branch testing, statement coverage, prime path testing, data flow testing, control flow testing, etc. In this kind of network forensic techniques, security can be evaluated through the internal structure, design, and coding of software, and it is also verified through the flow input and output, usability, and the security. Generally, white-box testing has three types of techniques: branch coverage, path coverage, and statement coverage. Branch coverage technique performs a series of tests for ensuring that all the branches should be tested at least once. Path coverage technique performs everything possible to cover testing including all branches as well as statements, whereas statement coverage performs on all programming statement with minimal test.

6.3.1.4 Double-Guard Detecting Techniques

Double-guard detection is used to detect the network behavior of user sessions across both the front-end web server and the back-end database (Figure 6.7). It helps to produce alert, identify a wide range of attacks, and monitor both web and database requests. Double-guard detection technique provides the user an isolation in which it makes them separate on web server. It seems like different web servers are assigned to different users, but actually web servers virtually act as multiple servers. Black box testing is a method for software security in which the software controls, its defenses and design of an application tested.

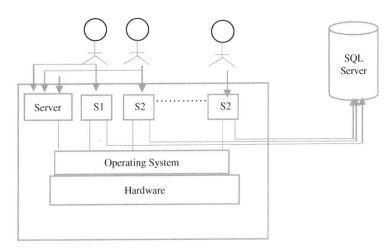

FIGURE 6.7
Double-guard detection system.

6.3.1.5 Hidden Markov Models

Attacks exploit web application vulnerabilities which are derived from the input validation. Hence, to detect these attacks, a new analysis is performed through Hidden Markov Model (HMM) which describes that they are very effective in detecting a wide range of either known or unknown attacks of web applications. HMM is applied mostly in host-based IDS to model system call sequences. HMMs are used to improve the performance that can be increased when a sequence of symbol is modeled by a group of HMM. It explicitly addresses the problem related to the presence of attacks inside the training set.

6.3.2 Honeypots and Honeynet

Honeypot is defined by Spitzner during 2002 as follows: "Honeypot is a security resource whose values lies in being probed, attacked or compromised". Honeypot is a system that is used for collecting high-value attack data and monitors the activity of an attacker on real-time operating systems. It also acts as an emulator to the services and operating system to detect the traffic that the system gets on the network. The main difference between honeypot system and other systems like intrusion detection system and firewall is that the honeypot captures a higher volume of data in real time, which means the security experts can have a high-value log file on the network.

Honeynet is a trapping system that allures the attacks for knowing the intention of attacker and their vulnerabilities. It is a network setup for inviting attacks for investigation of the latest attacks too.

6.3.2.1 Honeypot

Honeypot is a system set up to attract and trap the attackers. It acts as a decoy system posing itself to the Internet as a legitimate system offering services. Usually, honeypots are stand-alone systems, and any traffic directed to the honeypot is considered an attack or intrusion. If an outbound traffic is observed from a honeypot, it is an indication that the honeypot has been compromised and initiated to perform some activity. A honeypot could range from a simple port listening socket program to a full production system that could be emulated under various operating systems.

6.3.2.2 Honeynet

A honeynet is a network designed for the purpose of being compromised which could be used to observe the activities and behavior of the intruder. Honeypot is the part and parcel of a honeynet for the investigation of the latest attacks.

6.3.2.3 Classification of Honeypots

Honeypot can be classified into low- and high-interaction honeypots. They are explained as follows:

  Low-Interaction Honeypots: A limited number of configured services are available for an adversary to probe the system.

  High-Interaction Honeypots: An adversary can access all aspects of operating systems and launch further network attacks.

6.3.2.4 Honeywall

In order to protect nonhoneypot systems from attacks originating from a compromised honeypot, a honeywall could be set up with several data control and data capture features. It can also nullify the effect of malicious data packets that specifically target vulnerabilities on other systems. A honeywall can capture and monitor the data traffic entering, leaving, or inside the honeypot which could be then used to track the procedure adopted by the attacker to get hold of the honeypot. Encryption software is sometimes used by the attacker to encrypt the communication between the machine and honeypot, which couldn't be detected by honeywall. In such a case, a software called Sebek can be deployed which decrypts the data.

6.3.2.5 Architecture Types of Honeynet

The general architecture of honeypot can be serial and parallel. The types based on the architecture of the honeypot are the following.

6.3.2.5.1 Serial Architecture

In this architecture, the honeywall filters all the traffic intended to the firewall of the production system, and also all the traffic for the production system goes through the honeynet. If a honeynet is attacked, the production system is alerted about it. After collecting enough evidence, the honeynet is stopped, and analysis of the malicious packets starts.

Merit: It protects a production system from direct attacks.

Demerit: A delay would be suffered for every incoming and outgoing packet including the naïve traffic.

6.3.2.5.2 Parallel Architecture

This mainly aims at reducing the delay by exposing both production system and honeynets to the Internet. The function of the honeynet is now to analyze the malicious packets and then update the firewall about it which would then impose stringent conditions on the traffic.

Merit: Delay is reduced.

Demerit: This presents a high risk as the system is directly under attack.

6.3.3 Highly Efficient Techniques for Network Forensics

Cybercrimes are increasing day by day with the increase in the usage of the Internet. To prevent these crimes, there is a need for the good and efficient tools and techniques to investigate these crimes. Identifying the sources and destinations of all packets that appeared on a network and contained a certain excerpt of a payload, a process called *payload attribution* can be an extremely valuable tool to determine the perpetrators or the victims of a network event and to analyze security incidents in general. Here we present new methods for payload attribution which substantially improve over these state-of-the-art payload attribution systems. This approach constitutes a crucial component of a network forensic system that can be easily integrated into any existing network monitoring system. These techniques are capable of effectively querying for a small passage of a payload but can also be extended to handle the passage that spans several packets. The accuracy of attribution increases with the length of the passage and the specificity of the query. Then, the collected payload can be stored, and queries can be performed by an untrusted party without disclosing any payload information. Now, a short description about these techniques is represented below:

6.3.3.1 Bloom Filters

Bloom filters are space efficient probabilistic data structures supporting queries and are used in many networks and other applications. An empty bloom filter is a bit vector of m bits, all set to 0, that uses k different hash functions, each of which maps a key value to one of the m positions in the vector. To insert an element into the Bloom filter, we compute the k hash function values and set the bits at the corresponding k positions to 1. To test whether an element was inserted, we hash the element with these k hash functions and check if all corresponding bits are set to 1, in which case we say the element is in the filter. The space savings of a Bloom filter is achieved at the cost of introducing false positives; the greater the savings, the greater the probability of a query returning a false positive. While we use Bloom filters, our payload attribution techniques can be easily modified to use any data structure which allows insertion and querying for strings with no changes to the structural design and implementation of the attribution methods.

6.3.3.2 Rabin Fingerprinting

Rabin fingerprinting method was first proposed by a famous Israeli mathematician and computer scientist Michael Oser Rabin. Rabin fingerprinting is a method through which fingerprint can be implemented through finite field polynomial. It is a defined fingerprinting scheme for binary strings based on polynomials. Fingerprints are the short checksums of strings having the property that the probability of two different objects having the same fingerprint is very small. This scheme has found several applications, for example, defining block boundaries for identifying similar files and for web caching. Fingerprinting scheme is derived for the payload content and uses it to pick content-dependent boundaries for a priori unknown substrings of a payload.

6.3.3.3 Winnowing

Winnowing is an efficient fingerprinting algorithm enabling accurate detection of full and partial copies between documents. It works as follows: for each sequence of k consecutive characters in a document, we compute its hash value and store it in an array. Thus, the first item in the array is a hash of $c_1c_2\ldots c_k$, the second item is a hash of $c_2c_3\ldots c_{k+1}$, etc., where c_i are the characters in the document for $i=1,\ldots,n$. We then slide a window of size w through the array of hashes and select the minimum hash within each window. If there are more hashes with the minimum value, we choose the rightmost one. These selected hashes form the fingerprint of the document. They show that fingerprints selected by winnowing are better for document fingerprinting than the subset of Rabin fingerprints which contain hashes equal to 0 mod p, for some fixed p, because winnowing guarantees that in any window of size w, there is at least one hash selected. We will use this idea to select boundaries for blocks in packet payloads.

6.3.3.4 Attribution Systems

Various research studies have been made to design and implement feasible network traffic traceback systems to identify the machines that directly generate malicious traffic and the network path followed. But these approaches restrict the queries to network floods, connection chains, or the entire payload of a single packet in the best case. The Source Path Isolation Engine (SPIE) is a hash-based technique for IP traceback that generates audit trails for traffic within a network. It creates hash digests of packets based on the packet header and a payload fragment and stores them in Bloom filters in routers. The router creates a packet digest for every forwarded packet using the packet's non-mutable header fields and a short prefix of the payload and stores it in a Bloom filter for a predefined time. When an attack is detected by IDS, SPIE can be used to trace the packet attack path back to the source by querying SPIE devices along the path.

The Hierarchical Bloom Filter (HBF) is introduced by Shammuga Sundaram that is a compact hash-based payload digest data structure. For distributed forensics network, a payload attribution system based on HBF is a key module. The system achieves both low memory footprint and a reasonable processing speed at a low false positive rate. SPIE and HBF both are digesting techniques, but SPIE is a packet digesting scheme, while HBF is a payload digesting technique. An alternative approach to the payload attribution problem has been proposed called the Rolling Bloom Filter (RBF). This technique uses packet content fingerprints based on a generalization of the Rabin-Karp string-matching algorithm. Instead of aggregating queries in a hierarchy as an HBF, they aggregate query results linearly from multiple Bloom filters. They report performance similar to the best-case performance of the HBF. The RBF's performance is comparable to that of HBF, and RBF achieves low false positive rates only for small data reduction ratios.

When incorporated into a network forensic system, these techniques provide an efficient probabilistic query mechanism to answer queries for excerpts of a payload that passed through the network. These methods allow data reduction ratios greater than 100:1 while having a very low false positive rate. These techniques allow queries for very small excerpts of a payload and also for excerpts that span multiple packets. Moreover, privacy is achieved by one-way hashing with a secret key in a Bloom filter. Thus, even if the system is compromised, no raw traffic data are ever exposed, and querying the system is possible only with the knowledge of the secret key.

6.3.4 UDP Flooding Technique

The Internet is an important part of modern life. It is a collection of communicating computers. People connect over the Internet with each other and share the information. The Internet also facilitates the access to and utilization of the resources around the globe. Though the Internet has become very useful, it also has some disadvantages as it is vulnerable to various attacks. The information exchanges over the Internet are not secure, and the internet resources can be easily attacked. Sometimes, these resources are unavailable to the authorized users, because of denial of service (DoS) and distributed denial of service (DDoS) attacks. An attacker system (bot) floods the network with a large number of packets in a short span of time, which further causes DoS attack. The various types of flooding attacks such as HTTP, UDP, floods etc. are popular these days. Some of the deployed intrusion detection systems/firewalls are able to prevent these attacks. But the scenario can be different if we vary the flooding characteristics such as variation in packet size

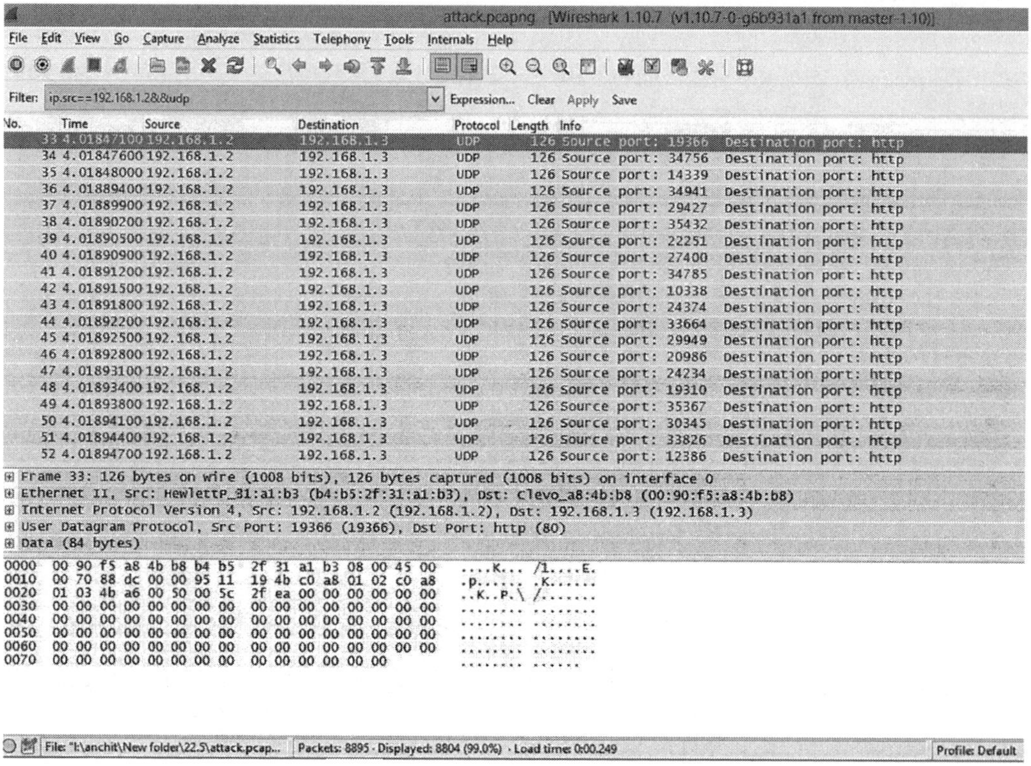

FIGURE 6.8
Flooding UDP datagrams sent by malicious web server.

(random-UDP flooding). Neither the IDS nor the firewall detects the flood because they work on the basis of threshold-based flooding criteria.

UDP flooding is a type of flooding attack in which multiple UDP datagrams are generated by a malicious system (bot) (Figure 6.8). These UDP datagrams flood across the network and when they reach at a system, cause congestion there. This further causes denial of service (DoS) attack. The flooding attack scenario becomes more hazardous, if there are slight changes in the characteristics of flood. The attacker system (bot) generates multiple UDP datagrams of different sizes. These UDP datagrams flood easily across the network without any restriction because every detection system works on the basis of two criteria: The first is signature-based detection, and the second is feature-based detection. Though they are UDP datagrams, their signature seems safe, and they easily pass the detection system. An intrusion detection system (IDS) also does the task of feature-based detection. In feature-based detection, it matches the features of packet flow to the feature of a safe packet flow. If they do not match, it stops those packets. Here, we have designed a malicious script by using a randomized function that runs on a bot. It sends the multiple UDP datagrams of different sizes to a victim system. The sizes of datagrams are different and less than the packet/datagram size threshold value (to prevent the restriction from the IDS/firewall). So, they pass the detection system easily. This type of flooding (random-UDP flooding) attack can be performed very easily.

Questions

Q.1. What do you understand by conventional network forensics techniques?

Q.2. Which network forensics technique comes under advanced network forensics techniques?

Q.3. What are the main differences between conventional and advanced network forensics techniques?

Q.4. Explain the IP takeback technique in detail.

Q.5. Explain packet marking techniques in detail.

Q.6. What do you understand by data fusion, alert generation, and correlation?

Q.7. What does the random-UDP flooding technique do? What is the role of randomizer function?

Q.8. What is winnowing? Explain the winnowing process in detail.

Q.9. Who proposed the Rabin fingerprinting method first? How does this method help to resolve the issues related to network forensics?

Q.10. What do you understand by honeypot? What are the main differences between low- and high-interaction honeypots?

Q.11. Explain the term "honeywall" in detail. Where does the bloom filter work? Explain.

References

C. Adams, "Internet X. 509 public key infrastructure certificate management protocols," RFC 2510, Available at http://www.ietf.org/.

A. Almulhem, "Network Forensics: Notion and Challenges," King Fahd University of Petroleum and Minerals, Dhahran.

A. Bijalwan, S. Sando, and M. Lemma, "An Anatomy for Recognizing Network Attack Intention," *International Journal of Recent Technology & Engineering*, vol. 8, no. 3, pp. 803–816, 2019.

A. Bijalwan, V. K. Solanki, and E. S. Pilli, "Botnet Forensic: Issues, Challenges and Good Practices," *Network Protocols & Algorithms*, vol. 10, no. 2, pp. 28–51, 2018.

A. Bijalwan, M. Wazid, E. S. Pilli, and R. C. Joshi, "Forensics of Random-UDP Flooding Attacks," *Journal of Networks*, vol. 10, no. 5, pp. 287–293, 2015.

F. Castanedo, "A Review of Data Fusion Techniques," The Scientific World Journal, vol. 2013, pp. 1-20 2013.

C. Y. Cho, S. Y. Lee, C. P. Tan, and Y. T. Tan, Network Forensics on Packet Fingerprints, *21st IFIP Information Security Conference (SEC 2006)*, Karlstad, Sweden, 2006.

I. Corona, D. Ariu, and G. Giacinto, HMM-Web: A Framework for the Detect ion of Attacks Against Web Applications, *IEEE International Conference on Communication* (pp. 1–6), IEEE, 2009.

Y. Guan, "Network forensics," in *Computer and Information Security Handbook*, Morgan Kaufmann, 2009.

C.-Y. Liu, C.-H. Peng et al. "A Survey of Botnet Architecture and Batnet Detection Techniques," *International Journal of Network Security*, vol. 16, no. 2, pp. 81–89, 2014.

N. Meghanathan, S. R. Allam, and L. A. Moore, "Tools and Techniques for Network Forensics," *International Journal of Network Security & Its Application (IJNSA)*, vol. 1, no. 1, arXiv preprint arXiv:1004.0570, 2010.

S. Mitropoulos, D. Pastos and C. Douligers, Network Forensics: Towards a Classification of Traceback Mechanisms, *Proceedings of the Workshop on Security and Privacy for Emerging Areas in Communication Networks* (pp. 9–16), 2005.

C. Modi, D. Patel, B. Borisaniya, H. Patel, A. Pater, and M. Rajarajan, "A Survey of Intrusion Detection Techniques in Cloud," *Journal of Network and Computer Applications*, vol. 36, pp. 42–57, 2013.

S. Parate and S. M. Nirkhi, "A Review of Network Forensics Techniques for the Analysis of Web Based Attack," *International Journal of Advanced Computer Research*, vol. 2, no. 6, pp. 114-119, 2012.

N. Qwasmi, F. Ahmed, and R. Liscano, Simulation of DDOS Attacks on P2P Networks, *IEEE International Conference on HPCC* (pp. 610–614), IEEE, 2011.

S. Rekhis and N. Boudriga, "A System for Formal Digital Forensic Investigation Aware of Anti-Forensic Attacks," *IEEE Transactions on Information Forensics and Security*, vol. 7, no. 2, pp. 635–650, 2012.

K. Shanmugasundaram, H. BrÄonnimann, and N. Memon, Payload Attribution via Hierarchical Bloom Filters, *Proceedings of ACM CCS*, 2004.

US Department of Commerce, Federal Information Processing Standards, Publication 198, The Keyed-Hash Message Authentication Code (HMAC), March 6 2002.

N. H. Vo and J. Pieprzyk, Protecting Web 2.0 Services from Botnet Exploitations, *Cybercrime and Trustworthy Computing Workshop* (pp. 18–28), IEEE, 2010.

S. Zaman and F. Karray, "Lightweight IDS Based on Features Selection and IDS Classification Scheme," *International Conference on Computational Science and Engineering*, vol. 3, pp. 365–370, 2009.

7

Detection of Vulnerabilities

LEARNING OBJECTIVES

This chapter focuses on different vulnerabilities and their detection. It also provides knowledge on the acquisition and identification of network vulnerabilities. After reading this chapter, you would

- Have knowledge about the vulnerabilities.
- Understand network forensic acquisition.
- Have practical knowledge of setting up an experiment for identifying the clues.
- Understand flooding attacks through practical knowledge.

7.1 Introduction

Vulnerability detection technique can also be evaluated by the combination of data fusion, alert generation, and applying correlation mechanism to find out the vulnerabilities. The literal meaning of fusion is to join more than two things together to form one entity, and this entity refers directly to the data that define data fusion as to combine all segregated information at one place for getting meaningful, relevant, and more intuitive results. This process provides concrete, consistent, and accurate information by collecting all information from multiple data sources. However, the terms data fusion and information fusion are quite similar, but it is quite noticeable that the term data fusion is for the raw data, whereas the information fusion belongs to the processed data. Data fusion is defined by the joint directors of laboratories (JDL) workshop as "A multi-level process dealing with association, correlation, combination of data and information from single and multiple sources to achieve refined position, identify estimates and complete and timely assessments of situations, threats and their significance" (Castanedo 2013). The same term data fusion is also defined by Hall as "Data fusion techniques combine data from multiple sensors and related information from associated databases to achieve improved accuracy and more specific interference than could be achieved by the use of a single sensor alone."

Generally, the data fusion technique is categorized into data association, state estimation, and the decision fusion technique. Data association is the technique which determines a set of measurements corresponding to each target. State estimation also refers to tracking technique in which all the target observations cannot be relevant every time. The estimation problem finds the value of vector such as its velocity, its size, and also its position that can be fit with the observed data. Decision fusion completely relies on knowledge of the perceived situation that can be taken by different sources in the data fusion domain. It makes high interference about the activities that are produced from the identified targets.

This correlation technique shows the strong relationship among the variables that extract outcome through statistical methods. The correlation technique is able to analyze the suspicious network vulnerabilities. This technique helps to extract more valuable reconstruction of events. Correlation analysis can be done through various methodologies. Flow correlation technique is one among them to analyze the network that can correlate traffic flow over input and output links. The flow-based correlation method can be divided into frequency- and time domain-based analyses.

7.2 Network Forensics Acquisition

Network forensics acquisition is a must as the nature of network forensics does not block all network-related crimes irrespective of collecting a profuse amount of evidences for identifying, detecting, and analyzing for forensics as well as for the future references. It makes it indispensable to law enforcement. The acquisition process also has to essentially preserve all the capture clues. These preserved data will produce more stringent findings for the forensics. Network forensics investigation is always a challenging task for the experts as the attacker keeps changing their location rapidly. The acquisition of network forensics is the first step to acquire all the evidence from the network. Preservation is also a tedious task to gather evidence in one place without any alteration.

Some of the forensics acquisition tools are already summarized in the previous chapter. Herein, the following acquisition tools help to investigate the digital forensics as well.

7.2.1 SIFT

In today's scenarios, the attackers are more stringent toward the technology that makes them compromise networks of any organization in which millions of users share much confidential information. This can cause the organization lose their trustworthiness, confidentiality, integrity, and financial reputation. They can lose important data, and millions of users may also be exposed. This kind of situation can be prevented by an efficient network forensics techniques and strong defense mechanism that can secure the network from outside intruders. SIFT is a distribution that includes many forensic tools. These tools are for the memory, file system, and network investigation to perform in-depth forensic investigation.

SIFT stands for SANS investigative toolkit (Figure 7.1). It is a forensic distribution developed by SANS forensic team for performing digital forensic. This distribution contains most of the tools required for forensics analysis and examination of incident response. It is an open-source tool kit which is publicly available on the Internet and open-source incident response platform that is available on Ubuntu. The digital forensic examination can be done through SIFT open-source incident response tool. The examination can be taken place by setting a variety of techniques. It can also match any type of forensics tool suit with incident response. This tool efficiently traces the results of intrusion through deep dive forensics and incident response technique that is updated periodically.

FIGURE 7.1
SANS image.

SIFT was freely available in 2007, and it was hard-coded for updating through download once the newer version arrived. New changes on SIFT came in 2014 in which it can be downloaded as a workstation. It was available as a robust package on Ubuntu. Later, in 2017, it had come with more advanced functionalities and provides abilities to the user for taking up leverages from other sources. It contains more than 200 tools from other parties in updated version. It is scriptable, has higher functionalities from others in terms of memory analysis, is efficient, and is stable than other versions.

7.2.2 CAINE

CAINE (Figure 7.2) stands for computer-aided investigation environment. This one is a complete package of Linux distro that gives a complete forensics platform. It is also referred to as an Italian Linux live distribution. It was started in 2008 to provide powerful scripts with graphical interface. It is a live Linux distribution and an open-source forensic platform that combines all components for making a software tool. This platform gives experts a complete package to follow their investigation from preservation, collection, and examination to the analysis process.

This tool can be booted through optical disk and removable drive and downloaded onto physical or virtual system. It also operates on data storage objects without having any supporting operating system to boot up. It carries umpteen software applications, libraries, and scripts which can also perform forensics-related task very easily. It consists of an add-on feature of forensics which can set blocked devices into read-only mode by default. CAINE provides user-friendly graphical interface with user-friendly tools in interoperable environment for digital experts by providing four phases of the digital investigation.

CAINE also supports network analysis, forensics, memory, and the databases through its software tools. It is having a bunch of software tools alongside the Linux distribution such as Autopsy, Sleuth kit, Tinfoleak, Wireshark, PhotoRec, Fsstate, RegRipper, etc.

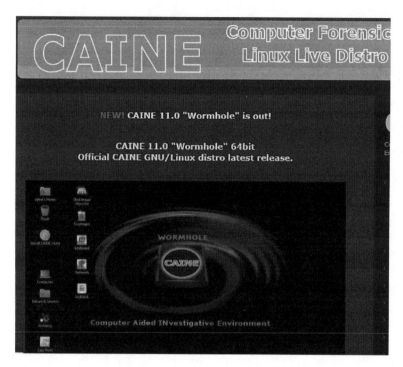

FIGURE 7.2
CAINE image.

7.2.3 Autopsy

Autopsy (Figure 7.3) is a forensic tool used for investigation on systems interfaced to the sleuth kit. This is an open-source platform often used to uncover the facts related to any intrusion. It can also trace the photos from the memory card of cameras. The investigator can flag pertinent underlying forensic information through its graphical user interface. It was first developed by Brian Carrier and his team for examining criminology. The main advantages of this software are as follows.

7.2.3.1 Extensible

It is extensible as its users can add the functionalities very easily. The users can analyze through the data sources by creating plugins.

7.2.3.2 Comfortable

This software does not have any requirement of reconfiguration. The browser of Autopsy software itself provides easy tools and wizards though which users can interact and repeat their phases without any reconfiguration.

7.2.3.3 Centralized

All modules and features can be accessed by the consistent mechanism of this software for investigating the matter.

FIGURE 7.3
Autopsy image.

7.2.3.4 Multiple Users

Many users of the company or a single user can interact with this software at a time.

Autopsy platform generally supports three types of data sources: disk image, local drive, and logical files. These data sources are explained in detail in the following.

7.2.3.4.1 Local Drive

The local drive in Autopsy can be analyzed without having any copy of it. There is no requirement of creating image first of it. To view all devices as an administrator certain points to be remembered:

- Pull down allows you to choose "local drive".
- Pull down list allows you to choose devices.
- Finally, choose any files.

7.2.3.4.2 Logical Files

The files and folders can be added on shared drive or local system without keeping into a disk image. It is useful if collection of files only requires to analyze. There is certain point is to be remembered for adding logical file:

- Pull down allows you to choose "logical file".
- Press the "Add" button.
- Navigate a file or folder to add.
- If sub folder is there, it is to be added too.
- Press "Add" and hold until all files have been selected.

7.2.3.4.3 Disk Image

Disk image is a single file or a set of files that copy byte for byte of media card or hard drive. It also adds the disk images. It supports disk images in many formats such as EnCase like .e01, e02, etc.; Raw Single like *.raw, *.dd, *.img, etc.; and Raw Split like *.01, *.02, *.ab, *.aa, etc. Adding disk image can be done through few steps.

FIGURE 7.4
Forensics acquisition website.

7.2.4 Forensics Acquisition Website

Forensics acquisition websites are also referred to as FAW (Figure 7.4). The websites keep much valuable information along with webpages that may be helpful to extract information for forensics investigators. Forensic acquisition website (FAW) is a software that is specifically made for forensics acquisition of webpages and law enforcement. FAW is a tool that can crystalize webpages effectively. It allows to capture the behavior of the content of multimedia pages. The onion router (TOR) network takes the webpages that exist on dark web. It also acquires webpages by allowing us to schedule at different times of the day. FAW crawler looks webpages that are linked to the main page. Crawler further extracts it from URL and hide to create an index from this process making it self-downloaded. FAW allows us to search social networks through login-protected areas on the websites. It also allows us to capture without changing metadata of the copied file of a complete website in SFTP and also in File Transfer Protocol (FTP) mode. It also controls fast capturing the list of webpages automatically, and it is acquired through P2P protocol from files and the server.

FAW also hashes the acquired objects. Further, it stores text and also stores checking file. This file determines any alteration in it. If it reflects that the list is altered, then it is checked again through the checking function of FAW. FAW acquires webpages for forensic purposes that are available on the Internet. It allows all webpages acquiring partially, fully, or with full resolution to trace. This software is helpful to trace users' activity if the users are violating the nonsolicitation clause by showing their project work on social media. It collects and preserves all evidences before it may be taken down by the user.

The Internet Evidence Finder (IEF) allows experts to view chat boxes, social networking sites, and all the webpages that can be stored into the system. Unlike IEF, the forensic acquisition website (FAW) captures all the evidences in a live environment. It also keeps loss of all incidents in real time that took place during acquisition. The experts can also perform multiple tasks at a time such as screenshots, recording, advertisement, and streaming of data. FAW is also useful to analyze the webpages if they are infected with any malicious code or are normal. Generally, the intruder launches malicious activity through JavaScript file with variant sizes of frames too. It can trace both files and frames with any size. It is made up of a built-in feature that recreates events easily. It captures the social networking post before deletion by the user.

7.2.5 Oxygen Forensic Suit

Oxygen forensic suit (Figure 7.5) is most preferable when the evidence has to be collected from a mobile phone for the investigation purposes, and then, gathering information is helpful through this tool. It is used to acquire information from any kind of mobile devices including pictures, cloud storage, WhatsApp logs, messenger logs, sim card, and the backups. It is user-friendly and capable to trace analytical things from the data. The graph, key evidences, can be traced with a proper timeline through an analytical section of oxygen forensic suit. The data can be traced by various techniques such as hashing, regular expression, keywords, etc. that can be further exported into different formats such as XLS, RTF, PDF, etc.

Currently, many organizations such as law enforcement, army, criminal investigation bureaus, national security organization, and many government and nongovernment organizations are using oxygen forensic suit for the investigation of all digital attacks especially on smart devices. These Internet of Things-related devices can be smart television, smart watches, smart refrigerator, smart-phones, drones, and many more. It can further be used for retrieving data from IoT-related devices like smart watches, refrigerator, and the television and cloud storages.

Oxygen Forensic Suit works on Windows 7, Windows 8, and Windows 10. It supports Bluetooth connections as well as USB cable. It can be installed by plug-in into system of its bundled package in a USB device.

7.2.6 Paladin Forensic Suit

Paladin forensic suit is a live modified Linux distribution that is based on Ubuntu. It simplifies many forensic tasks. This suit is available on both 32- and 64-bit versions. Paladin is available with more than 100 forensics open-source tools like hashing tools, hardware analysis, memory analysis, log analysis, mail analysis, encryption tools, database tools, file differential tools, etc. It is a bootable forensic Linux distribution whose boot process has been modified that assures no mounting or modification on the device's internal and external media.

FIGURE 7.5
Oxygen forensic suit.

Paladin is an open-source tool that can be used to perform various tasks. When paladin combines with autopsy, it allows the user to set up forensic exam from the starting to the final. Digital forensic examiners from different agencies like military, law enforcement, corporate, etc. take advantage of paladin. This suit combines many open-source forensic tools into easier interface that can be used by the user very easily.

Many forensics tasks are simplified by the paladin toolbox. It facilitates easier graphical user interface (GUI), so it is quite obvious that there is no requirement of command line interface. As paladin combines multiple tools, its engine also runs many applications that is being used by the forensics experts and the investigator.

7.2.7 ExifTool

EXIF stands for the exchangeable image file format and is developed by Phil Harvey. ExifTool is an open-source tool that is used for reading and writing, and it is utilized for the manipulation of images, audio, and video. It is a free and platform-independent software. Generally, it is a software program that is available as both command line application and Perl library. The advantage of ExifTool is that it supports different types of metadata like GeoTIFF, JFIF, XMP, IPTC, EXIF, FlashPix, and Photoshop IRB, and it works in many types of digital workflows. It is also used to parse metadata. The example of this software program is Flickr. It is an image hosting site that uses ExifTool to parse the metadata. It is done from the uploaded images.

ExifTool makes its own metadata by encapsulating information from different sources. Metadata contains a collection of information such as file size, file type, permissions, etc. This tool is written in Pearl and works in Linux, Mac, and also Windows operating systems. Extracting metadata from the file and the deployment of ExifTool is quite simple. The most used commands for working in ExifTool are the following:

1. The package can be easily installed through GitHub by:
   Sudo apt-get install lib-image-exiftool-perl
2. Cloning of the tool from GitHub by:
   git clone https://github.com/exiftool/exiftool.git
3. Extracting the entire metadata from the files:
   exiftool <filename>
4. Hexa-decimal format of Exif tags and ids:
   exiftool –H <filename>
5. Extraction of the most common metadata information:
   exiftool –common <filename.jpg>
6. Extraction of particular metadata information:
   exiftool –tagname –tagname <filename>
7. Extraction of metadata information with certain keywords:
   exiftool "-*keywords*" <filename>
8. Extraction of extended information that refers the comprehensive data about performing process:
   exiftool –v <filenames>
9. Commands for writing the metadata for manipulation on exif:
   exiftool -make=" Networkforensics"<filename>

10. Removing metadata from the information
    exiftool –all= <filename>

11. The output can be saved in the following ways:

    a. Saving ExifTool outcome in text file:
        exiftool (filename) > (outputexif.txt)

    b. Saving ExifTool outcome in html file
        exiftool –h (filename) > (output.html)

    c. Monitoring the output:
        cat <filenames>

7.2.8 CrowdResponse Tool

CrowdResponse tool is a free and an open-source tool that handles incident response by performing signature detection and the collection of the data. It is an automated tool that allows us to collect information incident response. It supports all Windows platforms and Mac operating systems. It provides information from basic utilities such as registry files, list of processes, folder and subfolder directory, rules scan, string extraction, and registry extraction.

CrowdResponse tool is developed by Mr. Robin Keir from CrowdStrike. It is a light-weight solution for the incident responder. It is an evidence collecting tool for the fast forensic. It is a new version of CrowdStrike that provides quick detection and ease to respond to the attacks. It has a feature to detect the adversaries easily. It parses both task scheduler 1.0 and task scheduler 1.2. Task scheduler 1.0 works with Windows XP, Windows server 2003, and below systems, whereas task scheduler 1.2 works with Windows vista and above systems. The CrowdResponse parses task scheduler including those created with At.exe applications. The main work of this process is to identify the malicious and suspicious attacks. CrowdResponse parses all complex information once any suspicious activity has been found.

7.2.9 BulkExtractor

All sensitive data can be easily searched by the BulkExtractor tool through a filesystem. It scans using parallel processing that makes it a faster tool. There is no fragmentation of the files in this tool. It is a complete package that exactly nothing else but a software program. It reveals information regarding credit card number, email addresses, URLs, etc. The BulkExtractor extracts the feature from the file by digital evidences. This tool is very helpful for the cyber investigation and helps to uncover the intention of the intrusion. It analyzes the password cracking identity and extracts the information related to the email addresses and credit card numbers by processing all compressed format data or incomplete or corrupted data.

BulkExtractor extracts much important information through files, directory, and disk images without parsing the file system. It also does not parse the system structure while extracting useful information from the disk images. The advantages of BulkExtractor tool are that the JPEG and all the encrypted RAR files can be dug out of fragment of compressed data. It can visualize the most common search keywords, domains, email addresses, and many other things on drive by creating a histogram. It also has a capability of making its own dictionary, i.e., a bunch of words that can help it for the password cracking in future too. Its multithreaded working behavior completes work in just half the time.

The BulkExtractor can be used by both command line and graphical user interface. The common syntax for using BulkExtractor is as follows:

1. To use basics using this tool from command line
   bulk_extractor −o <out_dir> -R <dir>
   Or we can use bulk_extractor −o <out_dir> <image>
   In this command o put the results in the <dir> directory and −R scan the <dir> directory recursively.
2. To display a commonly used parameter and options:
   bulk_extractor −h
   Some common option while using Bulkextactor tool:
   1. −i -It is for INFO mode
   2. −b<file> -It sets the banner file to the <file>
   3. −r<file> -It sets alerts list to the <file>
   4. −w<file> -It sets stop list to the <file>
   5. −F<file> - Reading a list of regular expression from the <file> to find
   6. −f<regex> -It finds the regex occurrence
   7. -q nn -It is a quiet rate. It only prints every nn status reports.
   8. -s frac[:passes] -set random sampling parameter.
   9. -W<num 1> : <num 2>- It extracts only words in length between <num 1> and <num 2>
   10. -E<scanner> -First enable the <scanner> and then disable all others
   11. −e<scanner> -It enable <scanner> of all the disabled scanners.
   12. −x<scanner> -It disables all scanners.
   13. −c<num> -It fix the context window to <num>
   14. −m<num> -It fix maximum number of the minutes to wait <num>
   15. −M<num> -It set the maximum recursive depth to the <num>
   16. −j<num> -It fix the number of threats to <num>
   17. −g<num> -It fix the margin to <num>
   18. −G<num> -It set the page size.

7.2.10 Xplico

The term Xplico has a Latin origin, and it is a Spanish word which means understanding. It is an open-source software and available free of cost. This forensic analysis tool is also used for data extraction from traffic. It can rebuild the stored contents with a packet sniffer. It has the ability to process huge amounts of data and also manages pcap files of many Gbytes and Tbytes. It can support the decoding of audio codec and MSTRA. Xplico software is developed by Gianluca Costa and Andrea de Franceschi, and it is written in Python, PHP, and C languages.

Explico is a network forensics sniffing tool that can extract all HTTP contents, email protocols, and VoIP call from the pcap files. This software supports SMTP, TCP, UDP, HTTP,

SIP, and many protocols. It has a capacity to work with multithreading behavior. It can easily create any kind of dispatcher that gives us more relevant and useful extracted data. It supports both IPV4 and IPV6 formats. The following are some commands that are important in using command line interface:

1. Installing xplico through command line
   apt_get install xpico or, sudo apt-get install
2. Decoding with real-time acquisition
   xplico –m rltm –I etho
3. Single pcap file decoding
   Xplico –m pcap –f xyz.pcap
4. No. of pcap file directory for decoding
   Xplico –m pcap –d/path/dir

7.3 Identification of Network Attacks

Denial of services attack results in erratic or complete inaccessibility of an Internet service. Due to this attack, the user of the services does not get access to the Internet service and resources. Generally, the attackers with the criminal intentions target the web services such as banks, payments gateways, and secret security information of a country or insider trade secret of a company. It is also observed that sometimes motives may not be financial gains, and the people with a criminal mindset may use it for different motives such as black mailing, tarnishing the image of popular personalities, etc. In denial of services, the attacker operates the attack with a remote distance with a machine made for spreading the infections. This machine sends the program code for spreading malicious activity. These program codes are sent to the user of Internet service. The objective of these codes is to infect and compromise the user machine and use the same machine to spread this infection further. The evidence symptoms of a denial of services are slow network inaccessibility to any website, nonconnectivity to WAN, abnormality-increased spam mails, etc.

DDoS attacks are quickly becoming the serious threats and pain point for the industries. With more and more advanced DDoS attacks, the organizations are finding it difficult to cope with it. If the organization and institution want to provide uninterruption to their customers, they must take this issue very seriously. The authorized Internet users may face difficulties in accessing the resources and services on the Internet due to denial of services (DoS) and distributed denial of services (DDoS) attacks. A DDoS attack is caused by an infected bot, which spreads a large number of packets in a very short period of time. HTTP, UDP, and some other protocols are utilized for executing different types of flooding attacks.

Such flooding attacks can be prevented with the help of intrusion detection and prevention system (IDS/IPS) and firewalls. But the complexities can increase, and the IDS/IPS and firewalls may fail to prevent the flooding attack if the botnet master introduces variations in the flooding characteristics and patterns, if by changes in the packet size, the current provisions and solutions are not sufficient and efficient enough for investigation of such flooding attacks as they are launched in very short-time intervals. Such random flood attacks have different types of attributes and IDS/IPS and firewalls both fail in detecting the attack as these appliances function on the threshold-based detection criteria.

7.3.1 UDP Flooding

A UDP (User Datagram Protocol) is a transport layer protocol distinct for exploit with the IP network layer protocol. UDP flood is a network flood and still a standout among the most widely recognized floods today. The attacker sends UDP packets, in generally huge numbers, to single destination or to arbitrary ports. In most cases, the attackers spoof the source IP which is easy to do because the UDP protocol is "connectionless" and does not have any type of handshake mechanism or session. This causes denial of service (DoS) attack. It is more risky if we disturb or try to change flood. In other cases, attackers use a chain of connections through many systems to cover their identity, for mitigation of this attack.

An infected system or bot generates multiple datagrams, which further causes the UDP flooding attack on the system security. This type of attack is executed by flooding the UDP datagram throughout the network, thereby causing congestion on the system which also causes denial of services (DoS) attack. The situation gets even worse by varying flood characteristics by the attacker.

By generating the multiple UDP datagrams of different varieties and sizes, the bot master ensures breach of network security by flooding these multicharacteristic UDP datagrams across the victim's network and gets success in doing so because all the security systems fail to identify and prevent this attack. Detection of these types of attacks is difficult because almost every detection system works on two basic conditions, i.e., signature- and feature-based detection systems. Being a UDP datagram, they easily evade the signature-based detection system. An intrusion detection system (IDS) also fails the feature-based detection. A feature-based detection system compares and matches the features of safe packet flows with the features of packets flowing in the network. In case of abnormalities, it detects the suspected packets flowing on the network and thereby ensures the security of the system.

Here, we have designed a malicious script by using a randomized function that runs on a bot. It sends multiple UDP datagrams of different sizes to a victim system. The sizes of datagrams are different and less than the packet/datagram size threshold value (to prevent the restriction from the IDS/firewall). So, they pass the detection system easily. This type of flooding (random-UDP flooding) attack can be performed very easily.

7.3.2 Random-UDP Flooding

The methodology shows the work in three scenarios, i.e., UDP datagram under normal flow, random-UDP bot flooding attack, and detection status of random-UDP flooding attack.

7.3.2.1 Normal Flow of UDP Datagrams

The user starts searching for the best tour and travel sites for issues in the services. So, the user requests for the webpage. All users get connected with the web server for their personal work.

After requesting the web services by the user, the user gets connected directly with the web server. Communication further starts from both sides. Similarly, other users can communicate with webserver from both sides.

For this purpose, we have created a scenario in which two users access various Internet-based services such as email, remote database access, etc. User 1 wants to book a tour package from an online booking website; he searches for that and gets a link (www.fasttoursandtravel.com) showing the cheapest rate, and he attracted toward that link and clicks on that. He successfully books the tour package. Figure 7.6 shows the request (HRQP-HTTP Request) for the webpage. Figure 7.7 shows the response (HRSP-HTTP Response) coming from the web server. Figure 7.8 shows the snapshot of the website (www.fasttoursandtravel.com/home.html) that opens in the browser of user 1.

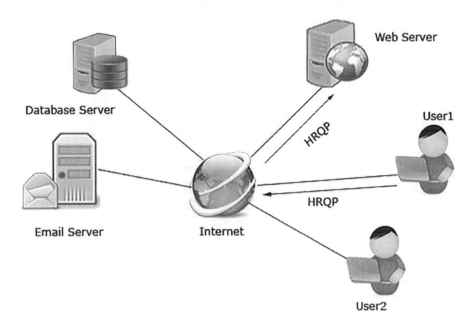

FIGURE 7.6
Request for a webpage.

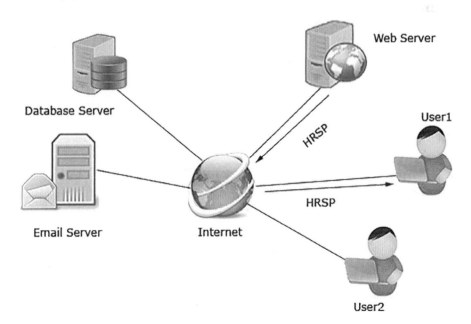

FIGURE 7.7
Response from the web server.

FIGURE 7.8
Web browser view of www.fasttoursandtravel.com.

7.3.2.2 Random-UDP Flooding Attack

This scenario shows that the malicious users send their link also through search engine. Normal users can send their request to the webserver and receive many best tour and travel websites along with the botmaster's link.

The methodology of random-UDP flooding attack shows how a user get trapped through the botmaster. Suppose the web server (www.fasttoursandtravel.com) becomes bot, the user 1 who wants to book a tour package can be easily victimized. User 1 sends HTTP request for the webpage. At web server (bot), a malicious script is run; it extracts the IP of the user 1 from the request and starts sending UDP datagrams of different sizes. Figure 7.9 shows the request (HRQP-HTTP Request) for the webpage. Figure 7.10 shows the response (HRSP-HTTP Response) flood coming from the web server. Figure 7.11 shows all the processes during UDP flooding.

The script which is implemented in BoNeSi is as follows:

```
#bonesi -i attack.txt -s {House, #5} -c {House, #5} -u
192.168.1.1:{House, #5}

# in case of range, else $RANDOM has random values
# number=$RANDOM
#let "number %= $RANGE"

PRANGE=500
payload=$RANDOM
let "payload %= $PRANGE"

CRANGE=100000
packets=$RANDOM
let "packets %= $CRANGE"
```

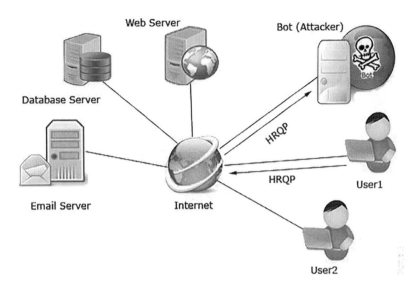

FIGURE 7.9
Request for a webpage.

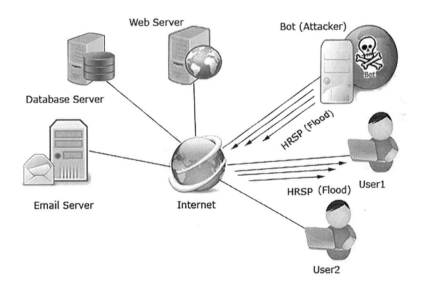

FIGURE 7.10
Flood response from the web server.

```
PORTRANGE=3000
ports=$RANDOM
let "ports %= $PORTRANGE"

SENDRATE=100000
sends=$RANDOM
let "sends %= $SENDRATE"
bonesi -i /home/test3/attack.txt -p udp -r $sends -s $payload -c $packets -u
10.10.63.51:$ports
```

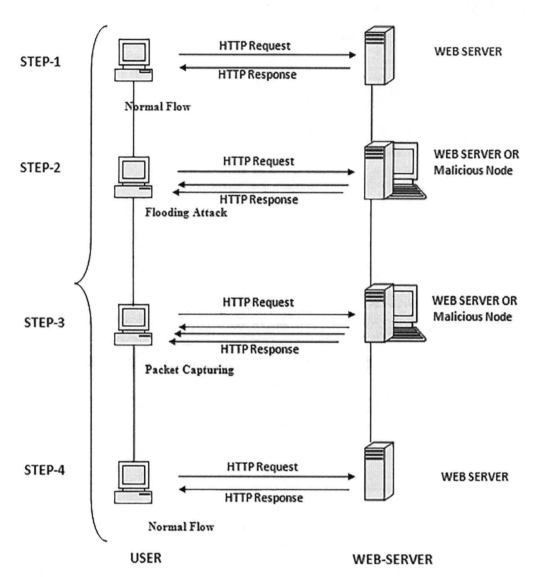

FIGURE 7.11
Execution of flooding attack.

7.3.2.3 Identification of Random-UDP Flooding Attack

The methodology for the identification of random-UDP flooding attack shows how we traced the results of bot clues and what kind of tools we used to get it. The random-UDP flooding attack is launched to the user 1's system. Now, there is a requirement of investigation of the flooding attack. For this purpose, we have started packet capturing using Wireshark tool. User 1 sends HTTP request for the webpage. At web server (bot), malicious script starts sending UDP datagrams of different sizes. These datagrams are captured and analyzed. Figure 7.9 shows the request (HRQP-HTTP Request) for the webpage.

Figure 7.10 shows the response (HRSP-HTTP Response) flood coming from the web server. User 1 has installed Wireshark which starts packet capturing.

Figure 7.12 presents random-UDP flooding attack steps. It shows the attacking scenario created by botmaster and execution process starts in the victim's system.

Figure 7.13 presents the process of capturing the bot clues in victim system and shows the steps involved in flooding packet capturing.

Figure 7.14 presents the analysis of captured record and shows the steps involved in flooding packet analysis.

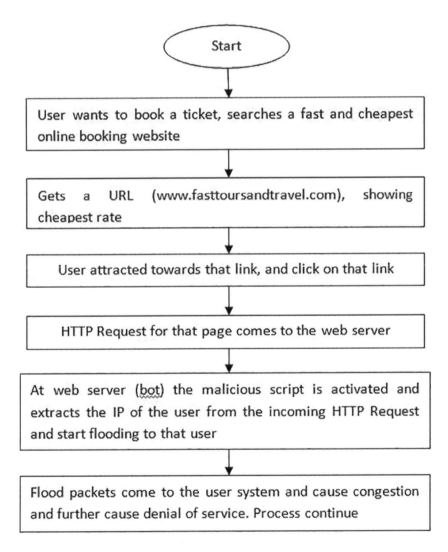

FIGURE 7.12
Random-UDP flooding attack.

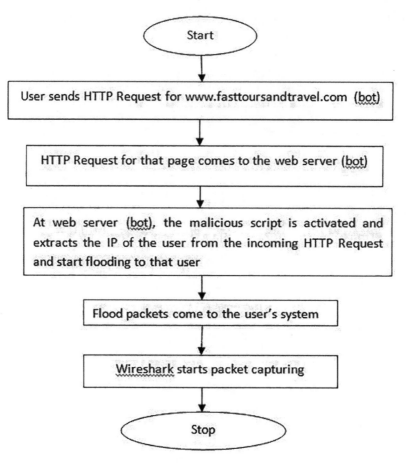

FIGURE 7.13
Flooding packets capturing.

Questions

Q.1. What do you understand by vulnerability? How can you detect the vulnerabilities?

Q.2. Explain the vulnerability detection techniques in detail.

Q.3. What do you understand by acquisition? Why is network forensic acquisition required?

Q.4. What is CAINE? What are roles of CAINE?

Q.5. Explain SIFT with its role in detail.

Q.6. What do you understand by flooding attack? Explain in detail.

Q.7. What is the role of CrowdResponse tool? Where does this tool give us advantage over other tools?

Q.8. Explain all ExifTool commands.

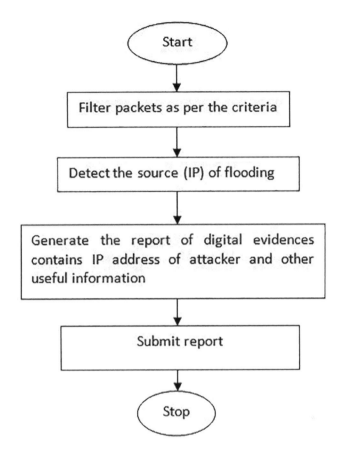

FIGURE 7.14
Flooding packets analysis.

Q.9. What is paladin forensic suit? What is the role of all tools under paladin forensic suit?

Q.10. How can we set the experiment for UDP flooding attack? How can randomizer function give advantages to the researcher?

Q.11. What do you understand by oxygen forensic suit? What is the role of this suit in forensics?

Q.12. What are the advantages of Autopsy software?

References

A. G. Bardas, L. Zomlot, Sathya Chandran Sundaramurthy, et al. Classification of UDP Traffic for DDoS Detection, *5th ACM USENIX Conference on Large - Scale Exploits and Emergent Threats (LEET)*, 2012.

A. Bijalwan, M. Wazid, E. S. Pilli, and R. C. Joshi, "Forensics of Random-UDP Flooding Attacks," *Journal of Networks*, vol. 10, no. 5, pp. 287–293, 2015.

F. Castanedo, "A Review of Data Fusion Techniques," The Scientific World Journal, vol. 2013, pp. 1-20, 2013.

X. Chuiyi, Z. Yizhi, B. Yuan, et al. A Distributed Intrusion Detection System against Flooding Denial of Services attacks, *13th IEEE International Conference on Advanced Communication Technology (ICACT)*, 2011.

S. M. Hussain and G. R. Beigh, Impact of DDoS Attack (UDP Flooding) on Queuing Models, *4th IEEE International Conference on Computer and Communication Technology (ICCCT)*, 2013.

H. Kim, B. Kim, D. Kim, et al. *Implementation of GESNIC for Web Server Protection against HTTP GET Flooding Attacks, Springer* LNCS, WISA, 2012. Information available at http://www.sans.org/top25-software-errors/

M. Li, J. Li, and W. Zhao, Simulation Study of Flood Attacking of DDOS, *International Conference on Internet Computing in Science and Engineering, ICICSE'08* (pp. 286–293), IEEE, 2008.

G. Mohay, E. Ahmed, S. Bhatia, et al. "Detection and mitigation of high-rate flooding attacks," in *An Investigation into the Detection and Mitigation of Denial of Service (DoS) Attacks*, Springer, 2011, pp. 131–181.

D. Moustis and P. Kotzanikolaou, Evaluating Security Controls Against HTTP-Based DDoS Attacks, *4th IEEE International Conference on Information, Intelligence, Systems and Applications (IISA)*, 2013.

S. S. C. Silva, R. M. P. Silva, and R. M. Salles, "Botnets: A Survey," *Elsevier Journal of Computer Networks*, vol. 57, no. 2, pp. 378–403, 2013.

Y. Tao and S. Yu, DDoS Attack Detection at Local Area Networks Using Information Theoretical Metrics, *12th IEEE International Conference on Trust, Security and Privacy in Computing and Communications (TrustCom)*, 2013.

Wireshark Information available at https://www.wireshark.org/

Part C

Network Forensics Attribution

8

Network Forensics Analysis

LEARNING OBJECTIVES

This chapter aims at explaining the analysis part of the network forensics. It discusses the process model for network forensics. It also explains the framework for network forensic analysis. It also imparts knowledge through the practical approach by setting up the experiment for the forensic analysis. After reading this chapter, you would

- Understand the development of the network forensic process.
- Have knowledge of network forensic process model.
- Understand how to set up the experiment for the analysis.
- Understand the analysis through various case studies through different datasets.

8.1 Introduction

Network forensics results in linking the diverse datasets have relevance to activities, habitually correlating the digital traces obtained in the different data sources such as webpages, logs, internet-related group, and online chat rooms. Network forensics process can be developed in two ways:

1. The first step is the susceptive use of conventional security devices like firewalls and intrusion detection system, analyzing the data, and then investigating it.
2. The other way is to eagerly trap the attacker by means of honeynets or greynets to observe the attack patterns, thus creating the observable profiles of attackers and their exploitation mechanisms.

In 1987, an intrusion detection model was proposed by Denning and team that lifted research contribution in the same area by the new researchers. After that in 1990, Ranum et al. defined the capture, recording, and analysis of the attacks that occurred. In 2002, Reith et al. proposed a new model referred to as an abstract digital forensic model which is predicated on the DFRW model. This model consists of seven stages which are key components of this model. These include identification, preservation, collection, examination, analysis, presentation, and decision in this given model.

In 2006, McGrath et al. interpreted network forensics after malicious data collection with the help of nonintrusive network traffic record system. Mandia et al. developed robust incident response methodology. His first phase, i.e., initial response, exhibited the formulation of a response and summed them up for an incident. The collection and analysis phase comes under the investigation phase which is defined in previous different models. In 2007, Frelling and Schwittay et al. proposed the model in which computer forensic and incident response processes can be utilized with management-oriented approach in the digital investigations.

In 2008, Abdullah, Mahmod, and Ghani et al. identified the five categories including framework, trustworthiness, data detection, data acquisition, and data recovery. Casey and Palmer et al. developed an investigative process model. It ensures the simplicity on previous tedious investigation processes and evidence handling and minimizes the chances of errors.

Umpteen authors contributed research in the field of network forensics and work done in an application of frequent sequence mining algorithm. The researcher Palomoa showed a novel theory approach for analyzing and visualizing network traffic data. It was predicated on growing hierarchical self-organizing maps (GHSOMs). This GHSOM was basically used to make cluster network traffic data and to present this sequentially. Zhong derived an a priori algorithm that is basically made for a kind of most sturdy mining Boolean association rule algorithm. The analysis of a priori algorithm on the mentioned procedure can improve the efficiency of evidence.

There are also many other researchers, scholars, and authors who have made research on the network forensics. They have presented their work using different tools and techniques. In 2002, Corey had described a network for monitoring the vulnerabilities. It is especially prepared to identify the configuration problem easily. The forensic analysis yields the convenient way to find out security vulnerability. This allows all the best possible scrutiny of security violations. Tools like tcpdump, gnutella, and netintercept have been used for the forensic analysis. In 2008, Wang had developed a novel graph-based approach toward the analysis for network forensics. This is the approach for developing a model related to evidence graph. This model ensures an automated reasoning and the presentation.

In 2012, Raftopoulos investigated the correlation of information based on four security parameters. These four security parameters are namely IDS alerts, examination and vulnerabilities reports, and unwanted filtered traffic through search engine to expedite manual forensics analysis of compromised systems. Tools like Nmap, NIC whois, nessus, and open vas have been used. Techniques like C4.5 decision tree-based algorithm, NIC whois querying, and TCP/UDP port scanning have been used. Comparison among the tree augmented naïve bayes (TAN), Bayesian tree classifier (BTC), and support vector machine (SVM) has been done for the forensics investigation.

In 2014, Shulman had reviewed the strongest procedure preventing cache positioning attacks on DNSSEC. This mechanism enables a posteriori analysis for the purpose of forensics. Detection of the attacks is used with ANYCAST technology, DNS cache poisoning by MiTm (man in the middle), and cache poisoning by subverting hosting infrastructure.

Internetwork is the root cause for distribution of cyber-attacks. But it is something that is much needed in almost every aspect of a country's economy, i.e., in banking, education, transportation (railways, airways, buses, and taxis), healthcare, business, and many more. With the growth of Internet, there is a need to protect the data. Though traditional protection techniques such as firewalls and antivirus software are not sufficient, it requires enhanced security measures. Protecting alone the system is not sufficient; rather, it is necessary to trace back to the criminals in case of cybercrime. Network forensics provides a mechanism to track the criminals. It also provides a mechanism to trace the malicious traffic and its analysis, thus helping in the investigation process.

Consider the cyber-attack at Giant company LinkedIn in 2012 where the password of nearly 6.5 million user accounts were stolen and again in 2016 about 100 million hashed passwords and email addresses were leaked both from the same source, i.e., Russian Cyber Criminals. There has also been breach in the security of Apple's iCloud leading to the stealing of 500 private pictures of celebrities in year 2014, though various scenarios and frameworks have been developed to prevent the attacks and identify its origin in case of attack. In spite of many existing virtuous frameworks and techniques for network forensics, there is need for continuous development in this area and to overcome challenges in existing models.

This chapter presents network forensic standard process model, framework for the analysis, analyzing network traffic through a dataset by showing one case study, and its behavior, and finally by another case study, it analyzes network traffic through another dataset. It presents network behavioral features that can be used to accomplish accurate malware detection. By analyzing and comparing known malware and normal processes, it successfully exploited differences in their network activity behavior and produced accurate and effective malware detection with minimal false positives and false negatives. This was accomplished by producing a set of behaviors which occurred most often in our analyzed malware samples during which two novel behaviors frequently used by malware were discovered.

8.2 Network Forensic Standard Process Model

A generic process model for network forensics incorporates the new phase of detection where fast evaluation is done to check the alleged outbreak of crime. This model aims to first authorize the investigator to perform the investigation process. It is important to preserve the evidence while making an initial assessment. Here, there is an option to abort the investigation if certain prerequisites are not fulfilled such as preinstalled sensor and network traffic collector tools such as NetIntercept or Xplico or others. In case further investigation is to be carried out, then a strategy is planned to reduce the network traffic collected and document them. Further analysis is done, and review is made through to check for further improvement. This standard network forensic process model is shown in Figure 8.1.

The detailed description of the standard network forensics model is as follows.

8.2.1 Authorization

This phase involves obtaining legal permissions from the concerned authority to initiate the investigation process as shown in Figure 8.1. Herein, Ciardhuain proposed the authorization phase to take consent from the internal and external organizations. The authorization phase may sometimes face the challenge of taking permission from external bodies located overseas, who may not permit due to their country's legal perspectives.

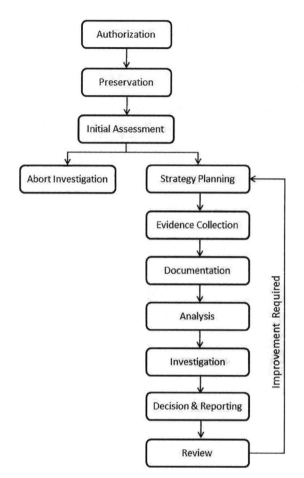

FIGURE 8.1
Standard network forensic process model.

8.2.2 Preservation

Preservation phase implicates the avoidance of tempering of network evidence. For example, in case a mobile device is involved in the crime, then it must be switched off to avoid mitigating of call and network logs. This is the second phase as shown in Figure 8.1.

8.2.3 Initial Assessment

In this stage, an initial judgment is made whether to continue or abort investigation. If there aren't preinstalled tools for network traffic collection, then the investigation is terminated. This phase has two outward links, out of which only one is selected as displayed in Figure 8.1.

8.2.4 Strategy Planning

This phase comprises to jot down the strategy to carry out further investigation, i.e., team members, duration of investigation, cost involved, and software use. This phase involves constructing a design strategy using design science that is given by Lutui giving more stress on efficacy and coherence.

8.2.5 Evidence Collection

Evidence is collected at this stage which may either involve automatic or manual network traffic collection. Further, the huge amount of data collected from the network can be reduced by eliminating superfluous data.

8.2.6 Documentation

Documentation is the process of writing all the relevant information required during the investigation process.

8.2.7 Analysis

Analysis phase involves determination of attack patterns by employing various machine learning techniques. This phase involves techniques such as PROLOG logic techniques to analyze the data.

8.2.8 Investigation

Further investigation is done to reconstruct the attack scenario and replay it at the investigator's end.

8.2.9 Decision and Reporting

A decision is made at this stage about the type of attack, and concerned authorities are informed to take appropriate actions.

8.2.10 Review

A review is done to check it for further improvement. In case any improvement is required, then the strategy is rescheduled by taking the novel parameters.

8.3 Network Forensic Framework for the Analysis

The amalgamations of standard network forensic framework phases along with the phases of the network forensic process model is most important for the analysis. In the framework shown in Figure 8.2, the network traffic is collected automatically and reduced to an extent by eliminating the superfluous data, and useful features are extracted and transferred to the next phase. The analysis of the derived features is carried through to obtain a pattern. The newly derived pattern can be matched with the patterns stored in the knowledgebase. If a match is found, then an initial quick response is made to the criminals stating warning to abort the attack. Further analysis is done to constantly deriving new patterns in case no match is found. The reconstruction phase involves design of attack scenario which is then replayed by the investigator in the next phase.

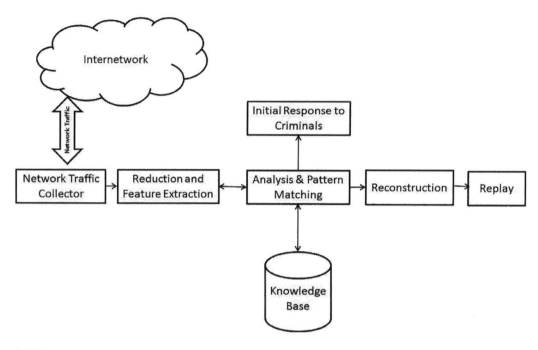

FIGURE 8.2
Standard network forensic framework.

8.3.1 Network Traffic Collector

The vast amount of traffic flows from the internet. The network traffic can be collected in one of the following three manners:

1. Automatic network traffic collection.
2. Collecting traffic on change in frequency at different intervals.
3. Manual network traffic collection.

This phase involves taking permissions from the concerned authority to perform forensics in the concerned intruded network and thus collect network traffic. After obtaining the authorization, the network traffic is collected, and the preservation phase involves keeping the data unaltered while examining the crime scenario. The three phases of process model act at the network traffic collector phase as shown in Figure 8.3. The automatic network data collection using distributed mobile agent's model fulfills the requirement as per this scenario. Initial assessment is done in order to check the feasibility of the assessment. If the initial judgment seems to be infeasible, then the investigation process is aborted.

8.3.2 Reduction and Feature Extraction

There are enormous data available on the network. Storing each and every bit of network traffic involves huge secondary storage media. This phase involves strategy planning to make the steps to reduce the data by eliminating the extraneous attributes. Similar kind of data can be represented using encoding techniques, e.g., all http packets using run-length encoding scheme, i.e., 100 http packets, can be represented as 100http. After reducing the

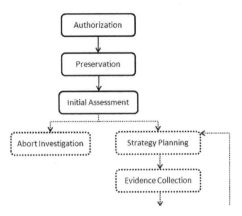

FIGURE 8.3
Three phases of process model acting at network traffic collector phase of framework.

FIGURE 8.4
Three phases of process model acting at reduction and feature extraction phase of framework.

data wherever possible, the important features can be extracted using various machine learning techniques. Relevant points are documented such as what kind of features to extract, who is responsible for this, and what algorithms to employ. Chen used a scalable network forensic method to reduce 97% of attack-irrelevant traffic of network resulting in reduced overhead and better accuracy for self-propagating stealth attacks. The strategy planning phase of standard network forensic process model acts at the reduction and feature extraction phase of network forensic framework as shown in Figure 8.4.

8.3.3 Analysis and Pattern Matching

In analysis and pattern matching phase, the reduced network traffic is further examined to determine the attack pattern. Dependency graphs can be used to show the order of occurrence of events. Attack patterns are obtained, which can then be matched with the existing patterns to find if any of them is stored in the database. If the current attack pattern matches with the prevailing pattern stored in the knowledgebase, then the investigator can move to the next phase. Thus, this helps in saving the investigator's time and fastens the examination process. If a new attack pattern is obtained during the analysis phase, then it is stored in the knowledgebase for future reference, and further analysis is done to obtain additional attack patterns. The analysis phase of process model as shown in Figure 8.1 acts at the analysis phase of framework Figure 8.2, and the amalgamation is shown in Figure 8.5.

8.3.4 Reconstruction

The pattern obtained from the analysis phase is reconstructed to generate the sequence of events. The patterns are scrutinized according to the flow of packet stream. A proper investigation is done of TCP connection in order to obtain knowledge about the inflow and outflow of packets. The investigation phase of process model acts at the reconstruction phase to framework to obtain the attack patterns as shown in Figure 8.6.

8.3.5 Replay

In this phase, the pattern created in the previous phase is replayed in order to obtain the crime scenario. The replay of the attack scenario is done on the investigator end without

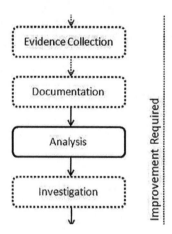

FIGURE 8.5
Analysis phase of process model acting at analysis and pattern matching phase of framework.

FIGURE 8.6
Investigation phase of process model acting at reconstruction phase of framework.

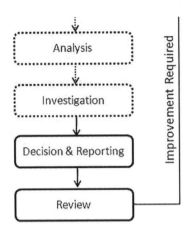

FIGURE 8.7
Two phases of process model acting at replay phase of framework.

harming the actual network. This is done using simulators to replay the constructed attack situation. The outcome of the simulation is compared with the actual attack scene, and reporting is done. It is based on reporting that a decision is made whether to include more parameters, and after exhaustive review of the replay process, the control goes back to the strategy planning phase if further improvements are required, which is shown in Figure 8.7.

8.4 Network Traffic Analysis

Humans have always aspired to develop techniques that could replace human efforts to a great extent. In this era, machine and deep learning is superseding other techniques. If one can train the machine using the data instead of explicitly programming the machine, that's where we need machine learning. Machine learning has empowered many domains such as web search, text recognition, speech recognition, medicine such as protein structure estimation, network traffic analysis and prediction, intrusion detection, etc. Network traffic analysis is one of the emerging domains. An attack can be predicted from the current network traffic flow, and it can stop the intruders before actually attacking the network. This can be done using machine learning by training the network. There are three categories of analyzing network traffic through machine learning, i.e., supervised, un-supervised, and semi-supervised. The first case we are taking up is on support vector machine (SVM) supervised machine learning technique for network traffic analysis. The analysis of network traffic classification using SVM can include two approaches, i.e., binary or two-way classification and multiclass classification.

1. The first approach works simply by classifying the network between normal and anomalous traffic.
2. The second approach can be applied using two subapproaches, i.e., (a) mapping multiple classes to individual binary classes.

8.4.1 Case Analysis

Numerous studies have been conducted for traffic analysis using KDD Cup'99 dataset. A computational efficient technique called novel multilevel hierarchical Kohonennet focuses on reduced feature and network size. The subset from KDD Cup'99 data is selected consisting of combination of normal and anomalous traffic records, which can be used to train the classifier. However, the test data consist of more attacks than available in train set and are used for testing the classifier. Evolutionary neural network-based novel approach for intrusion detection has been proposed over the same KDD dataset. This approach takes away less time to find the higher neural networks than the conventional neural network approaches by learning system-call orders. Network traffic classification using multiclass classifier 209 is another technique applied on KDD cup dataset that is a modified and improved version of C4.5 decision tree classifier. In this method, new rules are derived by evaluating the network traffic data and thereby applied to detect intrusion in the real time. Another technique applied on the modified version of KDD'99 dataset named NSLKDD aims to decrease the false rate and increase the detection rate by optimizing the weighted average function. A novel technique named density peaks nearest neighbors (DPNN) is applied on KDD'99 cup dataset to yield an improved accuracy over the SVM method. This approach detects unknown attacks, thus improving the subcategorical accuracy improvement of 15% on probe attacks and an overall efficiency improvement of 20.688%. This methodology used deep auto-encoder technique on KDD'99 cup dataset by constructing multilayer neurons showing improved accuracy over traditional attack identification techniques. It performed a two-way step on KDD'99 cup dataset: feature reduction using three different techniques, i.e., gain ratio, mutual information, correlation, and generated analysis score using Naïve Bayes, Random Forest, AdaBoost, SVM, bagging, kNN, and stacking. Their results showed the maximum performance given by SVM with 99.91% score and a closer performance score of 99.89 by Random Forest algorithm.

8.4.2 Dataset: KDD Cup 99 Case Study-I

The full train dataset consists of 4,898,431 records out of which 972,781 are normal records and 3,925,650 are attack records. In this full train dataset, a vast number of records are redundant, and after redundancy removal, the total records, normal and attack records become 1,074,992, 812,814 and 262,178, respectively. However, the 10% train dataset consists of total records of 494,021 out of which 97,278 are normal, whereas 396,743 are attack records. The test dataset consists of 311,027 records out of which 60,591 are normal records and 250,436 are attack records. In this test dataset, a vast number of records are redundant, and after redundancy removal, the total records, normal and attack records, become 77,289, 47,911, and 29,378, respectively. There were two invalid records found in the test dataset having a record number of 136,489 and 136,497 consisting of unacceptable value for service feature as ICMP and henceforth removed these two records from test dataset. KDD CUP'99 dataset includes four different categories of attacks which are further subcategorized into 22 categories. The methodology for the given dataset is shown in Figure 8.8.

The four classes of attacks present in train dataset are as follows:

1. Denial of Service (DoS),
2. User to Root (U2R),
3. Remote to Local (R2L),
4. Probe.

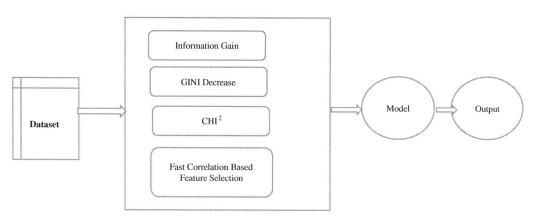

FIGURE 8.8
Methodology for case study-I.

Denial of service attack denies the user's genuine access to the machine by either flooding the network with excess traffic or making the system resources overutilized. In U2R, the unauthorized user gains access to the system's root directory, thereby attaining all rights of the super user.

R2L deals with getting local access of the machine from remote location by exploiting unknown vulnerability. Probe attack deals with gaining control of the system by security breach. Subcategories of the aforementioned attacks are depicted in Figure 8.8. The frequency of the number of attacks present in the particular train and test data-set files is mentioned clearly, though the redundancy has already been removed from both train and test datasets. Test dataset has unknown traffic category as well. Therefore, the total number of reduced records after redundancy removal in train dataset and test dataset is 1,074,992 and 77,289, respectively.

SVM is one of the most widely used classification techniques. A decade ago, it was typically used for binary classification; however, with the advent of its variants, multiclass classification is most frequently in use today. A hyper plane needs to be selected in Figure 8.8 both train and test network traffic data statistics (KDD Cup'99).

Network traffic classification using multiclass classifier 211 is used in such a way that it precisely separates between two classes of data. The wider the hyper plane width, the better it is. The width points of the hyper plane are decided from the closest points to the hyper plane line known as support vectors. In the context of network traffic data, there can be either normal traffic or anomalous traffic which comes under binary classification. Multiple subclasses of anomalous traffic can be determined using multiclass SVM. Binary classification is easy to implement as the classifier needs to learn either the traffic is normal or anomalous. In order to perform multiple-class classification, certain characterizations need to be considered, i.e., one versus one (OvO) and one versus rest (OvR). In OvR, one class separates from other classes if binary characteristics of one class distinguish it from the remaining set of classes. In OvO, each classifier forms a pair with every other classifier and learns from the relationship formed. Yet, there are many variants of SVM such as least squares SVM, v-SVM, nearly isotonic SVM, bounded SVM, NPSVM, and Twin SVM, but this chapter shall focus on multiclass categorization properties of SVM.

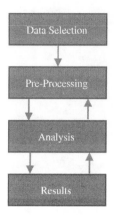

FIGURE 8.9
Data analysis phases.

8.4.3 Methodology

In order to perform the whole scenario, a formal step line has been followed. In general, it must follow four steps: data selection, preprocessing, analysis, and result evaluation as shown in Figure 8.9.

In nearly every data analytical domain, the generic flow model steps are followed meticulously. The steps may vary depending upon the unalike analysis requirements that are based on the generic model and the stair step followed as shown in Figure 8.9. The four steps are data selection, data preprocessing, analysis, and result, respectively, which further consists of substeps. Data selection may either include the primary dataset collected in hand or the secondary dataset selection from online repository. Data preprocessing is subdivided into three parts:

1. Removing redundancy
2. Feature selection
3. Data transformation.

Data analysis step involves extracting the relevant information from a vast amount of data. The people may use different methods for data analysis that is like a supervised machine learning technique (SVM) for multiclass classification that has been used. The final step is obtaining results and accuracy.

8.4.4 Case Study-I: Experimental Setup

The first-hand experiment is run on an Intel Core i5–5200U CPU @ 2.20 GHz computer with 8.00 GBRAMrunning operating system Linux (Ubuntu 16.04 LTS). Python 3.6 has been used for programming with scikit learn libraries such as Pandas and NumPy.

8.4.5 Data Selection

In data selection step, KDD CUP'99 is selected for data analysis. This first step could either be data collection or data selection. Data collection can be done by deploying network traffic collection tools such as tcpdump, NetIntercept, Snort, Bro, etc. Collecting data using these methods is called primary data collection. The collected data are stored as datasets having specific extension such as pcap. These datasets are most often available publicly to researchers. If a dataset is selected from these publicly available datasets, then it is called secondary dataset selection.

Data preprocessing means cleaning the data and making it readily available for further handling. In this step, the data in dataset is fine-tuned as per the input requirements to the model for processing. KDD Cup'99 dataset includes many redundant rows in training and testing datasets. There can be variant steps followed to preprocess the data. There is no generic step line for data preprocessing. Herein, a three-step process is followed to preprocess data that are removing redundancy, feature selection, and data transformation.

KDD Cup'99 dataset has two sets of train data and test data: complete dataset and 10% of complete dataset. The size of complete train and test dataset is 4,898,431 rows X 41 features and 311,031 rows X 41 features, respectively, whereas the size of 10% of complete train dataset is 494,021 rows X 41 features. Both the above complete and 10% of complete datasets consist of redundant rows. After redundancy removal from 10% of complete train dataset, the records become 145,586. The data redundancy may lead to the problem of biased results of the classifier toward frequently occurring records. Therefore, using a python script, the redundancy of training and testing dataset has been removed as a part of first step to data preprocessing. The second step to data preprocessing is feature extraction. Two widely used methods are used in combination and ranked the features accordingly.

Figure 8.10 shows the step line for data analysis network traffic classification using multiclass classifier 213. These methods are information gain and Gini covariance. The numeric values obtained using information gain method and Gini covariance method are in the range of 2.014–0.080 and 0.483–0.011, respectively, for all 41 features. Based on combined values of both the methods, rank is assigned to the respective feature. The highest ranked 26 features are selected for further analysis. The numeric value range for information gain method, and Gini covariance method is between 2.014–0.214 and 0.483–0.035, respectively, for all selected 26 features. The third step to data preprocessing is data transformation that involved two tasks: dataset file format conversion and symbolic conversion. The first subtask means to convert the dataset files in a format required by the machine learning model. Python with scikit learn libraries is used in this chapter for data conversion.

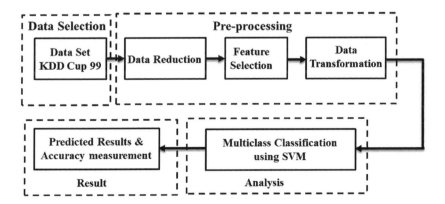

FIGURE 8.10
Case step line for data analysis.

Scikit-learn accepts data in csv (comma separated value) format for further analysis. Therefore, all the dataset files are converted to.csv format. The second subtask of data transformation is to convert the symbolic values with numeric values. Python code has been written for symbolic value conversion in the train and test dataset. Therefore, the data preprocessing step prepares the data for analysis in further steps. The authors have selected the subset of train set consisting of few attack sets from all four categories.

8.4.6 Analysis of the Case

Data analysis is the process of determining the relevant information by data modeling. Support vector machine (SVM) supervised the machine learning technique for modeling the network traffic data. Since SVM can be implemented for both binary class and multi-class classification, this has been implemented by using python programming with scikit learn libraries. A classifier known as support vector classifier has been used requiring a set of values to be passed as its parameters. The most relevant is the kernel which can take the values such as rbf, linear, etc., but the default kernel is set to radial basis function (rbf). Other parameters include C=1.0, cache_size, coef, class_weight, kernel, degree, gamma, decision_function_shape, verbose, etc. The parameter decision_function_shape can take either of the two values: ovr or ovo. The results using one vs. one value of decision_function_shape obtained categorically [DoS, U2R, R2L, normal] is 100, 66.66, 96, 98.12.

The results using one vs. rest value of decision_function_shape obtained categorically [DoS, U2R, R2L, normal] are 100, 60, 96, 98.53. However, the results are little improved when analysis is performed on the reduced feature dataset. In reduced feature dataset, the results using one vs. one value of decision_function_shape obtained categorically [DoS, U2R, R2L, normal] is 100, 67.6, 96.1, 98.12. The results using one vs. rest value of decision_ function_ shape obtained categorically [DoS, U2R, R2L, normal] are 100, 60.37, 96, 98.79. The above values are obtained by using Eq. (8.1). A substantial amount of computational time has decreased due to analysis being performed on reduced feature set data.

The aforementioned results in the analysis part are calculated using the simple accuracy formula of

$$\text{Accuracy} = \left(\text{Correct Prediction} / \text{Number of Test sample per category}\right) \times 100 \quad (8.1)$$

The number of testing sample per category is implied as the number of testing samples per category. For experimental purposes, the subset of the complete dataset is selected for analysis, and number of testing sample per category list holds the number of attacks categorically in the selected subset. The outcome of the machine learning model is compared with the actual data label which is stored in the list named the correct prediction implied as correct predictions obtained. However, it may be the chances that its accuracy can be improved if the following four notations are duly considered:

1. True Positives (TPs)
2. True Negatives (TNs)
3. False Positive (FPs)
4. False Negatives (FNs).

True positives are the correct predictions for correct traffic which is the most ideal case, and the focus remains on maximizing TPs. True negative is those results that shows model correctly predicted the negative class i.e. The data records of network traffic are appropriately labelled as normal. False positives, label as an attack to the normal record. False negative means considering attack traffic records as normal traffic records. Therefore, the measurement terms are as follows:

$$Accuracy = (TP + TN) / (TP + TN + FP + FN) \tag{8.2}$$

$$Error\ Rate = (FN + FP) / (TP + TN + FP + FN) \tag{8.3}$$

$$Precision = (TP) / (TP + FP) \tag{8.4}$$

$$Recall = TP / (TP + FN) \tag{8.5}$$

Eq. (8.2) is preferred over Eq. (8.1) while calculating the accuracy of the proposed machine learning model. The error rate, precision, and recall parameters are depicted in Eqs. (8.3), (8.4), and (8.5), respectively. Using Python programming, the values of TPs, TNs, FPs, and FNs are calculated and subsequently put in Eqs. (8.2)–(8.4) to obtain the values of different metrics. The accuracy, error rate, precision, and recall obtained categorically [DoS, U2R, R2L, normal] are: [1.0, 0.55, 1.0, 0.99], [0, 0.44, 0, 0.0020], [1., 1., 1., 1.], and [1., 0.99, 0.2, 1.], respectively.

8.5 Network Forensics Analysis with Case Study-2

This section presents an analysis of network behaviors of known malicious (including bots) and normal samples in an attempt to exploit differences to accomplish accurate behavior-based malware detection. The network behavior includes TCP, UDP, ICMP, and other network activities. Total number of DNS queries resembles the occurrence amounts for each collected sample of basic network function. In addition, other observations from the captured network activity are analyzed and correlated to identify network behaviors occurring mostly in malware. The classification algorithm of machine learning is to assess how effectively predicted network behavior can differentiate malware from the normal samples.

8.5.1 Analysis Methodology

This analysis is based on the dataset which contains malicious samples. The normal samples set covers a wide range of popular and daily used network applications including web browsers, FTP clients, social network clients, peer-to-peer (P2P) clients, and standard network tools. The dataset contains a broad range of malware types including bots, backdoors, malware downloaders, keyloggers, password stealers, and spyware, among others. For a testing set, this case study takes 31 malware samples from the ISCX dataset. These samples were reported as undetected by all antivirus software earlier. The sample of collected network traffic for each sample by executing it on a VMWare workstation with Ubuntu. The majority of malware samples had successful network activity during the collection period connecting with remote hosts and conducting malicious deeds. For each sample, we saved the traffic trace file, and we further analyzed each trace with filters in Windows network monitor.

8.5.2 Network Behavior

It shows the various network-based behaviors that can be exploited for malware detection. It defines each observation as O(n), where n is the identification number, and provides segregation of traffic dataset into malicious and normal traffic. The behavior in particular protocols is most important for the study. It includes the following.

8.5.2.1 Domain Name System

The domain name system (DNS) and network basic input/output system (NeBIOS) provide services to acquire IP addresses when a domain name is provided and vice versa. Reverse DNS (rDNS) queries are used to check if a certain IP address has a domain name associated with it. DNS and rDNS queries are used frequently by malware, especially bots, to establish a communication channel with external servers. It observed O1 issues a NetBIOS name request on a domain name that is not part of DNS or rDNS query.

8.5.2.2 Internet Control Message Protocol

The occurrence amounts of Internet Control Message Protocol (ICMP) activity, which focused on ICMP echo requests and replies, revealed an elevated usage by the malware samples in comparison to the normal traffic. Further analysis concluded that malware use ICMP echo requests in the same manner as the ping network utility to decide if a remote host is reachable, thus being a candidate for a connection attempt. The analysis shows that malware never attempted connections to IP addresses not receiving a reply to an ICMP echo request and almost always attempted to connect with IP addresses that did have a successful reply. Furthermore, the input IP address of the echo requests was never part of a DNS or rDNS query or NetBIOS name request. This may indicate that these IP addresses were hardwired, dynamically generated, or downloaded from a malware server. It refers two network behaviors based on the observation.

This encapsulates other less occurring activities, which is considered significant because they rarely occurred in the set samples or were implemented in a nonconventional way. These network activities are considered to be anomalous and not necessarily malicious behaviors. The value of recording the occurrences of behaviors is in those cases where a novel, never before observed or rarely used malicious behavior occurs in a malware sample. It is encompassed in this idea that it is rarely occurred network activity or a non-conventional protocol usage.

The percentage of samples with DNS queries, rDNS queries, and NetBIOS name requests appears in Table 8.1. While all normal samples issued DNS queries, only 79% of malware did so. This analysis revealed that malware used other network services, such as NetBIOS and ICMP, to acquire IP addresses. Several malware samples had failed DNS queries, which is due to malicious domain names that are either no longer active or previously discovered and shut down. NetBIOS name requests (NbtNs) were mostly used in malware (56%), while they were rarely used in normal samples (only 4%). We noticed that NetBIOS was issued on domains that have been either (a) previously used in a DNS query or (b) not previously used in DNS or rDNS queries. For normal samples, they were issued by two web browsers (Google Chrome and Firefox) on domains from the first category with some failing and others succeeding. On the other hand, most of the malware samples (50%) issued them on domain from the second category. We speculate that malware uses this approach to avoid detection by DNS-based methods, such as blacklists. Therefore, we conclude that this behavior can be used for detection and defined in Table 8.1.

TABLE 8.1

Segregation of Abnormal Traffic

SN	Parameter	Infected Content (%)	Normal Traffic (%)
1	DNS	79	100
2	rDNS	3	0
3	Observation 1	50	0
4	Observation 2	23	0
5	Observation 3	4	5
6	Observation 4	13	2

Observation 2, i.e., O2, ICMP-only activity, ICMP echoes requests for a specific nonlocal network IP address with no reply or a returned error message. Observation 3, i.e., O3, TCP/ICMP activity, TCP connection attempts to nonlocal IP addresses that received a successful reply to their ICMP echo requests. O3 occurred slightly more often in normal than malware, but it is the opposite for observation 4, i.e., O4. This supports our claim that malware frequently uses ICMP to identify IP addresses for connection attempts. These observations of O3 and O4 are provided in Table 8.1.

The selected Random Forest and BayesNet algorithm further classify to analyze the abnormalities. Several classification algorithms were applied on the test set with BayesNet and Random Forest. It is the most popular method used by many data scientists. All input is being taken down as a tree of the forest, and every tree provides its vote to classify the object. It is able to classify the large amount of data and provides high accuracy. It is an ensemble of classifier method that gives more accuracy than single classification algorithm. It is used to curtail the problem of large variance and biasness after averaging all learners and then make them balance.

Bayesian network is a statistical model that exhibits the random variables. It shows the probabilistic relationship between two factors. BayesNet classifier is one of the most effective classifiers to predict the performance with the state-of-the-art classifiers. Bayesian network classifier learns from the training set. This is the conditional probability of every attribute a_i given the class label cl. Supervised learning (classification) can be done by using Bayes rules to compute the probability of cl given the particular instance of $a_1, a_2 \ldots a_n$. Subsequently, it predicts the highest formal probability class. This computation exhibits feasibly by making a strong independence assumption. All the attributes a_i are conditionally independent given the value of the class c. By independence, we mean probabilistic independence, i.e., a is independent of b given c whenever $P(a|b;c)=P(a|c)$ for all possible values of a, b and c, whenever $P(c)>0$. This assumption is completely unrealistic. For solving such kind of issues, we have alternative machinery to comply and manipulate independence assertion known as Bayesian network.

Random Forest produces the best results as listed in Table 8.2. The false negative rates for all four algorithms were low ranging from 6% to 1%, and the false positives were also very low ranging between 0% and 1%. O3 with different IP addresses had successful network activity with remote hosts whose IP addresses were acquired through successful DNS queries.

Table 8.2 lists the amount of samples exhibiting the different types of observed network activity. TCP connection attempts to IP addresses which were not part of DNS, NetBIOS, or ICMP activity were the most prominent in this group with 10% in malware and only 2% in normal traffic. These malware samples, upon initial execution, immediately attempted connections to IP addresses ranging from a few to over 100 different addresses that appeared to have been hardwired or dynamically generated.

TABLE 8.2

Analysis Results

	Random Forest	Bayesian Net
FP	1	0
FN	3	2
FP rate	0.00	0.01
FN rate	0.006	0.01

8.5.3 Bot Analysis Using Classification

The effectiveness of an observed network behaviors can be evaluated by differentiating malware from normal samples. It can be used by clustering and classification algorithms analyzed through weka and orange suite. The referred dataset consisted of the occurrence amounts of network behaviors O1 through O4 for each malware and normal sample. The complete dataset is used for classification which is the combination of more than 600 training sets of malicious and normal traffic samples and the testing set containing the remaining samples. Some of the samples were not fitted in particular algorithm which further is not being used. Random Forest and BayesNet algorithm is used for the bot analysis.

Suppose that the set of features is M which includes edit distance algorithm. It defines the set of training examples as Tn and also its size in terms of the number of components as $|Tn|$. Subsequently, it defines the output value for each component $y^{(i)} = 1$, if it was labeled malicious or $Y^{(i)} = 0$ or otherwise. The output value $y^{(i)}$ for any component i2 Tn as a linear weighted sum of the values attained by each feature where the weights is given by β_j for each feature:

$$j \, \varepsilon \, F : y_i = \Sigma_{j \varepsilon F} \beta_j x_j + \beta_0$$

The following algorithm classifies a group of domains as malicious or legitimate by only looking at the domains within the group and is hence not reliant on definition of a database or distribution. The edit distance between two strings represents an integral value identifying the number of transformations required to transform one string to another. It is a symmetric measure and provides a measure of intra-domain entropy. The type of eligible transformations is addition, deletion, and modification. With reference to determining anomalous domains, we expect that all domain labels (or hostnames) which are randomized, will, on an average, have higher edit distance value. This algorithm gives the 100% accuracy to the experiment.

Algorithm 8.1: Dynamic Programming Algorithm for Finding the Edit Distance

Input: EditDistance(s1,s2)
Output:

1. *int m[i, j]=0*
2. **for** $I \leftarrow 1$ **to** $|s1|$
3. **do** *m[i, 0]=i*
4. **for** $j \leftarrow 1$ **to** $|s2|$
5. **do** *m[0,j]=j*

6. **for** $i \leftarrow 1$ **to** $|s1|$
7. **do for** $j \leftarrow 1$ **to** $|s2|$
8. **do** $m[i, j] = \min\{m[[i\text{-}1,j\text{-}1] + \text{if}(s1[i] = s2[j])$ then 0 else 1 fi, $m[i\text{-}1,j] + 1$, $m[i, j\text{-}1] + 1\}$
9. **return** $m[|s1|, |s2|]$

It is compared with the performance of each classifier based on their accuracy to predict classes of unknown instances. This case study is for the two classification techniques for analysis. These classification techniques are Random Forest and BayesNet algorithm which shows the ensemble classification (Figure 8.11).

Algorithm 8.2

Input:
D: dataset; tnd: training data; tsd: testing data point; cl: class label; f: feature; M: model
Output:

1. Obtaining tnd ($\text{tnd}_1 + \text{tnd}_2 + \text{tnd}_3 + \ldots\ldots + \text{tnd}_n$) and tsd ($\text{tsd}_1 + \text{tsd}_2 + \text{tsd}_3 + \ldots + \text{tsd}_n$) from D
2. Extracting f from tnd and tsd of D
3. Segregation on Normal and Botnet traffic
4. If no cl on botnet traffic then
5. Providing cl elseif
6. Go to next step
7. Segregation of Botnet from different observation
8. Test M_1 from knn, DT and svm
9. Frame M, test each M on cl data on tnd and tsd and obtain its accuracy
10. Test ensemble M_2 from multiple combinations
11. Compare results from step 8 and step 9
12. Predict the cl.

It compares the performance of each classifier based on its accuracy, precision, recall, and f-1 score to predict classes of unknown instances.

- **Accuracy:** Accuracy exhibits the description of systematic errors and the statistical bias. ISO defines the term trueness for the accuracy. The accuracy of a classifier

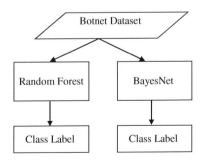

FIGURE 8.11
Ensemble classifier model.

on a given test set is the percentage of test set tuples that are correctly classified by the classifier.

$$\text{Accuracy / Recognition Rate} = TP + TN / P + N \qquad (8.6)$$

- **Precision:** Precision is the fraction of retrieved documents that are relevant to the query. The precision and recall measures are also widely used in classification. Precision can be thought of as a measure of exactness (i.e., what percentage of tuples labeled as positive are actually such), whereas recall is a measure of completeness (what percentage of positive tuples are labeled as such).

$$\text{Precision} = TP / TP + FP \qquad (8.7)$$

- **Recall:** Recall in information retrieval is the fraction of the documents that are relevant to the query that are successfully retrieved. In binary classification, recall is called sensitivity. So, it can be looked at as the probability that a relevant document is retrieved by the query.

$$\text{Recall} = TP / TP + FN = TP / P \qquad (8.8)$$

- **F_1:** F_1 score (also F-score or F-measure) is a measure of a test's accuracy. It considers both the precision p and the recall r of the test to compute the score. F_1 score is the harmonic mean of precision and recall.

$$F_1 = 2 \times ((p \times r) / (p + r)) \qquad (8.9)$$

Where p refers to the Positive tuple (tuples of the main class of interest), N-negative tuples (all other tuples).

True positives: True positive means the classifier correctly labeled the positive tuples. True positive is denoted by TP.

True negatives: True negative means the classifier correctly labeled the negative tuples. True negative is denoted by TN.

False positives: False positive means the negative tuples that are incorrectly labeled as positive. False positive is denoted by FP.

False negatives: False negative means that the positive tuples that were mislabeled as negative. False negative is denoted by FN.

Confusion Matrix: The confusion matrix is an important tool for analyzing how well your classifier can recognize tuples of different classes. TP and TN exhibit when the classifier is accepting right things. On the other hand, FP and FN exhibit when the classifier is accepting wrong things. Table 8.3 presents confusion matrix shown with total for positive and negative tuples.

According to this, results after observation, O1, occurred the most in the malware samples with 49% followed by O2 with 21% and O4 with 18%. All three are considered behaviors more likely to occur in malware than in normal traffic processes initially assumed anomalous and not necessarily malicious. Our analysis results successfully classified a diverse group of malwares and normal process with very high accuracy and minimal false positives and false negatives. Classification algorithms correctly detected newly introduced malware samples also with minimal false negatives and false positives. Most interestingly, our dataset that included 31 malware samples are not detected by any tools.

TABLE 8.3

Confusion Matrix

		Predicted Class		
		Yes	No	Total
Actual class	Yes	TP	FN	P
	NO	FP	TN	N
	Total	P'	N'	P+N

These undetected malwares were correctly identified using our analysis in classification algorithms with few exceptions. This provides strong evidence that our identified behaviors can be added to existing behavior-based bots and malware detection solutions to help stop zero-day attacks on a host machine.

Questions

Q.1. How can we develop a network forensics process? Explain in detail.

Q.2. Explain the evolution of network forensics analysis.

Q.3. Explain the generic process model of network forensics.

Q.4. Draw the network forensics framework and explain the suitability for investigating the attack.

Q.5. Is there any way to segregate the data from the dataset? Verify the statement.

Q.6. Explain network forensics analysis with any case study.

Q.7. What do you understand by confusion matrix? Why is it required?

Q.8. What do you understand by true positive and true negative?

Q.9. What is the meaning of false positive and false negative?

Q.10. Write a dynamic programming algorithm for finding the edit distance.

References

A. Bijalwan, "Botnet Forensic Analysis Using Machine Learning," *Security and Communication Networks*, vol. 2020, pp. 1-9, 2020.

A. Bijalwan and S. Harvinder, "Investigation of UDP Bot Flooding Attack," *Indian Journal of Science and Technology*, vol. 9, no. 21, pp. 1-6, 2016.

E. Casey, "Network Traffic as a Source of Evidence: Tool Strengths, Weakness, and Future Needs," *Digital Investigation*, vol. 1, pp. 28–43, 2004.

P. Kaur, A. Bijalwan, R. C. Joshi, and A. Awasthi, Network forensic process model and framework: an alternative scenario, in *Intelligent Communication, Control and Devices*, Springer, 2018, pp. 493–502.

P. Kaur, P. Chaudhary, A. Bijalwan, and A. Awasthi, Network Traffic Classification Using Multiclass Classifier, *International Conference on Advances in Computing and Data Sciences* (pp. 208–217), 2018.

H. Kim, B. Kim, D. Kim, I.-K. Kim, and T.-M. Chung, Implementation of GESNIC for web server protection against HTTP GET flooding attacks, in *Information Security Applications*, Springer, 2012, pp. 285–95.

M. D. Kohn, M. M. Eloff, and J. H. P. Eloff, "Integrated Digital Forensic Process Model," *Computer & Security*, vol. 38, pp. 103–115, 2013.

J. Kong, M. Mirza, J. Shu, C. Yoedhana, M. Gerla, and S. Lu, editors, Random Flow Network Modeling and Simulations for DDoS Attack Mitigation. *2003 ICC'03 IEEE International Conference on Communications*, IEEE, 2003.

C. Liu, A. Singhal, and D. Wijesekera, "A Logic-Based Network Forensic Model for Evidence Analysis," IFIP *Advances in Information and Communication Technology*, vol. 462, pp. 129–145, 2015.

R. Lutui, "A Multidisciplinary Digital Forensic Investigation Process Model," *Business Horizons*, vol. 59, pp. 593–604, 2016.

K. Mandia and C. Procise, *Incident Response and Computer Forensics*, Osborne McGraw-Hill, 2003.

E. S. Pilli, R. C. Joshi, and R. Niyogi, "Network Forensic Frameworks: Survey and Research Challenges," *Digital Investigation*, vol. 7, pp. 14–27, 2010.

P. Porras, H. Saidi, and V. Yegneswaran, "An Analysis of Conficker's Logic and RendezvousPoints," Tech. Rep., March 2009.

M. Reith, C. Carr, and G. Gunsch, "An Examination of Digital Forensic Models," *International Journal of Digital Evidence*, vol. 1, no. 3, 2002.

W. Ren and H. Jin, Distributed Agent-Based Real Time Network Intrusion Forensics System Architecture Design. *Proceedings of the International Conference on Advanced Information Networking and Applications* (pp. 177–182), IEEE Press, 2005.

9

Evidence and Incident Response

LEARNING OBJECTIVES

This chapter discusses about the traditional investigation methods for getting the evidence. It also reveals the sources of evidence and its incident response. After reading this chapter, you would

- Have knowledge about the sources of evidence.
- Understand handling the evidence and its various types.
- Understand the procedure of handling the evidence.
- Understand the botnets and its development year-wise.
- Have knowledge about the terminology of incident response.
- Understand the process of initial response and the incident classification.

9.1 Introduction

As we have studied in previous chapters, all the network events are captured, recorded, and further analyzed by the network forensics. This area of study discovers the facts related to all security attacks in the network. It is a postmortem of all the evidences. It captures the evidences for the incident response. It is a notitia criminis of the attack on the network. Over time, the strategy to investigate the crime and handle the evidences has changed. The general methodology for handling the evidence in the traditional investigation was somehow assumption based. These assumptions revolve around the data acquisition that differs from the modern strategy based on live forensics. Handling the evidence in traditional investigation was carried out by following way:

1. The source of evidence will be static. It is of fixed size which means no changes can be done on it.
2. The experts controlled completely on data collection which means the acquisition of evidences can be commanded by investigators.
3. There was no possibilities of alteration on the copies of evidences, and it can be used in a forensic manner.
4. All the copies can be compared with the original, and it is to be verified as and when required.

All these assumptions can satisfy when the sources of the evidence are within a network in which possible acquisition comes from fixed disk, removal media, and random-access memory (RAM). However, these assumptions do not feasibly fulfill the remote network.

When we talk about the evidence, it is a must to ensure that the investigation fulfills the properties for the evidence which is ardently required. It has to check genuinely if there is any alteration while seizing the data, either deliberately or unknowingly. When we acquire evidence and process it for further images, we must ensure that there should be authenticity while reproducing the evidences and also the system it is taken from.

9.2 Evidence and Its Sources

Evidence is a collection of facts that show whether the assumption and beliefs are true or valid. As we know through our previous chapters, the investigation can become successful when the evidence is carefully collected, preserved, and analyzed. It means handling of the evidences is most important as in other phases of network forensics. It is obvious that when we think about the evidence, i.e., a clue of the incidence, the consideration given below should be there. As per the aspiration defined by Sarah Mocas in 2003, three important considerations need to be maintained:

1. Technical Environment
2. Static Technical Environment
3. Dynamic Technical environment.

The technical environment states that the information is generally traced through the set of laboratory equipment in support of the investigation. The static technical environment states that only the investigative procedure is strongly liable to alter information for the investigation. The dynamic technical environment states that one or more components from where the information is traced have the potential to alter related to the investigation, independent of any changes to the system that might be introduced during the investigative process.

When we talk about the properties of evidence, we must check all the desirable properties while handling the evidence. These properties are as follows (Figure 9.1):

1. Integrity
2. Reproducibility
3. Authenticity
4. Minimization
5. Noninterference

The details on these desirable properties for handling the evidence are given below.

Integrity
As we know, the evidence is too fragile in nature. Due to this nature, it can be altered and destroyed very easily. So, integrity is a major concern in handling the evidence. Integrity refers to no changes in the evidence that means there should

FIGURE 9.1
Desirable properties for handling the evidence.

not be any changes in the evidence while collecting and securing it. It assures us that there is no alteration either knowingly or unknowingly or any damages on it. It also assures us that while making images from the originals, there will be no alteration in original evidence.

Reproducibility

Reproducibility is an ability to replicate the findings with the highest level of evaluating the evidence. It also validates the investigative claims by showing transparency of its methods, coding, and data (Figure 9.2). It assures us that the devices or the data through which examination took place are capable of reproducing more information. When the investigator performs the experiment, he sets up many experimental devices in the laboratory. The digital forensic investigator may have to deal with many experimental devices and tools. These arrangements may yield more complexity on the forensic settings. So, to ensure high quality of reproducibility capacity, high degree of formalization requires for providing best reproducible results on both setup devices and the process. It is a cyclic process of observation. Questions based on the observation may come for setting the hypothesis. It helps in formulating prediction that is based on the hypothesis. The prediction further testing it for the analysis and it is followed by the replication that again process it for the testing.

Authenticity

The authenticity of the evidence states that the information collected by the investigator is not compromised, altered, and damaged while handling the evidence. The system authentication means that all the acquired evidence taken by the set-up devices is flawless. The authenticity means that the action or the process of proving something is valid, genuine, and true. The term authentic means that the evidence must be evidentiarily proven, genuine, and admissible. The authentication of the system means that we are talking something about its IP addresses, identifiers, etc. The concept of authentication and the integrity is somehow similar but not completely the same. Once things are authenticated, it directly implies integrity, but its opposite is not always true.

FIGURE 9.2
Process of reproducibility.

Minimization

Minimization assures that the minimum data or information is already processed for the investigation from evidence. There is a set of protocols to the government by law to seize any item in which there is no evidentiary value. None of the authorized persons take out the things or seized items in nonevidentiary environment. It is acknowledged by the US Department of Justice in 2002 that it is not possible always with the digital evidence. It is quite obvious that whenever it possible, limit the information seized legally. For instance, the attacker launched attack on the network traffic that can directly compromise the network abruptly. So, in this case, we can, however, limit the amount of information seized in some cases, but it is not possible to reduce the amount of data processes from the hard disk. The amount of data can be reduced by the new technological development in sensor network that helps to segregate the information on good and bad files from a search.

Noninterference

Non-interference refers to the aspect of integrity and confidentiality. This property of handling the evidence refers to restricting the information flow from the system. Non-interference assures us that there should not be any change in original data or information, i.e., dataset, while acquiring and analyzing the digital evidence. If it does any changes on original dataset, it should be identifiable. There may be a chance of minimal changes while analyzation works proceeds on the digital devices. It may happen at some state of information when the operation is performed on the digital devices. However, the tools and the techniques applied to acquire the evidence and subsequently applied analysis do not alter or modify the original dataset like from the seized hard drive. On the other hand, when the forensic analysis takes place over network traffic connection, the investigator opts the strategy to disregard the investigation where the least changes occur. The National Institute of Justice, US in 2000 expressed that "One of the most important aspect of securing a crime scene is to preserve the scene with minimal contamination and disturbance of physical evidence."

Evidence handling can take place when a person knows the various sources of evidences which is important for the investigation. These evidences can be obtained from the following two ways.

9.2.1 Sources of Evidence within Network

Intruders not only try to compromise the host; in fact, they grab permeated information from all across the related environment. The investigator has to acquire all evidences not only from a random-access memory or from a hard disk, but they have to pay heed to all the connected components of the network (Figure 9.3). The following components are the sources of evidence within a network:

1. Network Traffic
2. Network and Device Logs
3. Random Access Memory
4. Fixed Drive
5. Removal Media, etc.

All these above components are the best sources of evidence within a network. Network traffic is the amount of data that travels into a network at a particular time period. The digital activities can be captured through the packet analysis of the traffic. Gathering evidence from the network traffic can be possible when the flow of data packets is to be focused. These packets can be observed through various tools that are already discussed in our previous chapters. Logs are the records of all the activities generated in the devices. It can also be performed by an outside user on the device. The logs can be generated by all the devices such as server, firewall, intrusion detection system, intrusion prevention system, and others. It captures all incoming and outgoing activities logged onto a system. The device-based logs can be the application log, operating system event logs, and others. We utilized hard drive in case of inaccessibility of any devices or computer system due to damages. The evidences can be retrieved through fixed hard drive of any device.

FIGURE 9.3
Sources of evidence.

9.2.2 Sources of Evidence in Remote Network

The following are the sources of remote network evidence:

1. Peer to Peer Network
2. Websites
3. FTP Servers.

9.3 Evidence Handling

Once we realize the sources of the evidence, the next step is how to handle the evidence. Protecting and making it intact is a primary concern. There should be an appropriate investigation process for the forensics that is also acceptable as per the law enforcement when it is used as per the terms. Thus, the investigator has to ensure that it does not contradict and follows the procedures. The investigator has to remind certain questions to meet the terms and agreements of the law as follows:

1. How, when, and where the evidence was received.
2. How and who deals with the evidence and for what purpose.
3. Where the evidence was stored before analyzing.
4. How the stored evidence will be given any appropriate result.
5. The images of the original collected evidence are the same or altered.
6. Proof of no alteration on image files.

The investigator has to ensure that he has the capability to handle the evidence for the analysis purpose. He should have a combination of three Cs denoting confidence, credibility, and cost. The meaning of three Cs is as follows:

Confidence
   The investigator should be more confident while handling the evidence as it is a matter of high secrecy. He should know how to deal with the others regarding evidence acquisition to the law enforcement. He should be well trained and have learned all facts to take an appropriate decision.

Credibility
   The investigator works with the investigation team while gathering evidence. This process is a time-taking process. The investigation must take place in the manner that the results are credible to a stranger to matter. He should consider the results, no matter it is not well desired.

Cost
   Every investigation is expensive in terms of time and money. The investigator has to fulfill expenditure while gathering the evidence because of unanticipated nature of work. There may be a chance of increasing of cost on evidence collection like original evidence, reproducing the images from original evidence and in evidence handling.

Digital evidence is volatile and fragile too, which means that any improper handling of evidence can alter it. There may be an easy chance of tampering in digital evidence, or there is a possible chance of getting destroyed as the characteristics of digital evidence itself are very fragile. Even though, while viewing or using, there is a chance of getting change in evidence. So it is a must to handle gently and keeping eyes on it so that no one can alter.

In the context of fragility and volatility of digital evidence, the protocol has to ensure and to followed it that the information should not get altered during handling. There are chances of it getting corrupted during access time, during collection, packaging time, transfer, and further storage. These protocols are notified when the evidence follows the steps. As per the Cyber Security Coalition, 2015, the response to the data breaches, unauthorized access to system, denial of service attacks, and other cybersecurity incidents include specific procedures. These procedures are followed to contain the incident, to investigate it, and for resolving the cybersecurity incident. There are two approaches to handle such kind of incidents as follows.

9.3.1 Recovery as Fast as Possible

The first way, i.e., recovery as fast as possible, ensures that we are coming out from the problems. Here, the investigator's tendency is to minimize the loss. It doesn't correlate with the preservation, but it emphasizes the prevention of the incident to minimize harm by the recovery. It is the primary concern of an investigator to get a fast response along with the recovery; otherwise, loss of the vital information might be possible.

9.3.2 Monitoring and Collecting Evidence

The second phase refers to monitoring the incidents and collecting more evidences. It ensures that collection of evidences is in a steady manner and more information about the incident is collected. This phase continuously monitors the behavior of an incident and provides details about it. The primary focus of this phase is to gather evidence irrespective of recovery. The investigator has to pay heed to the number of persons involved while handling the evidence. There should be a limitation on individuals who handle the evidences. There are certain protocols especially for the vulnerable evidences. The priority should be started from the most vulnerable to the least vulnerable evidence. The order of most volatility to the least volatility of evidence as per D. Brezinski and T. Killalia in 2002 for RFC 3227 is as follows:

1. Registers, Cache.
2. Routing Table, Address Resolution Protocol (ARP), Process Table, Memory, Kernel Statistics.
3. Temporary File Systems.
4. Disk.
5. Remote Logging and Monitoring Data.
6. Network Topology, Physical Configuration.
7. Archival Media.

9.4 Evidence-Handling Procedure

In earlier section, we have understood how evidence is the most important aspect of network forensics. Evidence handling is also a tedious process. There are four major phases in handling the digital evidence:

1. Identification of evidence
2. Collection of evidence
3. Analysis of evidence
4. Preservation and reporting of evidence.

The description of all above phases and the process in detail is as follows.

9.4.1 Identification of Evidence

Before starting the collection for the analysis of the crime, we should know the preliminary details of initial-phase evidence. Identification of an evidence is an important phase in which the investigator gets earlier clues of primary questions that are as follows:

1. What happened on the network?
2. Who is involved in this incident?
3. Where is the attack targeted?
4. When is the attack launched?
5. Who are the culprit and the victim behind this?
6. How does the attack take place?

These are the elementary questions that are necessary for the identification of an evidence. These questions give certain ideas to the investigator that how he should start working on the investigation process. It can exactly impact the investigator on how he has to follow up the case. These questions are exactly the same as we generally utilized in our traditional approach of investigation. In this scenario, the investigator approach is the same traditional investigation technique to identify the evidence. In such cases, they adopt procedures asking certain questions from the suspect, victim, and all the users who participate within a network or it can be the law enforcement investigations for identifying the evidence. This digital evidence can be identified from various sources such as computer, smartphone, hard drive, all the removal media, Internet of Things-related devices like smart watch, smart television, refrigerator, washing machine, etc. It is also possible to identify the attack from social media, different websites, different network Ips, and the logs too. If the cyber-crime is related to the fraudulent then the evidence can be identified through the seized storage media or from any seized devices.

9.4.2 Collection for the Evidence

The collection starts just after when the investigator identified the attack evidences. The incident can be secured when it is identified through observation, reported, and suspected. Collection phase includes all the available data and the resources from the network. This phase is not limited to the physical location; however, it covers the entire network within an organization or from where the incident took place. It collects evidence not only from the single digital device, but it also collects evidence from the server, multiple digital devices, and the systems. It can be more secure when all the identified evidence is to be preserved. Preservation is possible when none of the user interferes nearby the crime place, i.e., it should be protected from all the people. The crime place should be protected from any kind of contamination when it is identified by an investigator. It is to be well documented before the initiation of collection phase. The documentation will take place in the entire process of investigation. These documentations ensure the complete information that includes connections, serial numbers, number of devices, number of all consumable items, damages, and state of the system either on or off, etc.

The procedure of collecting evidence is completely hinged on the investigator. It is his choice whether he makes one team or a group of teams for the investigation process. The investigator starts investigation to collect the evidence with the coordination of law enforcement agencies. They may use any digital media device for collection once the consent nod comes from the law enforcement. These digital media devices can be internet-connected devices, computer, CPU, mobiles, server, or any other appliances. The investigator uses various tools to collect the evidence from the crime scene, but it should also be admissible by law court.

Collection of evidence from the remote network is quite different from collection within a network, as it is abstruse that remote network area comes under investigator's jurisdiction or control. It might be possible that the services are hosted from foreign countries, or the traffic in transit state between two different networks might also be possible. Then, it will be difficult for the investigator to collect evidence from any kind of remote services such as the FTP server, website, peer-to-peer network, and other areas. Again, the investigator will have to take permission from multiple law enforcement agencies to start the investigation of the collection of evidence. In such cases, the investigator has to ensure the verification of the integrity as well as authenticity while collecting evidence from the live network sources. The authenticity of collecting evidence from untrusted sources like the Internet is quite difficult as it can be manipulated very easily. In such case, finding the real origin of evidence is also obtuse. The following activity might invade the authenticity of the evidences:

1. IP spoofing
2. Email spoofing
3. Third party compromise
4. TCP relay
5. TCP proxy
6. Man in middle attacks
7. Session compromise
8. DoS attack
9. Anonymous repetitive mail
10. Web anonymizer
11. DNS cache poisoning

9.4.3 Acquisition and Analysis of Evidence

The third phase of the evidence-handling procedure is the analysis of acquired evidence. The conservation of evidence is indispensable in the postcollection phase. The major concern in the postcollection phase is to maintain integrity. The integrity of evidence is an issue for the data collection and also with the captured traffic. It may arise from the remote network services. The remote network service especially through the live network can put all the collected data into a stack, even though the devices and tools from which the evidence is acquired are also at risk. The malicious activities from the hostile network may harm any collection tool too. When the collection of data takes place in a live network, there may be more chances of harm rather than other scenarios. So, the investigator has to ensure maintaining integrity by preventing its devices and tools from any kind of anonymity. The experts can work on the image of collected file for maintaining the integrity of digital evidence. This analysis in search of evidence can be performed in two ways of data extraction as follows.

9.4.3.1 Physical Extraction

Physical extraction is a kind of extraction when the acquisition of the data for analysis is to be taken place within the location where the evidence resides such as a computer hard drive. This search is based within a device. It is to be conducted through file carving process like number of identifiers, header and footer. The investigator may use it through different keywords and analyzing the unallocated space.

9.4.3.2 Logical Extraction

Logical extraction is a kind of extraction when the acquisition of data for the analysis is to take place from the location relative to the file system of an operating system that is used to store the name and location of the files. It depends upon other components such as application on the device, operating system, file system, etc. There are chances of losing metadata from the file through logical extraction. The main advantage of the logical extraction is that it acquires evidence for the analysis from deleted files and through encrypted, decrypted, and compressed files. It also acquires data from the unused space and unallocated spaces, even though the file is locked with the password for the analysis.

There are few terms that might create confusion like active and passive acquisition and static and dynamic acquisition. In below statement, we can understand the term active and passive:

9.4.3.2.1 Active and Passive Analysis

When the evidence is gathered from the remote network server then we can refer it as an active, and when the evidence is collected from the network equipment such as hub switch or through air and across the cable can be referred as passive acquisition. The term passive generally, refers to the technologies such as Ethernet segments.

9.4.3.2.2 Static and Dynamic Analysis

Static analysis is a traditional approach for acquisition of evidence where data are not in a position to move. It can be analyzed by digital devices, memory dump, systems, hard drives, etc., whereas the dynamic analysis is an approach to collect, analyze, and maintain the report, even though the compromised system remains functional. We can clear these two terminologies with an example. When we talk about the websites and the network, we clearly state that the content in a website can remain for several years as per the requirement of the admin, but the content in the network cannot be retained for long. In such example, the data of the website is referred to as static, and the network is dynamic. The advantage of the dynamic analysis is that it provides integrity and consistency of forensic data that can be used as forensic evidence. The detailed information about the tools that have been utilized for analyzing evidence in static and dynamic modes is provided in Table 9.1.

TABLE 9.1

Static and Dynamic Tools for Analysis

Sr. No	Tool Name	Operating System	Static/Dynamic Analysis
1.	Registry Recon	Windows	Static
2.	SIFT (SANS Investigative Forensics Toolkit)	Ubuntu	Dynamic
3.	EnCase	Windows	Static
4.	Digital Forensics Framework	Windows/Linux/Mac OS	Static and Dynamic
5.	EPRB (Elcomsoft Password Recovery Bundle)	Windows	Dynamic
6.	PTK Forensics (Programmers Toolkit)	LAMP	Static and Dynamic
7.	FTK (Forensic Toolkit)	Windows	Static
8.	The Coroner's Toolkit	Unix	Static and Dynamic
9.	The Sleuth Kit	Unix/Windows	Dynamic
10.	COFEE (Computer online forensic evidence extractor)	Windows	Dynamic
11.	OCFA (Open Computer Forensics Architecture)	Linux	Dynamic
12.	OS Forensics	Windows	Dynamic
14.	SafeBack	Windows	Static
16.	X-Way Forensics	Windows	Static and Dynamic
17.	CAINE (Computer aided investigative environment)	Linux	Static and Dynamic
18.	Bulk Extractor	Windows, Linux	Dynamic
19.	IRCR (Incident Response Collection Report)	Windows	Dynamic
20.	Intella	Windows	Dynamic
21.	CMAT (Compile Memory Analysis Tool)	Windows	Dynamic
22.	WFT (Window Forensic Toolkit)	Windows	Dynamic
23.	Responder	Windows	Dynamic
24.	FRED (First Responder's Evidence Disk)	Windows	Dynamic
25.	Memoryze	Windows	Dynamic
26.	Windows SCOPE	Windows	Dynamic
27.	Second Look	Linux	Dynamic
28.	Volatility Framework	Volatility systems	Dynamic
29.	Volafox	Mac OS	Dynamic
30.	LiveWire	Windows	Dynamic
31.	Network Miner	Windows/Linux	Dynamic
32.	Net Intercept	Appliance	Static and Dynamic
33.	Tcp flow	Windows/Mac/Linux	Dynamic
34.	WireShark	Windows/Mac/Linux	Static and Dynamic
35.	Evidence Eliminator	Windows	Dynamic
36.	NetSleuth	Windows	Dynamic
37.	DECAF (Detect and Eliminate Computer Assisted Forensic)	Windows	Dynamic
38.	HashKeeper	Windows	Static

The acquisition methodology of collected evidence is different and depends on where the data are collected from. It completely hinges on the types of digital devices and the way of acquisition. For instance, the collected data are from the digital devices such as smart watch, smart phone, etc., and in another case, the collected data are taken from the damaged hard drive. When the analysis of evidence is extracted from the seized digital devices in the forensic lab, it is referred to as static acquisition. In this case, the investigator has to ensure to maintain the integrity of the evidence. There should not be any alteration on evidence inside of the forensic lab. The experts must set their tools and the technique in such a way that either the evidence shouldn't be tampered, or it minimizes the effects from any alteration. Eventually, the collected data from the seized devices are considered as a primary source of evidence for the investigator. There is a methodology to find out whether the image file is altered or it is the same as the original. It can be analyzed and calculated through the mathematical computation in which if the cryptographic hash value of image is similar to the original hash value, then it is observed to be of no alteration. If the hash value of image differs from the original value, then it is assumed that there is some modification on images.

9.4.4 Preservation and Reporting of Evidence

Preservation always protects the integrity while handling of evidence. It prevents from any kind of alteration on both original and the images of the file. Preservation of evidence is a continuous process from the beginning of the phases to the reporting. In preservation, it is a must to all those who are involved for identifying, collecting, acquiring, and analyzing of the evidence to demonstrate the details about no alteration on the processes. They have to maintain the chain of custody for the demonstration. It is a process to preserve the incident along with evidence by the investigator. The chain of custody works for the entire span of case. It provides all suitable answers that had been raised during the identification phase. It contains the complete information about the individuals and their detailed transactions with others during identification, collection, acquisition, and analysis phases for the documentation.

Evidence reporting is a well-written documentation in which all the processes and procedures are explained in brief. It primarily focusses on data recovery with the advisable facts. The report is always to be reviewed, cross examined, and critiqued. The outcome of the analysis is finally documented in a report. It is a must that the chain of custody document is enclosed with the report along with a detailed explanation of the methodology used, its steps, and all materials like figures, tables, tools, techniques, and its output. The report should be documented precisely and clearly. The purpose of investigation and its case under investigation should be clearly mentioned.

9.5 Incident Response and Its Methodology

Although an organization is functioning smoothly and its employees are happy with their daily routine hard work to uplift their knowledge as well as contribute to maximize the profit of their organization, all of sudden, a small mistake of an internal employee like downloading a ransomware intentionally or unintentionally can create gratuitous problem to the organization. This problem creates questions in everyone's mind that "How did it happen", "When will it resolve", and "How big is it". All the experts will try to determine what systems are affected by this incident and how it is being manipulated. Due to this problem, the experts have to further calculate the intensity of the damages by the effect of compromising the system and start the incident response.

The term incident response means a capability to facilitate response orderly. It is a process in which the experts manage the data breaches or any kind of attacks from the network. It also shows the way how the organization tackles the consequences of the incident. The main objective of the incident response is to manage the risk that arises through the attack so that the damages can be minimized and the collateral damage from the incident is kept minimum. It also keeps the recovery time and the cost due to the damages at minimal level.

Incident response is a crucial component of the organization that alerts when any incident takes place by the attacker. The organization has to build a capability to handle the incident by ensuring the working knowledge of the incident response processes. They have to keep in mind certain points:

1. In fact, the organization has to build a capability to handle the incident by ensuring the working knowledge of the incident response processes.
2. They have to build a core incident response team that is fully aware of the occurrence of incidents and able to minimize the damage, cost, and the recovery time.
3. After the formation of the incident response expert's team, the formulation of plan and related process should be implemented.
4. Further, the plan has to be evaluated and tested in every step of the framework. It should be structured orderly so that the organization takes the following procedure when such kind of incidents happen.

9.5.1 Process of Incident Response

There is a seven-step procedure to overcome the incident as follows:

1. Preparation
2. Identification of the incident
3. Detection of the incident
4. Analysis of the incident
5. Containment
6. Eradication and recovery from the damages
7. Postincident activity.

9.5.1.1 Preparation

Preparation is the most crucial phase of the incident response process (Figure 9.4). It refers to the preparation for unavoidable security breaches. Preparation also refers to the organization that in what extent the Computer Incident Response Team (CIRT) is ready for any kind of incident. In this phase, the security team makes the plan, their strategies, communication, and documentation to determine how to access the control, what tools are required for it, experts' details with their duties, what kind of training is required for all the team members, etc. It is impossible to succeed in incident response without having

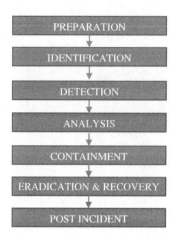

FIGURE 9.4
Process of incident response.

any good preparation. It also ensures if any other things are required apart from the present things like tools for both software and hardware forensics investigations. Training is the last sub-phase of the preparation that ensures that team members including the staffs of the organization are well trained so that in future they may combat with any future incidence.

9.5.1.2 Identification

Identification is the process through which the incidence can be identified. This phase ensures that the extract incident clues are really a security breach, or it is something else. The acquired data are further matched for the confirmation. This phase also makes sure to preserve the copy of the data so as to facilitate legal requirements, and as soon as the process is repeated on the original data, the results obtained after investigation are proved to be the same. If there is mismatch, it will proceed further for the detection phase of the incident response.

9.5.1.3 Detection

Detection is the process through which the incident gets confirmed noticed. This phase also calls for the rapid response so that the time, cost, and the damages can be minimized. Incident response team starts gathering the events, logs, and traffic, monitoring tools including intrusion detection system and intrusion prevention system, error messaging and the firewall to determine the scope of the incident response. The detection of any response depends upon the size of the organization. If the size of the organization is tool large, they may have millions of events per day. It means the security team have to face uphill task where they have day to day other activities too to perform. It will become a tedious job to detect the incident and take an appropriate decision.

9.5.1.4 Analysis

Once the detection phase detected the incident, the experts start their analysis on it to find the reason for the incidence. The analysis phase starts with the acquisition of data. This may take several days depending upon the size of the organization and ingress traffics.

Experts may try to acquire clues from the log files, software processes, network connections, etc. Once the acquisition phase is over, it is further forwarded for examination purpose. These analyses can be utilized through different tools and techniques. Finally, the analysis determines the root cause of the incident and provides a way to reconstruct the action of the threat actor.

9.5.1.5 Containment

The earlier phase gives full understanding of the incident and the system involved in this, and then the organization's team can further proceed for the containment phase. It is the priority of the incident response team to contain the clues just after analyzing the incidence. Containment phase keeps the attacks under control. It also ensures the policy to prevent the expansion of damages. The experts take the strategy to limit the damages and ensure further that there shouldn't be proliferation of the incidence onto another network resource. It might be possible that the proliferation can be stopped by plugging out the network cable from the firewall for locking down the ports from the infected machine.

9.5.1.6 Eradication and Recovery

Once the containment phase is over, eradication starts removing the threats from the system and starts restoring the affected system. It brings the affected system back to the initial state. This phase ensures that in the entire process, the data loss should be minimized, and the eradication process can obsolete the malicious content from the system.

Once the complete eradication process is initiated, the recovery is made by taking backups through efficient software. The damaged system can be reinstalled through a new operating system and applications. Experts can examine by their strategies if the recovered system has any previous account that can be activated when the system is connected with the internet again. This phase mainly works on testing, monitoring, and validating the system before reusing it in the organization.

9.5.1.7 Post Incidence

The post incident is a complete review of all the processes taken during the attacks. This phase ensures that the organizations prevent their network and the system from any anonymity or malicious attacks. It is an opportunity to update their incident response plan for the future that may have been missed at the initial level. It gives an idea about all positive and negative actions during incident response through which all the positive actions can be considered along with new ideas.

9.5.2 Incident Classification

We have seen in the earlier section that how important the incident response is for the organization. It not only corrects the system and all devices but also provides a healthy environment to the organization. The staff can feel confident in their work and contribute their efforts wholeheartedly. However, it is noticeable that the severity level of the threat and the level of incident somehow may vary in different scenarios. All the incidents can't be equal in severity level. For instance, if the attackers compromise the entire network of an organization, then the incident response team works differently irrespective of the virus that infects few systems or any active compromise in the server.

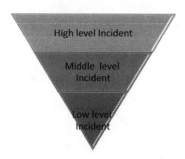

FIGURE 9.5
Level of incident classification schema.

The above discussion tells us that it is important to maintain the level of severity through classification. The classification of the incident response schema can be segregated into three phases as shown below and in Figure 9.5.:

1. High-level incident
2. Middle- or moderate-level incident
3. Low-level incident.

9.5.2.1 High-Level Incident

In high-level incidents, the organization is affected through a certain corruption, any kind of significant damages, loss of organization's staff or client information, loss of important data and the network resources, etc. It can also be a widespread loss of network devices or systems. High-level incidents can also severely affect the organization as follows:

- Loss of the system and flash drive that contain password-less data
- Physical compromise of the system
- Infection of sensitive information
- Intrusion on network
- Phishing attack
- Ransomware attack
- Possible damage on IT infrastructure.

There are also many other ways an organization can be affected. The intruder may compromise the website or mail of an organization and start malicious activity pretending like the stalwart of the company and start discussing with others.

9.5.2.2 Middle- or Moderate-Level Incident

In middle- or moderate-level incidents, the organization is affected without any compromise of the network by the intruder. Here, no misuse of the information happens, and irrespective of this, it leads to loss of information, damages, or corruption at certain levels. The middle- or moderate-level incidents affect the organization in the following manner:

- Chances of denial of services attacks
- Malicious software downloading
- Suspicious computer activity
- Malware infection
- Abnormal behavior of the system
- Unauthorized access
- Automated intrusion
- Limited malware infection.

9.5.2.3 Low-Level Incident

In low-level incidents, the organization is affected by unintentional activities. Sometimes it may be possible that the staff of the organization install the update that creates ruckus. The organization suffers unintentional damage that can be recovered by time in low-level incident. The main points through which the organization is affected due the low-level incident are as follows:

- Single system infection
- Pirated software installation
- Misplacing the device containing critical information
- Procedural violation during the execution
- Policy violation.

9.5.3 Role of CSIRT

The Computer Incident Response Team (CIRT) is also abbreviated as CSIRT and generally pronounced as "see-sirt" referred to as Computer Security Incident Response Team. Keeping eyes on the incidence is completely the responsibility of CSIRT experts. It is a must to notice the action taken on all the activities for complete cleaning of the incidence. If the team members belong to the security field, they may contribute more skills applying for the incidence response. The main role of the CSIRT is to expose the incident and avert this incidence targeting the organization.

The fundamental duty of this team is to focus on any incidence response to avert it from the organization. The main roles of the CSIRT are as follows:

1. Primary responsibility of the CSIRT team is to focus on prevention.
2. Healing security incident.
3. Identifying, detecting, and taking prompt action upon incident triggered.
4. Detail analysis of past incidents, opting 360° view.
5. Setting up all the procedures for the prevention.
6. Providing training to combat with the new threats.
7. Time-to-time audits.
8. Awareness program to the new tools, technologies, protocols, procedures, and policies.

9. Communication and the coordination.

10. Supervising during each and every phase of incidence response.

11. Pre- and postincident interactions.

12. Updating the incident plan on a regular basis.

13. Maintaining confidentiality.

As we have seen, the CSIR team has many responsibilities to prevent the organization from any kind of vulnerabilities. The escalation procedure itself signifies that one of the units in the organization should be responsible for clarification on the response process. The escalation process ensures that the CSIR team has been utilized effectively, and none of the maven people contacted with any member of the team. The process starts with the persons who have a close interaction with the system from where the call initiated if any anomaly was found. The escalation procedure indicates that if the containment of the malware is not possible at the elementary level, contact the CSSIR team by call. The member of the team will then take control through the staffs and start their process. They start their work for containing the malware in one system and then subsequently start the process of removing malware from the system. Similarly, if the cases belong to the network administrator side, where there is unidentified user account traced and they don't have a privilege to access it but are working. Then, the administrator calls the team to resolve this issue, and the team along with the coordinator immediately investigate things.

These incidents themselves show how the escalation process activates the CSIR team to resolve the issue created intentionally or unintentionally. The escalation process defines a set of responsibilities to the individuals through which they can alert to the team when any malicious activity is triggered. It also signifies involvement of stalwart of the organization with the team members in case high-level incidents happen.

Questions

Q.1. What do you understand by static acquisition?

Q.2. Explain the types of data extraction. How can an investigator perform the analysis on data extraction techniques?

Q.3. What do you understand by the chain of custody?

Q.4. Explain the terms static and dynamic with suitable examples.

Q.5. List at least five tools for both static and dynamic analyses.

Q.6. Why integrity is worrisome for the investigator?

Q.7. What do you understand by reproducibility? Explain the phases involved in reproducibility.

Q.8. What is incident response? Why is it required in an organization?

Q.9. Explain the process of incident response.

Q.10. Classify the incident response with the explanation.

Q.11. What is escalation procedure?

Q.12. What do you understand by CSIRT? Define the role of CSIRT.

References

A. Ahmad, J. Hadgkiss, and A. B. Ruighaver, "Incident Response Teamsâ€"Challenges in Supporting the Organisational Security Function," *Computers & Security*, vol. 31, pp. 643–652, 2012.

A. Bijalwan and P. Emmanuel, "Crime Psychology Using Network Forensics," *Journal of Computer Engineering & Information Technology (USA)*, vol. 3, 2, 2014.

S. Mocas, "Building Theoretical Underpinnings for Digital Forensics Research," *Digital Investigation*, vol. 1, pp. 61–68, 2004.

A. Moser and M. I. Cohen, "Hunting in the Enterprise: Forensic Triage and Incident Response," *Digital Investigation*, vol. 10, pp. 89–98, 2013.

National Center for Forensic Science. Digital evidence in the courtroom: a guide for preparing digital evidence for courtroom presentation. Washington, DC, US Department of Justice, National Institute of Justice; 2003. Draft document at http://www.ncfs.org/DE_courtroomdraft.pdf.

National Institute of Justice. Crime scene investigation: a guide for law enforcement. Washington, DC, US Department of Justice, National Institute of Justice; 2000a. NCJ 178280.

National Institute of Justice. Electronic crime scene investigation: a guide for law enforcement. Washington, DC, US Department of Justice, National Institute of Justice; 2000b. NCJ 187736.

10

Introduction to Botnet

LEARNING OBJECTIVES

This chapter reveals the in-depth knowledge of botnet and its evolutions. After reading this chapter, you would

- Have basic knowledge of botnet with some real examples.
- Understand the evolution of botnet and its lifecycle.
- Understand the structure of botnet.
- Have knowledge of all botnet security attacks including hacking and the terrorist attack.
- Have knowledge of all traditional botnet attacks.
- Have knowledge of all recent botnet attacks in depth.

10.1 Introduction

According to BBC News, on 19 July 2012, a huge spam botnet (Grum) was taken out by a security researcher. A botnet which experts believe sent out 18% of the world's spam emails has been shut down. Security company Fireeye and spam-tracking service SpamHaus worked with local internet service providers (ISP) to shut down the illegal network. The most popular botnets that engrossed in spam activity are Grum, Bobax, Pushdo, Rustock, Bagale, Mega-D, Maazben, Xarvester, Donbot, and Gheg. The previous study exhibited that 80% of all spam is sent by these ten botnets; they used to send 135 billion spam messages per day. These statistics are gradually becoming worse now. McAfee, the general malware threat, shows steady growth, which is grown up rapidly increased from 84 million in 2012 to 128 million in 2013. The new malware increased from 2 million in 2010 to 15 million in 2013.

According to McAfee global threat intelligence, Sql injection attacks are most common in the US followed by Taiwan, Spain, Venezuela, Germany, Brazil, and others. As per a security research company (Symantec), top botnet victims are China and the US. A 2016 survey shows that the US regained the largest 23% among all countries hosting the most malicious activity. South Korea dropped from the first place to the fourth in phishing website ranking, and China still holds the second place with 9% share of malicious computer activities.

DOI: 10.1201/9781003045908-13

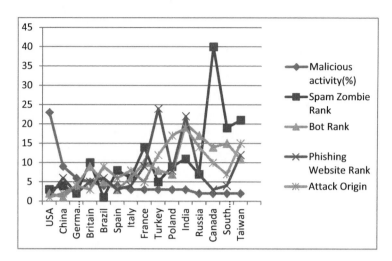

FIGURE 10.1
Malicious activity among countries.

Figure 10.1 shows the list of malicious activities in 15 countries in percentage, the rank of different countries for spam zombie attack, their bot rank, their phishing website rank, and their attack origin rank. If we see separately ransomware attack embattled India most. It is followed by Russia, Kazakhstan, Italy, Germany, Vietnam, Algeria, Brazil, Ukraine, and the US that suffered from the ransomware (Figure 10.2).

The most distributed denial of service (DDoS)-originated country in the world is China followed by the US, the UK, France, Korea, Singapore, Japan, Vietnam, and Germany. Figure 10.3 shows the most DDoS attack-originated countries in the world.

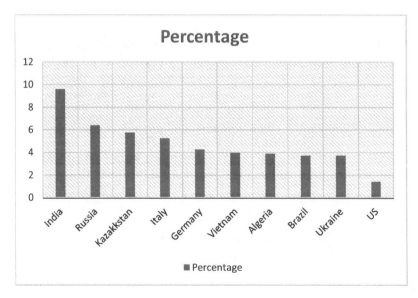

FIGURE 10.2
Ransomware-infected country.

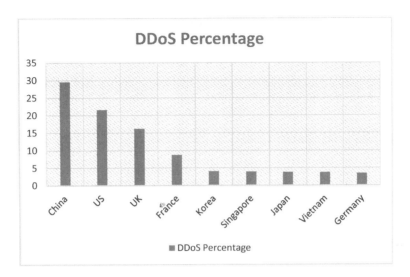

FIGURE 10.3
The most DDoS attack-originated country.

The term botnet originates from the word robot, which means to automate the task and perform all instructions given by their issuer, i.e., botmaster or botherder who performs from a remote location. The term bot is new as compared to virus, worm, and Trojan. Bot is a kind of malicious script that is launched in a victim's system to infect the system. It may be launched through websites (click fraud) or through different ways to steal personal information such as user name and password (phishing).

A botnet is some compromised and infected computers that are linked. Figure 10.4 shows how a botmaster connects and compromises other systems through a C&C server. The owners of the computer are not aware of the fact that their systems are compromised to spread the malicious activities such as spreading spam or viruses to infect other computers using the Internet. The DDoS attacks against individual user organization, institutions, the government body, or other are executed with the help of botnets most commonly by using polymorphism and rootkit techniques. Botnet node software is updated and reprogrammed. In the case of polymorphism, the malware code (botnet code) changes after every new infection so that it can cheat the antivirus and remain undetected, whereas in rootkit, an installed malware rootkit plays a significant role. Rootkit gets activated every time the system boots up. As the rootkit boots up before any system's operating system boots up, it becomes very difficult to trace (detect) it. Figure 10.1 is a diagrammatic representation of botnet and its attack. Bot can be classified in the following ways.

10.1.1 Spartan Dominition Robot (SD Bot)

Since 2002, the SD bot group of botnet has evolved and developed very well. It has also covered many variants and offshoots. Its development in open-source malware programs blessed this bot with the longevity. As the author of the SD bot released the bot code with his name and contact address, the public participations increased which led to further development of the code. The systems with strong security norms and complex (unique) passwords cannot be infected by the SD bot as the SD bot largely depends upon the networks utilizing blank or common passwords.

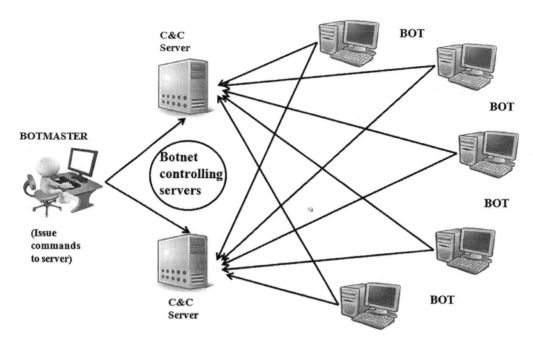

FIGURE 10.4
The botnet attacks.

10.1.2 AgoBot (aka Gaobot or Phatbot)

Modular functionality is the main characteristic of this bot. It infects the systems in three phases.

> Phase 1: In this stage, the Agobot attacks and conciliates the system with the bot client and release a back door, so that the botmaster can control and communicate with the system (machine).
>
> Phase II: The second phase aims at shutting down all the processes and programs related to antivirus and other related security programs.
>
> Phase III: In the third and final phase, it is made sure that the infected computer does not come to exposure of antivirus or security-related websites or the Internet.

10.1.3 Spybot

Spybot is the further extension of the SD bot. Spybot is more efficient than SD bot, as it has many other functions like spyware, for instance, email address harvesting key stroke logging and web surfing activities, etc.

10.1.4 Mytob

This group of viruses is a typical example of the advancement and use of hybrid technology in the field of malware. In mytob, the mass-mailing worms are collided (or combined) or associated with the functionality of bot hailing from SD bot group. A lethal combination of these two malwares results in a higher degree of damage at a very fast pace and compromises the system by making it lunatic after getting commands from the botmaster.

TABLE 10.1

Existence of a Botnet

S. No.	Botnet	Year	Channel/Protocol
1	SD bot	2002	C&C, Centralized
2	Agobot	2002	C&C, Centralized
3	Slapper	2002	C&C, Decentralized
4	Rbot	2003	C&C, Centralized
5	Spybot	2003	C&C, Centralized
6	Sinit	2003	C&C, Decentralized
7	Phatbot	2004	C&C, Centralized
8	Mytob	2005	C&C, Centralized
9	Nugache	2006	C&C, Decentralized
10	Rustock	2006	C&C, Centralized
11	Waledac	2007	C&C, Hybrid
12	Zeus	2007	C&C, Centralized
13	Blackenergy	2007	C&C, Centralized
14	Storm	2007	C&C, Decentralized
15	Trojan.peacomm	2007	C&C, Decentralized
16	Asprox	2008	C&C, Centralized
17	Koobface	2008	C&C, Centralized
18	Lethic	2008	C&C, Centralized
19	Kelihos	2010	C&C, Decentralized
20	Conficker	2010	C&C, Decentralized

10.1.5 Hybot

Hybot recovers the C&C channels in the event of destruction of most of the critical resources. Hybot ensures robustness and effectiveness by exploiting hybrid C&C structure, hybrid P2P, and URL flux.

There are some popular botnets, and their birth years are given in Table 10.1.

10.2 Evolution of Botnet

In the initial days of the Internet, i.e., the era between the 1970s and mid-1990s, the malicious activities on the network were not the serious cause for concern, as in the bulletin board systems days, such activities were done for the sake of fun. With the native nature of attacks, the detection and prevention measures were also very simple. By avoiding unsafe features and by protecting passwords, the security issues were easily resolved. During that time, the people connected with each other through local telephone lines and the connection also local in nature. Evolution of the TCP/IP protocol connected people, institutions, societies, groups, organizations, and nations across the globe. This paved the way for the growth of the Internet as a multiplying rate.

In 1988, the Morris was the first virus to be distributed via the Internet, which infected about 6,000 Unix machines. Ten years down the line, another powerful virus named Melissa spread like an epidemic infecting the computers worldwide, and day by day, the native viruses were replaced by a more complex and sophisticated attacks. The support of economic and political elements encouraged the development of more advanced and disruptive virus attacks.

In this series of malicious practices, the botnet is a new term. As the botnet provides a platform for launching other attacks such as Distributed Denial of Services (DoS) or spammer by using different communication channels in a centralized (Internet Relay Chat and Hypertext Transfer Protocol) or distributed framework (peer to peer), an attacker can easily infect the computer systems by sitting at a remote place. For this, the botmaster needs a covertly installed (malware) virus. Command and control servers come under the centralized architecture. By the botnet's utility in the terms of effectiveness, efficiency, and robustness, the taxonomy is proposed. Symantec said that a sharp rise in the bot attackes was observed in the year 2008. As per their observation, on average, around 75, 158 computers per day were traced. As bot infected in the year 2008, this was 31% more from 2007. Bot networks are responsible for the generation of 90% of spam or malicious activity. HTTP-based botnets are replacing the old classical IRC botnets gradually.

Jarkko Oikarinen worked on vested IRC in August 1988. IRC facilitates data dissemination and supports many types of communication which include multipoint and point-to-point communication, which further increases the vulnerability of the system security. Greg Lindahl in 1989 invented the bot from a single user code for running IRC operations on the local host to the code providing services to other users over the period the bots have developed into a comprehensive tool for operating IRC channel (operator). IRC's facilities of providing a platform to the users for running commands. Development of the more destructive IRC bots added fuel to the fire. By the late 1990s, the botmaster (attackers), who was connected to an IRC server, grouped a huge number of Trojan-infected computers and remotely controlled the activity. A new version of the subsevenTrojan, i.e., version 2.1, had distinctive features. It enabled the botmaster by facilitating some unique functions like key stroke logging, nondisclosure of identity, and password capsizing. It further allowed the attacker to remotely control the sub-seven server through an IRC channel. This association between IRC channels and Trojan server paved the way for the generation of even more detrimentally infected botnets in the coming days. In 2005, the honeynet project carried out a research on botnet for a period of 4 months. In this period, more than 10,000 computers were observed as the members of botnets. IRC-based botnets were the most dominating botnets among all the existing botnets for more than 10 years. As botnet detection and prevention techniques advance, the botnet attacks are also advancing accordingly. Classical protocols were replaced by HTTP and Fast Flux network based on DNS servers. Traditional topology was replaced by a group of interlinked IRC servers, which also have hybrid p2p functions. The most sophisticated and powerfull botnet, conficker, came in the picture in 2009. The DNS was implemented in a p2p C&C structure. The upcoming section examines and presents the most dominant IRC botnet and also covers other botnet technologies based on the protocol.

10.3 Botnet Lifecycle

The lifecycle of botnet includes five phases: preliminary infection phase, secondary injection phase, coupling or link phase (also called Rallying), malicious C&C phase, and update and continuance. Botnet forensics deals with detecting a compromised system on the network, where bot is basically a kind of malware that takes a complete command over the computer. The term bot came into existence from the word robot which works as a predefined function by the software program. It can be directed through command-and-control channel. Botnets are run by a malicious programmer known as botherder. Botherder sends the infection or viruses to the weak user's computer whose payload is a malicious application. It connects to the infected user's computer through a command-and-control server. A spammer purchases services from a botmaster, and the botmaster issues the updated command as shown in Figure 10.5. In preliminary infection, the attacker scans the aimed subnet for non-vulnerability and also infects the victim machine through the exploitation virus method.

In the secondary injection phase, a cell code that is a script is executed by the infected host (or machine) with the help of Hypertext Transfer Protocol (HTTP), Peer-to-Peer protocol (P2P), and File Transfer Protocol (FTP); the cell code traces the exact location, and from there, it fetches the images of the actual bot binary. Following this, the bot binary establishes itself on the targeted system that finally turns the targeted computer into "zombie" that spreads the infection to other systems on the Internet by running the malicious code (or malware).

The bot application starts automatically with rebooting the zombie every time. In the coupling or line phase, the bot programmers established the command and control (C&C) connection and connected the zombie to C&C server. This step comes in pictures when the bot restarts and facilitates command and control to the botmaster by linking him to the bot. Establishment of C&C channels makes the infected computers the part of botmaster's botnet army. The real commanding and controlling of botnets start post-coupling phase. The bot army of the botmaster receives the commands (or instructions) through or via the C&C channel. After receiving the command from the botmaster, the bot programs execute them. The updated binary is downloaded by the bots in the last phase; this means that this phase is about the upgradation and continuance of the botnet (or malware). To keep the attacker and his zombie army upgraded for new attacks, the maintenance cannot be overlooked or ignored. In a server migration process, the binary circulates (or moves) the

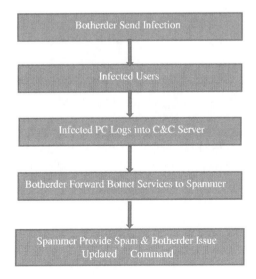

FIGURE 10.5
The botnet lifecycle.

bots to various C&C servers. With the help of dynamic (DDNS), the botmaster tries to keep botnet portable and invisible that helps the botmaster in updating and changing his server location frequently because of the short time to live (TTL) values; a changed IP address in the C&C server propagates immediately to bots. This further migrates (moves) the bots to a new C&C server so that it can stay alive.

For avoiding different network security systems (or codes), to escape detection, for avoiding the same repeated behavior, and for the addition of new features and sets of conditions along with different various C&C channels, the binary code for bot army is updated.

In the event of a repetition of the same behavior, the bots may be identified. Therefore, the botmaster keeps making frequent changes to avoid the monotony in the botnet behavior as fast and as frequent as possible. According to Leonard et al., the botnet's life cycle can be divided into four different phases:

- Formation phase
- Command and control phase
- Attack phase
- Post attack phase.

The attack phase of the botnet lifecycle refers to the active life of malware (bot) in which the bot engrosses into malicious activities by infecting other computers on the ground of the commands given by the botmaster. On the other hand, the post-attack phases such as scanning of new victims connecting to a C&C server, releasing orders, attack with DDoS, spreading spams, etc. have distinguished and different synchronization patterns. In the spread phase, the bot propagates and infects the systems.

The botmasters misguide the users so that they install the browser or application containing malware. Once the user installs the infected application, the malware gets active and starts infecting the computer (malware). In most of the cases, the attack is simply by the spam distribution that carries the malicious codes, and the size of the botnet increases when the attack is successful.

10.4 Botnet Structure

Botnet structure shows different procedures through which bot infects the system and updates the commands. The basic cause behind the existence of huge number of cyber securities is these botnets that are commanded and controlled by the botmasters instructions. Figure 10.6 shows the general structure of botnet in which botmaster continuously works to compromise the system and add their bot network through a command and control server.

10.4.1 Propagation and Compromise

A botnet-infected system can infect another machine connected to it. The system has evolved over the period, from installing a bot into the target machine and then spreading it with the single propagation vector that sometimes needed a physical coronation to the multiple computerized propagation vectors.

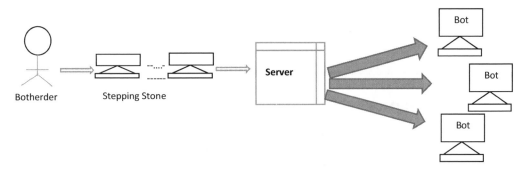

FIGURE 10.6
The general structure of a botnet.

   Slammer worm is a good example of classical bots. On the other hand, the SD bots are the example for the modern malware utilizing multiple mechanism consisting of open files sharing, P2P networks, providing backdoor and using it for commanding, and exploiting the resources of the machine (system).

10.4.2 Command and Control

Communication is the next major problem of the botnet attacker. Most attackers would communicate to bots but do not interact with the exposed bots. Botnet has three potential topologies to explore of various bot communication methods:

   1. Cetntalized
   2. P2P
   3. Hybrid,

10.4.2.1 Centralized

A topology is said to be centralized when a central point in that topology communicates with the rest of clients. HTTP botnet/malicious IRC botnets are the classic example of the centralized botnets. As multiple clients connect (switches) to common points, it can be easily detected and stopped by blocking C&C.

10.4.2.2 P2P

There is no C&C server in P2P topology. P2P topology does not have a centralized point for command and control. Instead of having a centralized point, a single node performs client as well as the server. Even after taking the node offline by the victim, the network remains under the control of the botmaster with this. It is clear that in P2P topology, the formal support (coordinates) does not require. An infectious command by botmaster is spread among another infected peer via intercommunication between them. P2P botnet's goal is to overcome the lacunas of the centralized networks. P2P communication system is much strong and complex. It does not grantee for the message delivery latency. Transferring command of P2P botnet is slow when compared with the centralized botnet. It overcomes the main limitation of centralized networks in which loss of one bot results into loss of entire botnet in a nutshell. In P2P, the entire botnet is not compromised due to compromisation of one bot.

10.4.2.3 Hybrid

A hybrid peer-to-peer botnet is hinged upon the unstructured P2P protocol. A hybrid bot is divided into servant and client bots. The botmaster gives instructions to the servant bot, which further forwards these sets of instructions to the client, for example, Nugache botnet.

10.4.3 Attacks and Theft

Extracting values from a malicious node is the biggest problem of botmasters. A botnet that was utilized for a simple Denial of Service (DoS) attack got evolved into multi-host distributed DDoS. A DDoS bot attack can be initiated by the command that is remotely executable and accessible with the help of SD botnet and Ago bot. The botmasters find out the information stored on infected computers/networks.

Stolen credit cards, social security numbers, banking details, and online transaction details can be utilized by the hackers so that they can use it in their favor. For example, SD bot is an advanced key logging technique that is used for collecting the personal data about the target (victim/potential victim).

Spreading (distributing) spam is also one of the key activities for which the botnet is used. A huge number of new mail servers are required for sending the spam and bot-infected host provides a platform for the same. The storm botnet has a remotely controllable interface which can be utilized for sending a huge number of spam messages. So, they are also used for phishing attacks.

10.5 Botnet Security Attacks

The growth in multiple strategies for launching of attacks provides a more chances for getting infected. It has become a serious cause of concern for almost all the countries around the world. According to Amorso (2012), there are five possible motives behind the cyber-attack.

10.5.1 Warfare Sponsored by the Country

It is similar to the physical warfare between two countries in which the attacking country aims the critical resources of the other country. In this case also, the botmasters from the attacking country target the national infrastructure of the opponent country. The intensity of such attacks largely depends upon the intension and resources of the attacking nation. To stand by the nation and for strengthening the national resources, the citizens sometimes donate their computing powers to the nation. This plays a very significant role in botnet attack facilitated by P2P.

10.5.2 Terrorist Attack

The terrorist groups execute this type of attack to accomplish their evil goals. In this type of attack, a normal Internet user can help this terrorist attack simply by donating his computer equipment to the attacker. It simply means that involving in a terror attack without acquiring any formal training, expertise, knowledge or skills.

10.5.3 Commercially Motivated Attack

Such botnet attacks are motivated with the intension of hampering the market reputation and finances of the rival company. In such attacks, the competing company attacks the cyber infrastructure of the rival company. Such attacks are more evident in the e-commerce business.

10.5.4 Financially Driven Criminal Attack

Such attacks intend to harm the user financially. In such a type of botnet attacks, the botmaster targets to attack the financial data such as particular's banking details, mode of making payments online, and similar other financial services. Such attacks are up to individuals, and they target companies as well by giving them threat for their online infrastructure.

10.5.5 Hacking

Hacking is a practice by an individual or a group seeking pleasure from such notorious activities and looking for some extra attention on the Internet. Eggdrop bot was the first botnet that introduced in 1993. It was designed in 1993 by Robey Pointer using Tool Command Language (TCL language). Eggdrop bot was a benign bot program designed to assist managers with IRC channel management. From 1999, when Mobman designed the backdoor program SubSeven V2.1 that used the IRC communications protocol for bot control, bot technology began to be adopted by hackers for malicious purposes and bot programs using the IRC communications protocol as a C&C method started to become mainstream. Botnets are usually used to send spam. Kamluk (2008) indicated that the annual average earnings of a spammer total USD 50,000–1,00,000. Generally speaking, the IP address from which spam is sent is usually blacklisted, or the messages are auto-tagged as spam by the mail server. The enormous scale of a botnet helps spammers to solve this problem, as a botnet includes a large number of IP addresses of infected computers, which allows spammers to send successfully a lot of messages within a short period.

10.6 Traditional Botnet Attacks

There are a number of attacks that are caused by botnets. Distributed Denial of Services (DDoS), spam, and personal information theft are the most common among them. The general traditional botnet attacks are as follows.

10.6.1 Distributed Denial of Service Attack

Distributed Denial of Service (DDoS) attacks are the most common attacks caused by a botnet, and it usually leads to a large quantity of financial loss. The concept of distributed denial of services is to paralyze the operation of certain services that belongs to an organization.

In a DDoS attack, the botnet consumes (exploits) the bandwidth and thereby disables the network services of the victim; for instance, a botmaster may connect to the IRC channel of the target and then send him millions of service requests from the botnet. The target IRC network is taken down (hacked) in such type of attacks. As per records, the Transmission Control Protocol (TCP) flooding, Synchronise (SYN) flooding, and User Datagram Protocol (UDP) flooding attacks are the most commonly implemented. To prevent a DDOS attack, the number of infected systems must be controlled along with disabling the remote-control mechanism. However, apart from these measures, even more advanced and efficient techniques are required for avoiding such attacks.

In the computation resource consumption, SYN flood is most common and easy to implement. SYN flood happened when the attacker used the vulnerability of TCP protocol. In the TCP protocol, the three-way handshake is needed to ensure the integrity of data which are transmitted. The process of the three-way handshake is that the user has to send a request to the server with an SYN packet, which is used to inform the server that a user needs to connect to it. Then, the server will send an SYN/ACK packet back, which means that the connection is approved. Finally, the user has to send an ACK packet to the server, and it means the start of the connection. Via a three-way handshake in the TCP protocol, data are transmitted more safely. SYN flood happened when the attacker sent a large number of SYN packets to the server to request a connection. With too much SYN packets, the server cannot handle too much requests. If a legal user has to connect to the victim, the server will have too much requests to deal with the legal user, and it will be out of connection because it is full of SYN packets. In the bandwidth consumption, the most common attacks are UDP flood, Internet Control Message Protocol (ICMP) flood, and Hypertext Transfer Protocol (HTTP) flood. It is similar to computation resource consumption, which paralyzes the victim by sending a large number of packets. But there is still some differences between them because of the transmission protocol. UDP protocol (User Datagram Protocol) is not as rigorous as TCP protocol that needs three-way handshake to ensure the establishment of the connection. Compared with the TCP protocol, the header is much simpler, which only has the port of source and destination, length, checksum, and data. Although the reliability of the UDP protocol is not as high as TCP, it can transmit data in a massive and quick way. Thus, the selection of protocol is important to enhance the security or efficiency of the network. Because the UDP protocol is connectionless, which means that it does not check whether the data are received correctly, some attackers use the vulnerability of UDP protocol to launch a Distributed Denial of Service (DDoS) attack, which is called UDP flood. The attack model of UDP flood is shown in Chapter 7. Different from SYN flood, UDP flood attacks the victim by sending a large number of packets to a random host that the port is open for certain services.

If the number of members that belong to the botnet is larger, the scale of UDP flood will be larger. The characteristic of UDP flood, the bandwidth of the victim, is huge due to the massive transmission of the packet. After the Bots receive the command from the Botmaster, the Bots send the packet with high capacity to paralyze the bandwidth that the victim owns. If the victim encounters UDP flood, the change of network traffic is very obvious and that makes the victim unable to connect to the Internet. ICMP flood is also a commonly distributed denial of service attack that belongs to bandwidth consumption. The purpose of the ICMP flood is to saturate the network by sending numeric ICMP packets. ICMP protocol (Internet Control Message Protocol) is used to reply the connection status between two hosts. Round-trip delay time is calculated by the number of successfulreply and the time between them. It can check whether the destination host exists or not and compute the transmission time between source and destination host. Through "echo request" and "echo rely on" sending by the ICMP protocol, the reply time can check the connection status between two hosts. ICMP flood is similar to UDP flood, and it launches an attack by sending numeric ICMP flood that makes the victim cannot afford to process it. If the victim receives too much ICMP flood, the bandwidth will be paralyzed. The effect is same as UDP flood, which intercepts the connection ability of the victim.

10.6.2 Spam

Spam is also a serious problem that still exists in the current network environment. Internet security industry is concerned with the growing number of spams; as per their observation, it is nearly about 70%–90% of the times. The botnets are the cause behind these spams. The report further reveals that when bots open socks v4/v5 proxy (TCP/IP RFC 1928) on a compromised malicious or infected bot, the infected machines can be utilized for spreading spams. Some bots by using their special functions are capable of gathering electronic mail addresses.This characteristic of the bots is utilized by the botmasters for spreading a huge number of spams. To overcome the concerns caused by spams with the help of botnets, the researchers and scientists have to come up with the trinity. Trinity is a proposed distributed content-independent spam classification system that is expected to resolve the spanning problems. Bots responsible for spamming spread mass emails within a fraction of a second; therefore, sending a message from such infected addresses may further lead to spreading more spam. As the trinity is still under trial, its effectiveness cannot be completely trusted upon.

Xie et al. have propounded AutoREFramework (a spam signature generation framework) so that the aggregate (average) behavior of the bot responsible for spam generation can be studied. It further aims at investigating the potential benefits from their detection in future. Their study further reveled various features of spamming botnet such as

1. Spammer's letters contain some random and legitimate URLs so that the detection can be prevented.
2. Botnet IP addresses are distributed over many autonomous devices; it is with a small number of machines (system) in every autonomous system.
3. The target victims with the same email address may get the spam with different contents.

The fruitful utilization of these features for detecting botnets and preventing the spams is the matter of investigation shortly.

Due to the development of a botnet, spam has become harder to solve because of its scale. Spam is also called junk mail, which attracts the click and links to the malicious website. These kinds of websites will make the victim infect with the botnet by downloading malicious software. Mail spam has some properties like the content has a malicious link or some attractive software. Mail spam usually sends by batch, which means that spam sends numeric emails to the users in a way that is designed previously. Through the control by the command, the bots will send an email to the receiver at certain time. The content usually has some links and attracts users to click. In spam, four characters are discussed, which are a spammer, a spam receiver, and a spam-filtering service. The spammer is the unit that launches the spam attack, which tries to gain some profit from it. The spam receiver is the victim who receives a larger number of spam mails. If the spam receiver cannot resist the attraction of the content in spam mails, some losses will happen, like personal information theft and infecting with the botnet. Spam filtering service is used to filter spam mails in some rules, and it is installed in client or mail server. By filtering mails with the spam-filtering service, spam mails cannot be sent to the end user easily. Some researchers and reports suggested that the mails received from senders who are not in the friend list should not be opened. According to the current network environment, if the sender is infected with a botnet, which means the botmaster can totally control it, the mail from the infected sender is not safe. Due to the behavioral model of spam from a botnet, the spam mail is sent by a command from botmaster, and it makes the scale of spam grow quickly. Once the receiver clicks the links or downloads the file in it, it is possible that the user will post some private data to the server which the botmaster owns. If the receiver downloads a malicious software from a spam mail, it is possible that the infection happens. The receiver will become a member of the botnet and wait for the command from the botmaster.

10.6.3 Personal Information Theft

Some of the bots make the security networks lunatic and thereby control and command the victim's systems. The botmaster with the help of such malicious code can retrieve the useful and sensitive information from the infected machines such as user password, banking details, etc. The list of incidents also indicates that botnet has become a major cause of concern for the corporate and industry as well. The bots are capable in bypassing the security systems and by making the host as well as the network system to include in its zombie army. The botmaster thieve the sensitive and significant financial and strategical information through its army. The infected systems are beyond the security scan and therefore are difficult to be caught. Inner attackers can be prevented with the key login. As such bots read the activity on the keyboard and report the botmaster who in return commands these bots so that the personal information can be stolen from the infected machine. In this condition, key login can prevent such theft of personal data.

Besides Distributed Denial of Service (DDoS) and mail spam, one of the serious troubles from a botnet is personal information theft. Personal information is valuable, like name, email, address, account password, etc. This personal information is stored in the memory, and it is easy to be gotten by the botmaster. As mentioned above in the behavioral model of a botnet, some malicious software is injected into the victim's computer, and the botmaster will control the victim via the control and command server. The purpose of personal information theft is just information gathering and gets financial profit from selling personal information. The personal information is stolen by two ways, which are uploading and recording. Uploading is that the infected user uploads some insensitive data to the botmaster. Some information stores in a cookie when the user saves their data intentionally or otherwise. Such file that is stored in the memory usually has some insensitive data, like account and password. If the file that stores sensitive data is usurped, it is possible that the data inside can be extracted by information techniques. Besides uploading, recording is also a method to steal personal information. Through the injected malicious software, it can record the input character when the infected user enters some sensitive data, like account, password, email, or address. By recording illicitly by the software, the input data is gotten by the botmaster, and among them, "Spyeye" is one of the famous malicious software that steals personal information. It is hard to detect and monitor the victim to record the data from it. Some famous websites, like Google, Yahoo, eBay, and Twitter, have stolen personal information by Spyeye. It monitors the victim by forcing them to download a configuration file and records the input illegally. If the personal information theft occurs in the bank, it will be very severe because the stolen data are extremely sensitive. With more personal information that thefts from a botnet, the botmaster can have more financial benefit by selling to certain organizations.

10.6.4 Click Fraud

Click fraud is a new term coined in the encyclopedia of a botnet. This is a very interesting form of the bot in which a bot creates a fake impression of being an advertisement sometimes manually or automatically. The user clicks on such advertisement and gets into the loop. Online advertisement business is the worst hit by the click fraud. It basically aims at increasing the revenue by having maximum clicks on the content. But now people in the adtech industry are gradually recognizing it and are looking for the ways to overcome the issue. According to Andrew Goode, Chief Operating Officer (COO), Project Sun block, a click fraud creates a false impression in the minds of the advertisers that their content is the most hit one. It also gives a fake hike to the advertisement as the content seems to be hit a huge number of times.

Click fraud can be operated in two ways, i.e., manually and automatically. The click fraud is done manually. The botmaster manual hits the site or the ad, whereas in the case of automatic click fraud, a software or malicious code is utilized which keeps hitting the advertisement without any manual support. The objective of both is to inflate the economic value of the ad by increasing the number of hits. In the case of manually operated click fraud, it is difficult to trace the difference between the actual people and the fraud hitting the ads. Many companies employ workers to hit their ads and click the link manually to inflate their value. Niall Hogan, Integral Ad science, managing director U.K., has beautifully explained how the bots are utilized for making click fraud. He states that without the information to the user, a malware is downloaded to their system. The moment the bit is installed, it starts functioning according to the commands. Given by botmasters, it builds a lucrative cookie profile, which further generates the fake impression on a site, and in this way, by inflating the traffic network, the revenue is generated through automated click fraud.

The activity of utilizing bots to one lac, for click fraud, is known as "click farm" as the single machine with a single bot is not that hazardous, but in practice, it is observed that thousands of bots operate together for generating a fake impression, which is more dangerous. However, James Collier, Ad Truth, general manager, EMEA has come with a solution; according to him, telltale signs can be utilized for identifying the fraud click. According to him, the environment with very low or very high conversations must be subject to investigation. High rates of conversion can be single for click fraud, which can be detected by training the user who shows a pattern of the frequent visit and continuous hitting on the same site.

Bot attackers utilize botnets for installing advertisement add-on and browser helper objects (BHOs) so that by providing a maximum hit to an ad or link, its economic value can be inflated. Such bots are capable of generating higher clicks through CTR. The same as Google's Ad Sense program to get higher CTR, the botnet helps in clicking the link artificially.

10.6.5 Identity Theft

Identify fraud that is also known as identity theft is one of the fastest growing cybercrimes on the Internet. An identity theft takes place when a fraudulent person with the unethical means accesses to the personal information about an individual with the intention of utilizing it for fraudulent practices. This information may include name, address, educational testimonials, address details, etc. This is one of the most dangerous threats in the cyber world as the personal information of an individual may be utilized for creating a fake identity card or fake passport for a terrorist attack. The user or the victim is unaware about his identity information being stolen and the kind of fraud it is utilized for.

Generally, the botnet is utilized for committing identity theft. Phishing mail is a classic example of such id theft. In such case, the botherder compromises server and the network that creates a malicious Uniform Resource Locator (URL) and encourages the user to submit his personal information using that URL. Huge spams are sent to the user's mail address with the help of botnet. There is another way of fetching the personal data of user, i.e., creating a fake website. Identity fraud is the serious cause of concern for all as the stolen confidential information about an individual can be utilized for several criminal offenses like a financial fraud by opening a bank account and obtaining loan and other facilities on that account, or criminal offenses by making fake passport, fake driving license, fake identity card, etc. on the victim's name.

10.7 Recent Botnet Attacks

Following are the recent botnet attacks.

10.7.1 StealRat Botnet

The advent of stealRat brought many security issues along with it. StealRat (Torre 2013) has a high level of technically compressed and sophisticated group of bots. These bots are specialized in hiding the malware. Hiding can be replaced with covering. The steal-Rat minimizes the interaction between server and spam messages; therefore, it is able to overcome almost all the network security systems of the organization. With the help of one infected system and the two compromised or malicious websites, the stealRat hides its operations in three different layers. As per an estimate by Trend Micro (Torre 2013), the botherder sent the malicious spam to seven million users. The botmaster utilized 85,000 internet protocol addresses (IP addresses). The stealRat is one more step ahead in the evolution of the botnet.

10.7.2 Citadel Botnet

Citadel botnet is another type of botnet utilized for malicious activities. This botnet not only harms the computers but also has an amazing capability to fail the network security systems and overcome the antivirus software's bot detection process.

The secret behind the success of citadel botnet is that it breaks the link between network security system (Antivirus software) and the user. By prohibiting access to the malware detection software, it infects the users' machine. This was also proved during initial investigations on the citadel botnets. A group engrossed in the malicious activities is spreading the citadel botnet, by pre-installing it on a pirated Windows XP operating system (OS).

The government together with the IT industry is trying its best to overcome the citadel issue as this botnet has affected not only Microsoft and Federal Bureau of Investigation (FBI), but also the American marshal services.

10.7.3 Andromeda Botnet

The Andromeda botnet was introduced in 2011 with some new functions added it reemerged in 2013. The Andromeda botnet is spread with the help of spams, which links it with the malicious websites hosting Blackhole exploit kit (BHEK) code. It operates in four modules:

1. Grabbers module
2. SOCKS4 proxy module
3. Keyloggers module
4. Rootkits module.

It has all the characteristics of the classical looks. It also has a back-door function like Zeus, and it can also update itself and can download and execute the files and exit if required.

10.7.4 Attacks on WordPress Targeting "Admin" Password

WordPress is an open-source blogging tool which is utilized to strengthen the powers of websites. In 2013, the WorldPress admin account faced a brute force attack (Press 2013). According to Gilbertson (2013), this attack was more powerful and destructive just because 90,000 unique IP addresses were used by the botmasters in this attack.

10.7.5 Android Master Key Vulnerability

The new threat has come in the form of Android-based devices. The advent of the Android-based technology has also brought some serious security issues. These devices can easily link to any company's network and fetch the confidential information of the companies. Such vulnerability in the android's security models was recognized by the blue box security team (Forristal 2013). This lacuna of androids allows the botmaster to change the APK code without damaging application's encrypted signature, which in turn converts the legitimate application into an infected malware, which is identified by the device or the user of the device. As android's vulnerability evades the security system and facilitates access to the database or the personal information of the user, it is posing a threat for both the corporate and individual users. The degree of risk increases when the applications designed by vendors or the company working in collaboration with vendor give a special feature that allows access to a system's UID.

Questions

Q.1. Define the term 'botnet'.
Q.2. Explain the botnet attacks in detail.
Q.3. Explain all kinds of bots in detail.
Q.4. List the evolution charts of all bots.
Q.5. Explain the botnet lifecycle with figures.

Q.6. Write down the botnet structure with an appropriate diagram.

Q.7. Is there any difference between traditional botnet attacks and the advanced botnet attacks? Explain in brief.

Q.8. Explain the botnet security attacks in detail.

Q.9. Is hacking a legal term in the context of botnet terminology?

Q.10. Explain the distributed denial of services. Is there any difference between distributed denial of service and denial of service attacks?

References

M. Abu Rajab, J. Zarfoss, F. Monrose, and A. Terzis, A Multifaceted Approach to Understanding the Botnet Phenomenon, *6th ACM SIGCOMM Conference on Internet Measurement* (pp. 41–52), ACM, 2006.

P. Bacher, T. Holz, M. Kotter, and G. Wicherski, "Know your enemy: tracking botnets," 2005, Available: https://www.honeynet.org/papers/bots, 2008.

A. Bijalwan and P. Emmanuel, Understanding Botnet on Internet, *IEEE Conference on Computational Intelligence and Computing Research*, Coimbatore, Tamilnadu, 2014.

A. Bijalwan, V. K. Solanki, and E. S. Pilli, "Botnet Forensic: Issues, Challenges and Good Practices," *Network Protocols and Algorithms*, vol. 10, no. 2, 2018.

A. Bijalwan, M. Thapaliyal, E. S. Pilli, and R. C. Joshi, "Survey and Research Challenges of Botnet Forensics," *International Journal of Computer Applications*, vol. 75, pp. 43-50, 2013.

D. Cook, J. Hartnett, K. Manderson, and J. Scanlan, Catching Spam Before It Arrives: Domain Specific Dynamic Blacklists, *Australasian Workshops on Grid Computing and e-Research-Volume 54* (pp. 193–202), Australian Computer Society, Inc., 2006.

T. Dubendorfer and B. Plattner, "Analysis of Internet Relay Chat Usage by DDoS Zombies," Ph.D thesis, Department of Information Technology and Electrical Engineering, Swiss Federal Institute of Technology Zurich (ETH), 2004.

M. Feily, A. Shahrestani, and S. Ramadass, "A survey of botnet and botnet detection," in *Third International Conference on Emerging Security Information, Systems and Technologies* Athens, Glyfada: IEEE, 2009, pp. 268–273.

Forristal, J. (2013) Android: One Root to own them all.

T. Holz and S. Marechal, "New Threats and Attacks on the World Wide Web," *IEEE Security & Privacy*, no. 2, vol. 4, pp. 72–75, 2006.

J. Jung and E. Sit, An Empirical Study of Spam Traffic and the Use of DNS Black Lists, *Proceedings of the 4th ACM SIGCOMM Conference on Internet Measurement* (pp. 370–375), 2004.

E. Levy, "The Making of a Spam Zombie Army: Dissecting the soBig Worms," *IEEE Security & Privacy*, no. 4, vol. 1, pp. 58–59, 2003.

C.-Y. Liu, C.-H. Peng, and I.-C. Lin, "A Survey of Botnet Architecture and Batnet Detection Techniques," *International Journal of Network Security*, vol. 16, no. 2, pp. 81–89, 2014.

J. Liu, Y. Xiao, K. Ghaboosi, H. Deng, and J. Zhang, "Botnet: Classification, Attacks, Detection, Tracing, and Preventive Measures," *EURASIP Journal on Wireless Communications and Networking*, vol. 2009, pp. 1184–1187, 2009.

M. Prince, "The ddos that almost broke the internet," in *CloudFlare blog*, March 27, 2013, p. 2013.

R. Puri, "Bots & botnet: an overview," 2003, Available: file:///C:/Users/Skynet_1/Downloads/bots.pdf

M. A. Rajab, J. Zarfoss, F. Monrose, and A. Terzis, "My botnet is bigger than yours (maybe, better than yours): why size estimates remain challenging," in *HotBots'07*, Washington, DC: USENIX Association, 2007, p. 5.

B. Saha and A. Gairola, "Botnet: an overview," *CERT-In White Paper, CIWP-2005-05*, vol. 240, 2005.

F. Sullivan, "Enterprises harness social networking for increased agility and responsiveness, finds Frost & Sullivan [Pressemitteilung]," [Online]. Available: http://www.frost.com/prod/servlet/press-release.pag, 2014.

Y. Wang, Z. Jin, and W. Zhang, Analysis of Botnet Attack and Defense Technology, *International Conference on Computer Science and Service System (CSSS) TBD Nanjing*, China, 2011.

Z. Zhu, G. Lu, Y. Chen, Z. J. Fu, P. Roberts, and K. Han, Botnet Research Survey, *32nd Annual IEEE International Computer Software and Applications Conference* (pp. 967–972), IEEE, 2008.

11

Botnet Forensics

LEARNING OBJECTIVES

This chapter focuses on imparting the knowledge of botnet forensics. After reading this chapter, you would

- Have knowledge of the concepts of botnet forensics.
- Have knowledge of the methodology related to botnet forensics.
- Understand the features, forensic cycle, and classification of botnet forensics.
- Understand the botnets and its development year-wise.
- Have knowledge of the framework and identification of botnet forensics.
- Understand the inquisition model for botnet forensics and its analysis.
- Understand the analysis by a practical approach through the case study.

11.1 Introduction

An intelligent learning system can read the users' actions and behaviors in the cyber world. It can easily detect the behavioral nature and aspect of every activity on social media. However, the black hat community works only in the self-interest and focuses on propagating malicious activities. The botnet is one of the most emerging threats for the digital society.

As we have studied in the previous chapter, botnet is a collection of zombie networks whose tendency is to propagate bot continuously. A bot is a malicious program that acts upon botherder's command. Botherder executes these bots illegally further for their self-interest, which is called bot attack. Bot attack is difficult to handle as botnet rapidly germinates in order to get off the detection process. Due to this dynamic behavior, the value of botnet information degrades quickly.

Botnet forensics refers to the usage of the bot clues left after an attack, determining how an attack occurred and what an attacker did to the network. Using network forensics, we can analyze and investigate every possible attack. However, using botnet forensics, we can analyze and investigate the botnet attack. It is the science so as to easily recover and investigate all the data found in the digital artifacts. Digital artifacts can include storage devices, electronic documents, computer systems, computer network, and the sequence of data packets transmitted across a computer network. Using botnet forensics is like using a bot network time machine, which allows us to go back to a particular time and reshape the catenation of all actions that occur at the time of the rapture. The term botnet forensics was first coined by Anchit Bijalwan in 2013.

Botnet forensics is a new technology used to investigate different bot attacks on the network. It is an extended phase of network forensics that specially focuses on bot attack, and further network forensics is an extended phase of the network security, so this technology helps us to solve various network security issues, e.g., access control, system log, and router log. It is also used to resolve all the connection issues related to the network. Botnet forensics is used as a tool for monitoring the activities, specifying, analyzing, and detecting the source of attacks. It is a technique to collect, identify, examine, correlate, analyze, and document digital evidence of an attack. The goal of this field is to detect an attack, investigate them, recover the information about the incident, and document them.

Botnet forensics is a real-time analysis of the network traffic. It can be done through continuous monitoring of the network by using significant resources. It is a process of detecting intruders as they break into sensitive networks by focusing on the analysis and monitoring of the anomalous network traffic. Botnet forensics analyzes the network traffic, identifies the logs, then collects packets and data that it stores, which move throughout the network, further stores it for some period, and also locates the suspicious systems. It captures digital evidence during an investigation before any specific event takes place.

Generally, botnet forensics has two uses as follows:

- It is related to the security that involves detecting the traffic and identifying the intrusions.
- It is related to law enforcement that involves capturing and analyzing the network traffic, and it can also include various tasks such as searching for the keywords and reassembling the transferred files.

Network forensics has two other uses that are general purpose: collecting the information about the working of the computer system so as to optimize their performance and debug them as required, and also in the case of any hardware and software failures, recovering the data.

Botnet forensics deals with a botnet and its associated vulnerabilities. Botnet is an emerging threat facing computing asset through which it is used for illegal activities such as sending spam, different unwanted emails (Trojan, phishing, spyware, adware, fast flux, etc.), media, software, stealing information or computing resource, click fraud, denial-of-service attacks, etc. It is a collection of compromised computers. When a computer is conciliated by an attacker, there is often a code within the malware (a computer program that is made to harm the system) that commands it to become a part of a botnet. It is the most dangerous threat against cyber security as they provided a distributed platform for many activities. A malicious botnet is a network conciliated by the botmaster or botherder. Inter-related chat (IRC) network is specially used by the attacker for managing and controlling the infected hosts because IRC is a most easily available network or server.

11.2 Methodology Used in Botnet Forensics

Botnet forensics deals with detecting compromised system on the network where bot is a kind of malware that take a complete command of the computer. The term bot is derived from the word robot which carries out a predefined function by a software program. It can be directed through a command-and-control channel. Botnets are run by a malicious programmer known as botherder. Botherder sends the infection or viruses to a weak user's computer whose payload is a malicious application. It connects to the infected user's computer through a command-and-control server. The spammer purchases services from the botmaster, and the botmaster issues the updated command. Generally, the methodology used in botnet forensics involves the following three steps

11.2.1 Collection of Malwares

It follows a "catch-it-as-you-can" system. In this, all the packets that pass through an exacting traffic point are captured. It is followed by a consequent analysis process that further demands massive storage. Every piece of bot packet is examined exclusively, and then it is stored in a definite memory for future reference.

11.2.2 Malware Analysis

After malware collection, the next process starts, i.e., malware analysis. The botnet forensic system is a security device with hardware and pre-installed software. It is defined as behavior-based analysis. The researcher often uses machine learning approach to analyze the malware collection. Different tools can be used for the malware analysis such as weka, Hadoop, and course era.

In the final phase, a simulation technique is adopted for mitigating the problem. The extracted information from malware collection interferes with the control channel of the botnet network that tracks what kind of attack has occurred.

Botnet forensics is a science that determines the scope of breach and applies the methodology to find out the types of infection. Botnet forensics is the investigation of botnet attacks that includes collection, identification, detection, acquisition, and attribution. It is the postmortem activities for the botnet.

11.3 Nature of Botnet Forensics

Prevention is better than cure, i.e., attack is the main mantra of the botnet forensics. It is an approach of proactive in nature rather than reactive and corrective after the event of malicious activity. Botnet forensics engages the attackers in such a way that they spend more time and energy in covering their tracks while making an attack. It is the criminal psychology that they would like to ensure their safety first. It prohibits and discourage the attackers from engrossing into a malicious activity, hence thereby it ensures the efficiency and provides the network security. Internet service providers are equally accountable for the use, abuse, or misuse of the Internet on their networks. Nowadays, companies engaged in e-commerce are also under the regulatory frameworks, and it is mandatory for them to disclose their security breaches and to have an updated network security system with them.

For understanding botnet attack, we should understand its nature and build and design a botnet lab to deploy a botnet monitoring system. An effective botnet monitoring system needs continuous, comprehensive, concrete, and convenient work for achieving the desired output or the target.

11.3.1 Continuous

To escape from the detection, botnet changes its location very rapidly. So, it might be possible to maintain continuously the botnet log and update the changes.

11.3.2 Comprise

The system should understand the propagation of the botnet and the technique used for propagation.

11.3.3 Concrete

The system requires providing concrete information as early as possible because botnet constantly changes their place. So, the information of botnet and its values also degrade quickly.

11.3.4 Convenient

The system should get this information within a time so that the value cannot change.

However, it is a requirement of individuals to have domain knowledge and its analysis. The system will collect the information about various aspects of botnet including its flooding, i.e., denial-of-service, communication infrastructure, propagation technique, identities of compromise host, and details of activities that participated in.

11.4 Background

As you know the term "bot" that came into existence from the word robot, which carries out a predefined function by a software program. It can be directed through a command-and-control channel. Botnets are run by a malicious programmer known as botherder or botmaster. The botherder sends the infection or viruses to the feeble user's computer whose payload is malicious application. It connects through a command-and-control server. The spammer purchases services from the botmaster, and the botmaster itself issues the updated command.

Botnet forensics is a very young science. The term botnet forensics came into existence after few terminologies such as static forensics, malware forensics, and network forensics. Static forensics is a traditional and foundation approach for digital forensics. This analysis is used to identify all deleted files and determine whether they are encrypted files or any other. Static forensics obtains clues from identified files that are helpful for previous event results. On the other hand, live forensics deals with those evidence that is not collected by

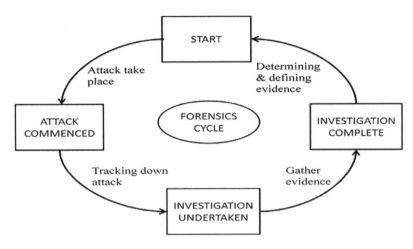

FIGURE 11.1
Forensics cycle.

traditional forensics. We can collect all evidence from running system through live forensics. Malware forensics is the analysis of malware. It is directly associated with the malicious activities caused by DDoS, phishing, spam, etc. The forensic investigation is needed to get rid of this problem. Figure 11.1 refers to a forensics cycle that consists of four phases, namely, start, attack commenced, investigation undertaken, and investigation completed.

In recent times, the network forensics has drawn tremendous significance for ensuring the organization's network security. Network forensics facilitates the detailed analysis of both the outside attacks and the insider's abuse. By investigating both kinds of attacks, it ensures detection of attacks and their prevention in the future, which avoids financial loss and saves the reputation of the organization.

Network security and network forensics are two different technologies. Security products that are utilized for avoiding intrusion provide data for forensic analysis and investigations. Unlike network forensics, network security prevents the attack on the system. Network security has a proactive approach as it keeps a close observation on the network and is constantly looking for any abnormal behavior in the context of potential security attack. It is a preventive measure to avoid the malicious activities by bots. Network forensics is a reactive approach, in which the investigation is usually done after the attack. It is like an autopsy, i.e., postmortem investigation. Most often it is observed that it is specific and focused on the type of attack and addresses only the issues related to the attack.

Ranum coined the term network forensics. According to Schwartz (2010), network forensics can be defined as "the reconstruction of network event to provide definitive insight into action and behavior of users, applications as well as devices." However, network forensics is about utilizing the scientific method and tools for collecting, identifying, collaborating, examining, analyzing, and generating the document using digital information from live network sessions.

Pilli et al. defined the concept of network forensics as "it deals with data found across a network connection mostly ingress and egress traffic from one host to another." He further defined network forensics as it goes beyond network security as it not only detects the attack but also records the evidence. There are certain attacks that do not breach network security policies but may be legally prosecutable. These crimes can be handled only by network forensics. Forensic systems act as a deterrent, as attackers become cautious.

They spend more time and energy to cover the tracks in order to avoid prosecution. The network forensics is a scientifically proven technique for collecting, identifying, examining, fusing, analyzing, and documenting all evidences for the purpose of revealing the facts.

11.5 Botnet Forensics Classification

Botnet forensics involves capturing (fetching) the network traffic and retrieving the evidence after reconnaissance from multiple devices, systems, processes, and other resources. The information given by botnet forensics is utilized to strengthen the security tools by understanding the modus operandi of the attacks. The available observations can also be utilized in future to prevent a potential threat to network security. Botnet forensics is both a proactive and reactive approach. It not only ensures the network security but also facilitates the law enforcement. The prime objective of botnet forensics is to measure the level of intrusions, investigating them and providing information to recover from an intrusion so as to strengthen system security and retrievable evidence presentation.

Botnet forensics is the science of mitigating, characterizing, trace backing investigating, and identifying the clues of bot. Botnet forensics is a technique that assists to ameliorate the system through an analysis of the bot attack and detect them. It focuses on the preservation and acquisition of the digital evidence from the various sources to be used as a bot clues for the investigation. Botnet forensics is of great importance nowadays, as it assists and prevents the organization from the outside and inside network attacks. It helps to detect the attack and to mitigate the damage occurred by determining who is responsible for an attack, and it can also determine the path from an affected network or system to the point from where an attack is originated. Table 11.1 lists major botnets and their establishment.

Broadly, the whole botnet forensics can be classified as shown in Figure 11.2.

11.5.1 Payload Classification

In payload-based traffic classification, packets are classified into the field of the payload. Payload uses classification techniques like deep packet inspection (DPI) for verification and classification of traffic. For understanding and verifying various applications, DPI utilizes the signature analysis. In most of the applications, a unique pattern of signatures exists. There are different signature analysis methods such as pattern analysis, protocol analysis, heuristic analysis, numerical analysis, and behavioral analysis.

In pattern analysis, applications have some patterns in the payload of the packets, which can be used to identify the protocols. These patterns may be present in any position in the packet, and the classification is possible after this only. Numerical analysis includes numerical characteristics of the packet, for example, payload size, the number of response packets, etc. Behavioral and heuristic analyses go simultaneously, and several antiviruses utilize both techniques for identifying viruses and infections. In protocol analysis, protocols are a set of rules of a particular action.

There are many traffic classification techniques proposed by many researchers in which one of the common techniques is based on the particular port number of a particular protocol to find the network application. It was proved ineffective for these port

TABLE 11.1

Major Botnets and Their Establishment

Types of Protocol	Bot Name	Discovered	Propagation Mechanism
HTTP	Rusktock	2006	Propagation through spam and infection.
HTTP	Blackenergy	2007	Propagation through infection.
HTTP	Zues	2007	Propagation by downloads.
HTTP	Waledac	2007	Propagation through spam
HTTP	Koobface	2008	Propagation through social networking sites.
HTTP	Lethic	2008	Worm, virus Propagation through spam.
HTTP	Mirai	2016	Targets on consumer devices through scanning.
IRC	GTbot	2000	Involvement for UDP/SYN flood
IRC	Sdbot	2002	Involvement for UDP/ICMP flood.
IRC	Gaobot(Agobot)	2002	Involvement for dos, spam, brute force attack
IRC	Rbot	2003	Involvement for DDoS attack.
IRC	Spybot	2003	Involvement for spam, file deletion and UDP flooding.
IRC	MaXiTE	2003	500–1,000 server bot. TCL script
IRC	phatbot	2004	Involvement for DDoS attack, spamming and sniffing traffic
IRC	Mytob	2005	Propagation through email attachment extension.
IRC	Dorkbot	2011	
P2P	Slapper	2002	Involvement in DDoS, spamming and harvest email account.
P2P	Sinit	2003	Installed in OS, exploit the browser and redirect the website.
P2P	Nugache	2006	Involvement in DDoS attack using decentralized custom protocol
P2P	Peacomm	2007	Spamming, DDoS, disable the firewall and attach with mail.
P2P	Conficker	2009	Spamming, through dictionary attack stealing data.
P2P	Kelihos	2010	Spamming, DDoS and embed links through hidden social networking.
P2P	Necurs	2016	Distributor of many piece of malware. Email attachment with Javascript or through macros.

number-based traffic classifications because of some reasons like new growth of peer-to-peer network application, the dynamic port number for some applications, or wrapping different services into a particular application. Machine learning algorithm utilizes classification and clustering on particular set of a payload content for the identification. It had tried to detect the P2P traffic rather than particular P2P application. Shortage of sharable dataset and inappropriate metrics became the main reason for the failure of comparison between the mentioned methods.

11.5.2 Signature-Based Classification

The main objective of the signature-based classifier is to detect, investigate the nature, and find out the feature of a bit string operating in the given payload. There are so many applications that use primary protocol like in three way handshaking (TCP) protocol three way handshaking. This classifier is utilized on fredezone, a free network service provider (Wi-Fi) operated by the city of Fredericton. It also reconnoiter on the theoretical bounds for

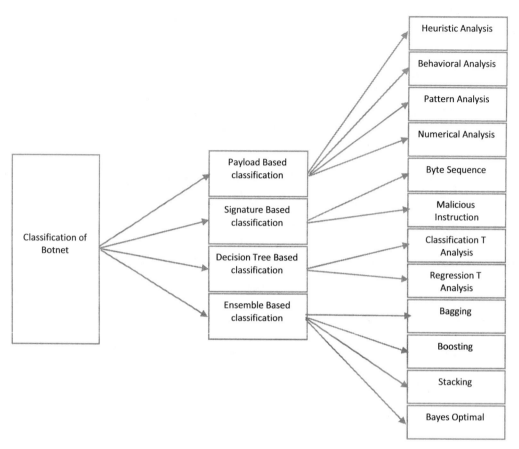

FIGURE 11.2
Botnet forensics classification.

learning signatures using an existing theory showing a framework for online extraction of signatures using a supervised classifier system.

11.5.3 Decision Tree-Based Classification

The structure of decision tree-based classification looks like a tree. By splitting the dataset into smaller subsets, the decision tree also developed simultaneously, and the outcome is presented in the form of a tree that has decision nodes and leaf nodes. It is a better method for classifying the unknown traffic. It can be further utilized for classification of traffic by initiating from roots of the tree and moving up to complete classification till the leaf node that defines a simple and efficient model for classification of unknown applications into different categories.

11.5.4 Ensemble-Based Classification

Ensemble method is used to improve the quality and robustness of supervised and unsupervised learning algorithms. Initially, the researcher used a bagging method for ensemble learning. Meta-algorithm of model averaging was built for classification initially. It used the multiple training set by utilizing bootstrap, and it used many versions of training set. Through combining both averaging and voting output of the model can produce a single output in the case of regression and classification. Each version of dataset is utilized for training of different models. Through averaging and voting output of the model combined and then create a single output in case of regression and classification.

Ensemble classifier is a methodology to lift several other classifiers. Ensemble classifier combines different classifiers in order to obtain the output for improving the accuracy. For this purpose, we can select any different pairs of individual classifiers and combine them for the improvement of the algorithm. Generally, there are two ways to generate ensemble classifier, i.e., data independent and data dependent. Data dependent can also further classify as implicit dependent and explicit dependent too.

11.6 Botnet Forensic Framework

Unethical hacking of sites, probing, click frauds, phishing, denial-of-service attack, and many such malicious practices affects the organizational integrity and sovereignty. Such activities are direct attacks on the safety, security, and confidentiality of the organization. These activities put organizational privacy at stake. Botnet forensics is broadly categorized into three phase: framework, identification, and analysis. This study shows a generic framework for botnet forensics based on existing models and studies (Figure 11.3). The first phase of generic framework is malware that is the combination of propagation, infection, communication, and attack that shows the stages of malware. As we know, botnet has become a common phenomenon on the Internet. It is a collection of infected machines, or in other words, it is a kind of army of infected bots targeted at spreading malicious activities and expansion of bot army. The botmaster controls and communicates through C&C channels. IRC is the most commonly and widely utilized channel. This portion shows the kind of malware whether it is botnet or other kind of malware. The second phase of the generic framework is botnet forensic identifier. This botnet forensic identifier focuses on identifying whether the system is compromised or it may get infected. If it is compromised, it will identify whether it is bot attack or any other kind of attack. Botnet forensic identifier searches the bot through the reconnaissance of traffic, attribution, automotive passive, and malware sample. Our botnet forensic identifier tries to locate and concentrates on spam email because 80% of email traffic is just because of spam. Botnet forensic identifier also covers the attribution, automotive passive, and malware sample.

The third phase of the generic framework is botnet forensic analyzer that analyzes the results generated from the identifier. Botnet forensic analyzer works to search after crime investigation. When identifier insures the malware, the analyzer seeks what type of malware it is and where it infected. At this stage, the analyzer finds out the clues with actual information and forwards it to botnet evidence phase. It is observed by different phases such as analysis, investigation, examination, collection, and preservation. It includes analysis, investigation, examination, collection, and preservation of all collected clues. The fourth stage is botnet evidence that collected all information from the various previous stages and forwards it to incident response phase III.

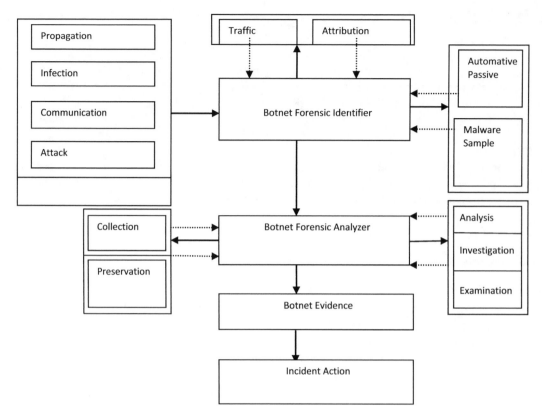

FIGURE 11.3
Botnet forensics framework.

11.6.1 Botnet Forensic Identification

Botnet forensic identification refers to the system involvement in bot malicious activities. This is the initial phase where the researcher may get the possibilities of any malicious activities specific to the botnet. Few researchers also showed a novel technique for the automatic identification of botnets used to deliver malicious emails. The author showed a referential implementation system for presenting this technique. This developed system can be deployed in a live environment.

According to the botnet forensic identification survey, we classified the whole identification of botnet forensic process into traffic, attribution, TCP fingerprint, malware, and automotive passive identification (Figure 11.4).

The whole traffic can be classified into bot traffic, data adaptive network traffic, and machine learning traffic identification. Machine learning traffic identification is classified into naïve classification, Bayesian classification, and J48 classification. Automotive passive identification is classified into spam, which includes the heuristic, Bayesian analysis, and embed URL. In anti-spam classification, it focuses on isolation, conflicts, clustering, and durability. In malware sample, it shows the sample, proactive heuristic sample, action, and tracing malware. Methodology is diversified, analyzed, and the structure is traced, captured, and analyzed. In TCP fingerprint identification, it can arrange into dataset which show the traces of the data. the TCP stack collects attributes passively from remote devices. TCP fingerprint identification can be traced during communication in transport layer.

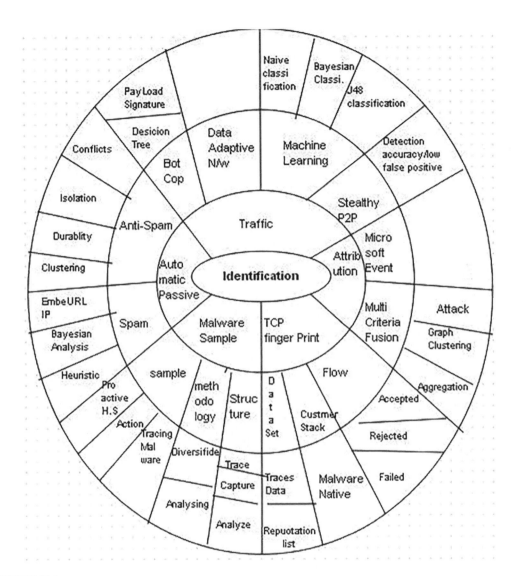

FIGURE 11.4
Identification of botnet forensics.

11.7 Botnet Forensic Analysis

In order to detect and analyze the botnet attack, the dataset that is completely implemented in a physical testbed environment has been taken. It uses real devices for generating the real traffic. This dataset contains both training set for real traces and testing set for normal and botnet traffic.

Botnet analysis is utilized for detecting the nature and kind of attack. This can be executed by disparate machine learning algorithms. These machine learning models may give different results, but the model with comparatively better result can be taken as the best-fitted model.

11.7.1 Botnet Inquisition Model

There are two ways of evaluating the network security aspects, i.e., prevention and detection. The prevention mechanism is being done by firewall and intrusion prevention system (IPS), and the detection can be done by intrusion detection system (IDS). Botnet forensics uses postmortem techniques to collect, identify, detect, examine, analyze, and incident response document for bot shreds of evidence from digital sources. It uses network security tools to uncover facts related to the cybercrimes specifically on the botnet. The major challenge of the botnet forensics is to analyze digital evidence of cybercrime.

Generally, botnet forensic analysis faces many challenges. It requires an efficient repository, which can be obtained through the passive deployment of vulnerable systems to be compromised. Attackers can use encrypted malware traffic by modifying web traffic for the detection and analysis aberration, reconstruction, attack behavior, etc. Normally it has to monitor full traces of malicious behavior in order to get through the nature of the attack. The classification and clustering process can be applied when there is a protocol's complexity. Furthermore, the reconstruction method is used to understand the purpose of attack and to resolve the convoluted shreds of evidence.

This inquisition model is able to refurbish the quality of results of the malicious evidence analysis specifically for a botnet. It incorporates all the information at different levels of the model by tracing and detecting the anomaly and by applying the forensics. These results curtail the time duration of the decision made in the botnet investigation phase. In general, most of the frameworks hinge upon distance, feature, or probabilistic measurements. However, this inquisition model is often used in the alert correlation techniques, which depends on the attack attributes.

The model primarily focuses on investigating the various kinds of botnet attacks. It helps in identification, detection, and classification of botnet and analyzes the attack intentions. It further visualizes and generates the report so that such bot attacks can be prevented in future. The entire process requires deep investigation and analysis of various factors, and therefore the term "inquisition" is referred for the title of the model.

The model analyzes various attacks including cybercrime on the networks. It computes the probability for detecting accuracy values of the attack intentions and it is calculated with the help of various algorithms like attack intention analysis (AIA). It also gives a list of probability attack intentions depending on the relevant evidences. The Dempster–Shafer (D–S) evidence theory with causal networks can also be used to get a better estimation of the attack purpose. This evidence theory is used to compute the probability of attack intentions as it provides better values and better accuracy. Figure 11.5 represents the inquisition model for detecting the network.

11.7.1.1 Data Sources

This is the first phase of the botnet forensics model, which is utilized for collecting all the data traffic and packets from the network or the system. It is responsible for collecting all the ingress and egress packets from the network. Furthermore, it captured and monitored all the data traffic and the packets from the network and then analyzed the entire network traffic. This was done by using different botnet forensic analyses and monitoring tools such as Wireshark, Tcpdump, and Silent Runner.

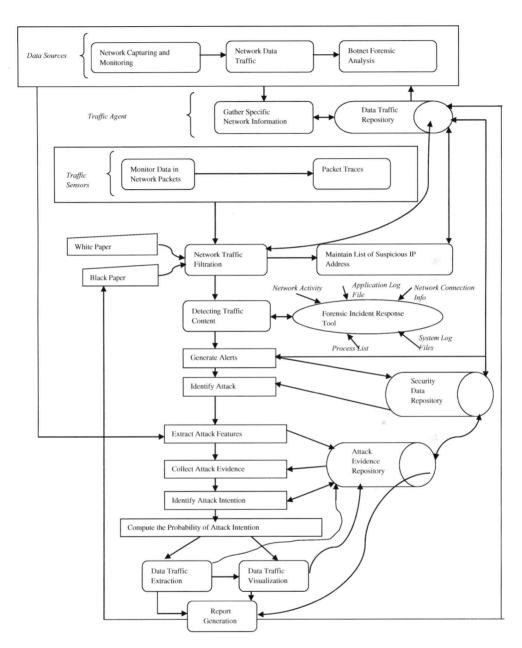

FIGURE 11.5
Inquisition model for botnet forensics.

11.7.1.2 Traffic Agents

The specific information collected in the previous phase is gathered. The information that is useful in detecting the attacks and collecting all the packet traces to identify the attack intentions is gathered. All the information and packet traces are collected in the data traffic repository so that no crucial information can be lost. The data traffic repository can be utilized for future use and can retrieve the data or the packets as and when required.

11.7.1.3 Traffic Sensors

All those network packet traces or the required information that is gathered in the previous phase using different network monitoring tools like packet capturing, fingerprinting, IDS, pattern matching, and statistics such as Ngrep, Bro, Snort, Argus, Wireshark, etc. are monitored. These packets analyzed to collect the traces of the attack and to identify the intentions of the attacker.

11.7.1.4 Network Traffic Filtration

In this phase, all the packets that have been captured in the earlier phase are filtered. It gives full concentration on unwanted packets, thus resulting in the reduced workload. There are two ways of doing it, i.e., the whitelist and blacklist filtering.

11.7.1.5 Whitelist

The whitelist is the set of packets that are not infectious in nature. For an instance, windows update, antivirus update, and a list of known sites are examples of whitelist.

11.7.1.6 Blacklist

In this section of network traffic filtration, blacklist filtering weeds out the infectious packets. These details can be utilized for filtering out the malware and detecting that whether they are bots or not in the next phase. After filtering out those packets, a list of all the suspicious IP addresses that make the work easier is also maintained. This helps in finding out all the malicious activities done on the network or the system. Furthermore, it can also easily identify the attack intentions. A list from the data traffic repository can be maintained and can be saved. In the future, same facilitates an easy identification of the malicious activities on the network.

11.7.1.7 Detecting Malicious Traffic Content

This phase mainly aims at identification and detection of unknown packets or the infected data traffics that goes through the blacklist filtration. The forensic incident response tool is utilized for infected packet detection. The forensic incident response tool facilitates network connection info, application log, system log, process list, and many other functions. It is followed by detection and identification of the organization's policy, legal issues, and business constraints. The role of the incident response tool is vital in deciding whether to carry on the investigation and collect more traces or to abort the process.

Furthermore, alert generator generates the alerts in order to enable the network forensic investigation. A copy of the captured data is analyzed to identify the attack alerts. Alerts are generated on the basis of matching the pattern of the known or unknown packets, which are collected in the previous phase. After generating the alerts, all the malicious packets or unknown data that could be malicious in nature are saved to the security data repository so that these packets could not be lost as they are very crucial for attack intentions in botnet forensic inquisition. This information can be used from the security data to identify whether it is an attack or not. This identification is done on the generated alerts. This can also use the data saved in the data traffic repository to generate the alerts and to identify an attack. These repositories are linked together for finding an attack and saving the data traffic securely.

Feature extraction is used after identifying the attack alert. The attack evidence can be collected and saved in the attack evidence repository for the future use. After collecting the evidence, all the attack features like how the attack has occurred, who was involved in that attack, duration of the exploit, and the methodology used in the attack can be extracted. Each and every possible feature of the attack is extracted so that the attack intentions can be identified, which is the main purpose in this proposed framework for botnet forensic inquisition. Attack evidence and security data repository are linked together to collect the evidence and save them securely for the future. Various machine learning algorithms can be applied for detecting malignant and benign data. For this work, ensemble-based classification technique has been applied for detecting malicious and benign data.

11.7.1.8 Attack Intention

The attack intention probability is computed with either the Dempster–Shafer evidence theory or AIA algorithm. All the values are associated with a relevant attack to generate the value of the attack intention. This is the main aim and specialty of the framework, which differentiates it from the other existing frameworks. It employs probability values to approximate the attack intentions to determine the similarity of new attacks with the other predefined intentions.

There is already a defined set of values that contains all the previous attacks and another set of values that contains the attack intentions for all the predefined attacks. Using any given algorithms, estimating the similarity of values between the new attack intentions and the others is necessary. It identifies the attacks that contain one or more attack intentions and compute the sum of all the probability values of the attack intentions that are relevant. Different techniques differentiate the stage of the attack and determine the target. The stage of attack segregates into, increased access based, the disclosure of information based and denial of services. Furthermore, it can be observed through targets such as a file, a computer, or a network and analyzed through intruder skills, capability, and tools. It determines the threat estimation, intention list, and attack probability.

11.7.1.9 Data Traffic Extraction/Visualization

The circumstances of attack and motive can be explained and proved by extracting the relevant information from the collected values. Data visualization helps in presenting the situation. Complete information about that attack is maintained in a log that validates those packets or collected information. It takes all the required information from the attack evidence repository and maintains an attack log by taking those values. Furthermore, this attack log and evidence are used to identify the attack intention for botnet forensic inquisition. Visualization can be done by separating the normal traffic and botnet traffic. Furthermore, botnet traffic is used to analyze through the ensemble classifier algorithm and tools such as NetMate and Orange.

Report generation is the final phase of the framework in which observations are presented in an understandable format, providing an explanation of the various procedures to arrive at the conclusion of detection of attacks and identify an intention of the attack. The required information has been taken from the attack evidence repository and the attack log maintained in it and generated a document or a report based on those shreds of evidence. It also updates the data traffic repository for finding out the new malicious packets as well as for updating the list of suspicious IP addresses. A detailed review of an entire case documentation is done for future examination, detection, and identification of the attack intentions.

The inquisition model exhibits computing probability of attack intention using the Dempster–Shafer theory or attack intention analysis (AIA). The result will find out new vulnerabilities that help improving the decision-making process. The inquisition model also provides better results and accuracy for detection and identification of the attack intention. The dependencies of packet attribute from various tools and reconnaissance of attributes from different hosts validate an attack.

11.7.2 Botnet Analysis Using Ensemble of Classifier

Botnet inquisition framework provides the details of botnet detection and its analysis through a step-by-step process. It is obvious to analyze the botnet when botnet identification process gets completed. There is a different way to get the feature extracted and to analyze them. This machine learning model refers to the classification technique to analyze the data and has taken the ensemble of classifier and machine learning algorithm to improve the accuracy in detecting the botnet. The work particularly deals with a specific kind of botnet dataset which infiltrates the network from inside denial-of-service (DoS), distributed denial-of-service (DDoS), and brute force data. Collected botnet traffic is the ingestion of SSH, HTTP, and SMTP traffic that refers to the user's behavior. It is further classified and characterized through a set of attributes that distinguish the malicious traffic from normal traffic. Botnet analysis is explained through one case study that is taken from ISCX dataset that is next filtered into normal traffic and botnet traffic and select botnet traffic sample for further analysis. This process has been extracted 42 attributes, provided labels to every instance, and bifurcated it into training and testing datasets.

In this case study, maximum attributes are extracted from TCP/UDP headers directly such as Source IP and Destination IP. These extracted 42 attributes are srcip (source IP address), srcport (source port no.), dstip (destination IP address), dstport (destination port no.), proto (protocol), total_fpackets (total packets in forward direction), total_fvolume (total bytes in forward direction), total_bpackets (total packets in backward direction), total_bvolume (total bytes in backward direction), min_fpktl (minimum packet size in forward direction), mean_fpktl (mean packet size in forward direction), max_fpktl (maximum packet size in forward direction), std_fpktl (standard deviation of packet length in forward direction), min_bpktl (minimum packet size in backward direction), mean_bpktl (mean packet size in backward direction), max_bpktl (maximum packet size in backward direction), std_bpktl (standard deviation of packet length in backward direction), min_fiat (minimum time between two packet in forward direction), mean_fiat (mean time between two packet in forward direction), max_fiat (maximum time between two packet in forward direction), numroot (no. of root accesses), rootshell (if root shell is generated), numcompromised (no. of compromised condition), suattempted (attempted su root command), hot (no. of hot indicators), num_le_creation (operation on the number of file creation), aglaud (average payload packet length), numaccess_les (no. of operation on access control file), count (in the last two sec no. of connection), duration (no. of establishment), std_fiat (standard deviation time between two packets in forward direction), min_biat (minimum time between two packets in backward direction), mean_biat (mean time between two packets in backward direction), max_biat (maximum time between two packets in backward direction), std_biat (standard deviation time between two packets in backward direction), sflow_fbytes (subflow of forward direction in average no. of bytes), sflow_bpacket (subflow of backward direction in average no. of packets), sflow_bbytes (subflow of backward direction in average no. of bytes), sflow_fpackets (subflow of forward direction in average no. of packets), total_fhlen (total size of forward packet), total_bhlen (total size of backward packet), and mean active (mean time of flow active before idle state).

Attributes are extracted by two types of segregations: host-based and flow-based. Network flow refers to the set of attributes extraction. P2P and non-P2P traffics are obtained from these attributes by link flows. Flow vectors are utilized and inserted into NateMate and Orange tool for extracting 42 different attributes. Furthermore, it is labeled into normal traffic and P2P botnet traffic. Normal traffic is a legitimate traffic.

Figure 11.6 shows that how the botnet analysis model works. The dataset was extracted into normal and malicious traffic. In this study, malicious traffic was taken for further machine learning analysis. For this purpose, the training and testing set is used for extraction, and all inputs were given to the model. The classification model was applied in this study for further analysis. On the other hand, quality metric which shows the error differences were also set with the machine algorithm and applied to the classification, model, intended to the final output. Normal traffic is a legitimate traffic, so the process hasn't paid heed on it, especially for normal P2P traffic. P2P botnet traffic is basically fraught with different bot traces. Therefore, this process has not used both collected traffic.

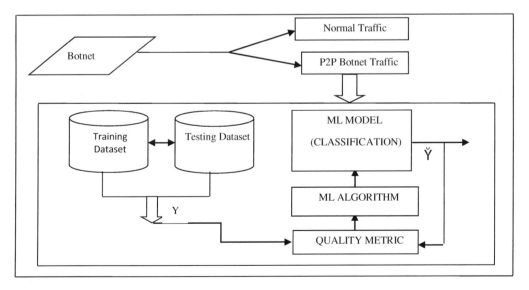

FIGURE 11.6
Botnet forensic analysis model.

Algorithm 11.1

Input:
D: dataset; tnd: training data; tsd: testing data point; cl: class label; f: feature; M: model
Output:

1. Obtaining tnd (tnd$_1$ +tnd$_2$+.........+tnd$_n$) and tsd (tsd$_1$+tsd$_2$+....+tsd$_n$) from D
2. Extracting f from tnd and tsd of D
3. Segregation on Normal and Botnet traffic
4. If no cl on botnet traffic then
5. Providing cl elseif
6. Goto next step
7. Frame M, test each M on cl data on tnd and tsd and obtain its accuracy
8. Test M$_1$ from knn, DT and svm
9. Test ensemble M$_2$ from multiple combinations
10. Compare step 8 and step 9
11. M ← best from M1 & M2 models based on accuracy
12. Predict the cl

Machine learning ensemble of classifier algorithm refers to the multiple combinations of the single classifier, so that the power of detecting botnet clues can be increased. This model is a combination of bagging, AdaBoost, and Soft-Voting method of ensemble-based classifier. It also compared the performance of each classifier based on their accuracy to predict classes of unknown instances.
Let an example E of N classifier, i.e. $\{E_1, E_2, E_3..., E_N\}$.
Ensemble E is actually having two levels ensemble itself, so each classifier E$_x$ in the ensemble E is actually a collection of (ensemble) of N classifiers.
Each classifier E$_i$ is at the middle level. The lowest level contains the actual classifier.
Suppose that all middle-level ensemble E$_i$ is trained with r followed wedges. As soon as new chunk appeared, it is necessary to train the next middle-level ensemble till E$_N$.
Let data wedge $W = \{W_x, W_{x-1}, ..., W_{x-r+1}\}$, where W is randomly divided into n equal ports,
i.e. $\{W, W_1, W_2, ..., W_n\}$, where all ports will have the same no. of positive and negative example.
Next build E$_x$ with n classifier=$\{E_{X(1)}, E_{X(2)}, ... , E_{x(n)}\}$, where each classifier E$_{X(j)}$ is trained with the dataset and computed the expected error. The expected error of ensemble E$_x$ by may be obtained by testing each classifier E$_{X(j)}$ on W$_j$ and averaging their error. Thereafter, updated the upper-level ensemble E by replacing middle level.
All the classifiers trained on instance sample were taken with replacement from the training set. Some instances have represented many times. Figure 11.7 describes the flow diagram of an ensemble classifier.
A confusion matrix is an important tool for analyzing how well the classifier can recognize tuples of different classes. True positive (TP) and true negative (TN) exhibit when the classifier is accepting right things. On the other hand, false positive (FP) and false negative (FN) exhibit when the classifier is accepting the wrong things. Table 11.2 shows the confusion matrix shown with totals of positive and negative tuples. It shows the parameters taken for evaluation.

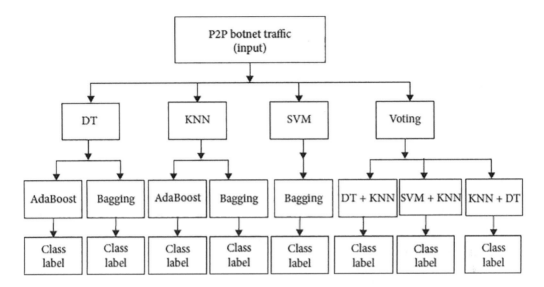

FIGURE 11.7
Ensemble of classifier model.

TABLE 11.2

Confusion Matrix

		Predicted Class		
		YES	NO	TOTAL
Actual Class	YES	TP	FN	P
	NO	FP	TN	N
	Total	P	N	P+N

11.7.3 Results and Discussion

The results and discussion from the above case studies are as follows.

11.7.3.1 Single Classifier

The botnet is a large network of compromised computers which are instructed by a both-erder. The reactive approach refers to the evidence that should be preserved in one place for postmortem. This evidence is further applied for the analysis of botnet traffic and to retrieve the relevant information from it. For this purpose, machine learning model 1 has been taken that reveals the analysis using a single classifier.

Table 11.3 presents the table for a single classifier. In this table, the decision tree algorithm shows 93.7% accuracy, 92.09% precision, 93.48% recall, and 94.76% F1 score. In the case of KNN algorithm, 94.65% accuracy, 95.0% precision, 93.48% recall, and 94.76% F1 score are observed. Subsequently SVM shows 75.99% accuracy, 81.07% precision, 76.05% recall, and 66.78% F1 score.

TABLE 11.3

Single Classifier

Classifiers	Decision Tree	KNN	SVM
Accuracy	93.7	94.65	75.99
Precision	92.09	95.0	81.07
Recall	93.48	95.0	76.05
F1-score	94.76	95.0	66.78

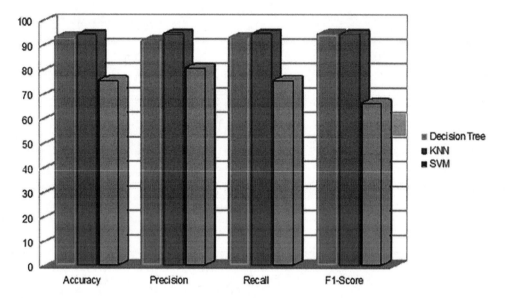

FIGURE 11.8
Comparison among single classifier.

Figure 11.8 shows the comparison chart among single classifier. The red column exhibits the decision tree, the blue column exhibits the KNN, and subsequently, the green column shows SVM.

11.7.3.2 Ensemble of Classifier

Ada-Boost Decision tree also increases accuracy from 93.7% to 98.36% improving learning process of a decision tree, and the highest accuracy is achieved by using soft-voting rule because it merges the power of two algorithms and gives more weight to the decision of better-performing algorithm. The output of a single classifier does not give perfect bot findings. The performance of bot evidence using the ensemble of a classifier is better than the single classifier.

Table 11.4 shows the comparison chart of different ensembles of classifiers. As we can see in such case study in which the performance of bagging KNN, i.e., 94.77% in Table 11.4 is better than KNN, i.e., 94.65% in Table 11.2. An ensemble of classifier reduces the variance in input data and avoids overfitting. It gives ensemble classifier better than single classifier and the highest accuracy, i.e., 98.36% for AdaBoost-DT, 94.65% for AdaBoost-KNN, 95.30% for Bagging-DT, 94.77% for Bagging-KNN, 75.99% for Bagging-SVM, 95.47% for

TABLE 11.4

Comparison Chart of Ensemble of Classifier

Classifier	AdaBoost-DT	AdaBoost-KNN	Bagging-DT	Bagging-KNN	Bagging-SVM	Voting-KNN+DT	Voting-DT+SVM	Voting-SVM+KNN
Accuracy	98.36	94.65	95.30	94.77	75.99	95.47	85.06	94.65
Precision	98.85	95.0	95.25	94.89	81.07	96.0	87.0	95.0
Recall	98.23	95.0	95.48	95.0	76.05	95.78	85.0	95.0
F1-score	98.54	95.0	95.76	94.42	66.78	95.23	83.0	95.0

Voting-KNN+DT, 85.06% for Voting-DT+SVM, and 94.65% for Voting-SVM+KNN. First, the AdaBoost with SVM decreases the performance because SVM is a strong learner, while AdaBoost is used mainly to boost up weak learners. Second, AdaBoost provides sampling to train the instance according to their complexity to classify, i.e. more weight is given to the instances, which are hard to classify.

Figure 11.9 shows the comparison of the ensemble of classifier where the white-bar chart refers the combining power of AdaBoost and decision tree, the red bar shows the AdaBoost with KNN, the green bar shows Bagging with DT, the grey bar shows Bagging with KNN, the blue bar shows Bagging with SVM, and the yellow bar shows voting, KNN with DT.

11.7.3.3 Discussion

The results show that ensemble-based classifier provides better results because it is made up by combining multiple algorithms for botnet analysis. Observation showed that decision trees are very flexible, easy to understand, and easy to debug. Simple decision trees tend to overfit the training data more so that other techniques which mean generally have

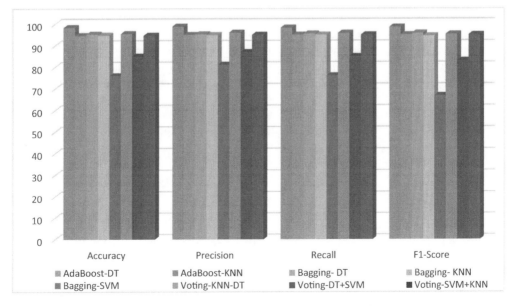

FIGURE 11.9
Ensemble comparison.

to do tree pruning and tune the pruning procedures. KNN keeps all the training data. Through KNN, calculations comparatively goes large and complexity is higher when a dimension is very low. A KNN calculation goes largely because it calculates similarity from its nearest neighbors, and after sorting them, it applies majority voting on top K neighbors to predict the class of data point. Therefore, complexity is directly proportional to the value of K.

When all features give continuous real value, KNN provides the good result. When a number of features are very large as compared with the training samples, SVM cannot work efficiently. SVM should not be taken in the case of multiple classes. In this study, binary classifier can be taken and can use the voting method to classify any one of the class.

This model is also compared with the performance of each classifier based on their accuracy, precision, recall, and F-1 score to predict classes of unknown instances. The accuracy of the results shows that all the proportions of observed prediction are correctly taken, which is a sign of a good model. In this study, the results exhibit that ensemble of classifier model can detect botnet traffic more accurately than a single classification model. Precision refers to the proportion of all positive observations that are correct. F1 score refers to the harmonic mean (average) of both precision and recall.

11.8 Challenges

Botnet forensics uses scientific techniques to collect, examine, analyze, and document digital bot shreds of evidence from digital sources and network security tools. It uncovers facts related to the cybercrimes specific to the botnet. Inquisition model shows the mechanism for applying forensics on botnet traffic after passing from various phases. The existing classifiers have been combined in an ensemble model for detecting the botnet traffic. This ensemble of different classifiers performs better because it is made up by combining the power of multiple algorithms. It segregated the features into class, i.e., on normal traffic and botnet traffic and provide labeling. Thereafter by using data mining tool, ensemble of classifier algorithm has been applied. This result shows that the ensemble model improved various parameters like accuracy, precision, recall, and F1 score in detecting the botnet traffic as compared with the previous single classification algorithm. However, the inquisition model can be implemented for botnet forensics in future. Machine learning technique can be used analyzing big data of botnet attacks with the combinations of ensemble classifier. The challenges obtained through research gaps in this case study on investigation of botnet attack are as follows.

11.8.1 Collection

Collection is an important process of botnet forensics in which case study collects all information from network and further sends for different works. Without the loss or drop of packets, capturing real-time data is an important challenge. Capturing all packet information gives very large amount of data. Collecting information from the network and the collection of useful data are also challenging. Filtration process requires to separate only those data which are needed.

11.8.2 Preservation

Collected data are to be preserved for future. Traces of data and logs are stored on a backup device. The original security traffic data are unaffected for legal requirements. To keep secure, these data are also an important challenge.

11.8.3 Identification

Packet captures are to be examined to identify protocol features that are manipulated. This information is correlated with attack events, and the compromise is validated. Validation of attack takes the process to the investigation phase. Packets are reorganized into individual transport-layer connections between machines, and the attack behavior is analyzed by replaying the attack.

11.8.4 Traffic Analysis

The analysis of identified sources is also an important challenge of research. To get the dataset for analysis purpose is also a tedious job check. To classify dataset, feature extraction is required. Algorithm may be tested for improving the accuracy. Irrespective of single classifier, ensemble-based classifier can be analyzed for improving the results.

11.8.5 Investigation

Botnet forensics is targeted to define communication pathway between an infected machine and back to the origin point of attack. Incident response and prosecution of the attacker are used to identify the attacker, the tough measurement of the botnet. IP spoofing and stepping stone attack are still prevalent techniques of the attacker to hide himself.

11.9 Summary

Botnet forensics is a new technology to investigate different bot attacks on the network. It is an extended phase of network forensics that specially focuses on bot attack, and further network forensics is an extended phase of the network security, so this technology helps us to solve various network security issues, i.e., access control, system log, and router log. The other challenges involved while setting up and building botnet lab, i.e., botnet monitoring system, are as follows.

- The passive deployment of malware and waiting for the compromising system require good lab infrastructure.
- Botnet monitoring system requires simulator with latest binaries and data set that are tedious job to get from security agencies.
- Malware spread through a web browser. Malware is hosted on the webserver, and when a victim visits the page, the victim machine is compromised through vulnerability in the browser. To obtain such malware, need to capture malware, i.e., installed through social engineering technique.

- We need to study various steps involved in the propagation of malware. Malware is often hosted on compromised webserver. Attackers first seek vulnerable webservers and then start compromising it. Then, thereafter the attackers advertise links to compromise servers to infect victims that visit the link. New tools are required to detect how attackers find and compromise webservers, and to monitor the propagation of malware links.
- Denial-of-service requires the high storage capacity and the processor with high bandwidth to deploy and process effectively.
- It is a very tedious job to get dataset from the companies.

Questions

Q.1.   What do you understand by the term "botnet forensics"?

Q.2.   What are the methodologies used in botnet forensics? Explain in details.

Q.3.   Explain the meaning of statement "prevention is better than cure"? How can it fit in the term botnet forensics? Elaborate.

Q.4.   Explain the features of botnet forensics in detail?

Q.5.   Explain the inquisition model for the botnet forensics in detail?

Q.6.   Draw the diagram for the inquisition model and explain any feature is to be more fit in any area that can make it more refine?

Q.7.   Draw a diagram for botnet forensic analysis model?

Q.8.   Explain the botnet analysis model in detail that incorporates all phases of it?

Q.9.   How can we filter the malicious traffic into normal and botnet traffic? Define the process?

Q.10.   What do you understand by ensemble classifier? How ensemble classifier makes it better than others?

References

A. Bijalwan, "Botnet Forensic Analysis Using Machine Learning Approach," *Security and Communication Networks*, vol. 2020, 2020.

A. Bijalwan, N. Chand, E. S. Pilli, and C. R. Krishna, "Botnet analysis using ensemble classifier," *Perspectives in Science*, Elsevier, pp. 1-9, 2016.

A. Bijalwan, S. Sando, and M. Lemma, "An Anatomy for Recognizing Network Attack Intention", *International Journal of Recent Technology & Engineering*, vol. 8, 2019.

A. Bijalwan, V. K. Solanki, and E. S. Pilli, "Botnet Forensic: Issues, Challenges and Good Practices," *Network Protocols and Algorithms*, vol. 10, no. 2, 2018.

S. Noh, G. Jung, K. Choi, and C. Lee, "Compiling Network Traffic into Rules Using Soft Computing Methods for the Detection of Flooding Attacks," *Applied Soft Computing*, vol. 8, no. 3, pp. 1200–1210, 2008.

J.-S. Park and M.-S. Kim, "Design and implementation of an SNMP-based traffic flooding attack detection system," in *Challenges for Next Generation Network Operations and Service Management*, Springer, 2008, pp. 380–389.

L. Rokach, "Ensemble-Based Classifiers," *Artificial Intelligence Review*, vol. 33, no. 1–2, pp. 1–39, 2010.

H. Safa, M. Chouman, H. Artail, and M. Karam, "A Collaborative Defense Mechanism Against SYN Flooding Attacks in IP Networks," *Journal of Network and Computer Applications*, vol. 31, no. 4, pp. 509–534, 2008.

E. Schwartz, "Network Packet Forensics," *Cyber Forensics*, 2010, pp. 85-101. doi.org/10.1007/978-1-60761-772-3_7

K. Takemori, M. Fujinaga, T. Sayama, and M. Nishigaki, IP Traceback Using DNS Logs Against Bots," *International Symposium on Computer Science and its Applications, CSA'08* (pp. 84–89), IEEE, 2008.

P. Wu, Y. Shuping, and C. Junhua, "Recognizing Intrusive Intention and Assessing Threat Based on Attack Path Analysis," *International Conference on Multimedia Information Networking and Security, MINES'09* (vol. 2, pp. 450–453), IEEE, 2009.

P. Wu, W. Zhigang, and C. Junhua, "Research on Attack Intention Recognition Based on Graphical Model, *Fifth International Conference on Information Assurance and Security*, 2009. IAS'09 (vol. 1, pp. 360–363), IEEE, 2009.

12

System Investigation and Ethical Issues

This chapter focuses on imparting the knowledge about live system investigation on both Windows and Unix operating systems and its ethical issues. After reading this chapter, you would

- Have knowledge about all the types of computer crimes and challenges while deterring a crime.
- Have knowledge about computer laws such as patent, copyright, trademark, trade secret, etc.
- Understand the concept of live system and its analysis.
- Understand Windows- and Unix-based analyses.
- Have knowledge about ethical issues.

12.1 Introduction

This chapter includes crimes and the issues, challenges, responsibilities, and obligations of an investigator. When we talk about ethics, we pre-assume that we are talking about moral values. Ethics is a branch of knowledge that shows the moral principles of individuals and how to conduct the activities. Ethics is concerned with positive and negative behaviors of a person that reflect the individual's personality at various situations. It is a branch of philosophy that shows the interrelationship of persons with each other. It reflects whether the action is right or wrong, good or bad, or acceptable or unacceptable. As we know, investigating a crime that is committed within the network and its branches is known as network forensics. This chapter is about the moral values and the behaviors related to investigating the crime. Earlier cyber ethics was also known as computer ethics as most of the work and crime was related to the computer. Ethical behavior requires diligence, honesty, sense of communication, proficiency, consistency, and goodwill while investigating a crime. When we talk about the forensic investigation, we may concentrate on two basic things, i.e., post-mortem analysis and examination of evidence.

DOI: 10.1201/9781003045908-15

12.1.1 Postmortem Analysis

The postmortem analysis is the investigation that occurs after the crime. Postmortem analysis is also a reconstruction of an attack. It provides a detailed analysis to connect all the evidence and further it tested for reconstructing the event. Sometimes this approach demands or reveals further evidence.

12.1.2 Examination of Computer

Examination of computer is essential to find out some sort of criminal violation. It means that the investigator starts examination from the same tool and techniques which criminal use for the attacks

Forensic examiners analyze and examine the investigative process from a computer. These computers may be having any operating system, i.e., either Windows operating system or Unix operating system.

12.2 Crimes

Criminal activities are very rapidly increasing on network and its connected computers. An attacker uses various methodologies to compromise the computers. These attackers are accountable for the huge financial loss and many other adverse impacts on people. Crimes on computer are any kind of criminal activities carried out in a network and its computers by a tool that proliferates their activity. It is so widespread, so identifying the target is very cumbersome. As per the Certified Information System Security Professional (CISSP), we can bifurcate computer crimes into crimeassociated with the prevalence of the computer and computer as incidental to other crimes.

Crime is associated with the prevalence of the computer where crimes are not possible without computer. It is traditional by nature, but its target is ever evolving. The example of crime associated with the prevalence of the computer is piracy, copyright violation including software, programs, black marketing of the all the equipment associated with the computer, and piracy of movie. Computer is incidental to other crimes where the computer is not a direct device to commit the crime. whereas, computer is a necessary device to facilitate any kind of crimes and helps it to undetectable. Money laundering is the best example of computer as incidental to other crimes. Money laundering can be defined as the introduction of illegally produced funds from the authentic financial marketplace.

12.2.1 Computer Crime

In the previous chapters, we have categorized network attacks into active and passive attacks. However, the following are few important computer crimes that can impact an organization's or individual's personality and behaviors:

- Intelligence attacks
- Financial attacks
- Business attacks
- Terrorist attacks

- Fun attacks
- Grudge attacks
- Thrill attacks.

12.2.1.1 Intelligence Attacks

The criminal agents can acquire sensitive files and information illicitly from the police offices, ministerial offices, or from the military base. These agents can be foreign intelligent agents, traitors of the country, or any other criminals. Sometimes the government of any particular country launches such kind of attacks during conflict and war.

12.2.1.2 Financial Attacks

The victims of this kind of attack can be a large corporate sector, banking sector, or any e-commerce websites. The attacker can compromise all of these areas just for the sake of money, any financial information, devastate individual's financial status, their business and credit or debit card details, etc.

12.2.1.3 Business Attacks

Sometimes, stiff competition among all corporate sector makes them to use the malicious way to be the winner. Hence, businesses are becoming soft targets for computer attacks and internet attacks. These attacks can be through phishing, denial of services, some intelligent attacks, or any other kind of attacks that hamper the businesses drastically.

12.2.1.4 Terrorist Attacks

Terrorism can be in different forms using the Internet. Sometimes it may be used for tarnishing a country's image through social networking sites. We might have seen umpteen times the conflict between Chinese and US governments. In early 2000, the Chinese hackers utilized their strategies to get down the US reconnaissance plane while landing on Hainan Island.

12.2.1.5 Fun Attack

This category of attacks do not make any harm to the computer; however, this also comes under illegal activities. It is created due to curiosity or excitement. These types of attacks are easier to detect and prosecute than other types of attacks. It is often found in public social networking sites where a small group of friends interact with each other.

12.2.1.6 Grudge Attack

In this type of attacks, the attacker due to some personal conflicts, executes malicious activity to individual's computer or executes malicious intent to organization. Grudge attack is a personal attack motivated for taking revenge. The victim user is a well-known person of the attacker. In such kind of attack, the attacker may delete all the information from the organization's computer, steal the data, and delete and steal the secret information, and they may also launch a logic bomb on critical systems.

12.2.1.7 Thrill Attacks

Like grudge, the victim is often a well-known person of the attacker, but unlike grudge, it is not made for the revenge. The attacker wants to show their credibility in front of others. It is done by the attacker to challenge the victim or to boast themselves.

12.2.2 Challenges on Deterring Crime

However, there is still lacuna to cope with these kinds of crimes that include the following:

- Inadequate laws
- Lack of understanding
- Lack of evidence
- Rules of evidence
- Casual approach
- Lack of knowledge
- Lack of tangible assets.
- Loss of data
- Multiple roles.

12.2.2.1 Inadequate Laws

Attackers are always trying to learn new tools and technologies for launching the attacks at different ways so that they can compromise the system and get maximum profits from them, whereas changes on laws are very slow. It fails to keep the pace with the changes on the technology.

12.2.2.2 Lack of Understanding

All the top-notch officials including judges, attorneys, law enforcement team, etc. are not able to tackle with the new technologies that the attackers use. They take more time to become familiar with the issues related to crimes.

12.2.2.3 Lack of Evidence

Identifying and detecting the clues sometimes makes haphazard situation to collect the evidence. The wrong interpretation can cause lack of evidence that may lead to more loss. The expert attackers use malicious codes to compromise the network from different countries and keep change their location for lurking.

12.2.2.4 Rules of Evidence

Computer and its peripheral or the data that reside on the drive are the actual evidence. Sometimes, it is difficult to present original documents in court, because it is presented with hearsay basis that must also meet certain requirements to be admissible in the court.

12.2.2.5 Casual Approach

Sometimes people's casual approach toward handling transactions and other things makes them vulnerable. The attackers watch the ordinary user, and when they get the chance, they start their malicious activities.

12.2.2.6 Lack of Knowledge

Sometimes unknowingly people are allured by advertisement links given by the attacker and get compromised. For instance, the attacker sends a message of getting 50,000USD to many users. An ordinary user may get tempted and click on that message. When he clicks on it, he gets compromised. This is one example of getting compromised; there are so many ways the attackers can proliferate their intention.

12.2.2.7 Lack of Tangible Assets

It is very difficult to quantify the things related to the network where the crime occurs. The computer resources, data, bandwidth, or any other things are often the assets at issue. The asset valuation process definitely provides key information.

12.2.2.8 Loss of Data

When an attacker changes the original data, it somewhere loses its integrity. To readjust the coordination of any communication is a herculean task once the confidentiality and the integrity of the data are lost.

12.2.2.9 Multiple Roles

The investigator who applies forensics also engrosses with other roles of an organization. These multiple roles often make errors while investigating the crimes. On the other hand, the attackers' tendency is only to launch malicious codes that make them savvy on their work.

12.3 Computer Law

Computer law is a bunch of laws that are made for securing the electronic information, software, computer programs, its peripheral, piracy-related matter, and many other things that are closely associated with the computers. Computer law covers the entire range that includes computer security, its constitutional law and individual property rights, etc. However, all these rules are made for an organization to secure their data and associated matters. The different areas where these laws are applied are as follows.

12.3.1 Privacy

The information that can be easily received at a click on the Internet while keeping all these information private is an important issue. The lawyers mull over how to make all the information private and how to keep the customer information safe. Lawyers implement policies for securing information from any breach. They set policies about at what stage the information should be broadcast and at what level the information should be reserved. The privacy is controlled and governed by certain protection and privacy laws. There are many legislation forms to handle the private information through certain jurisdictions. If we see, all these works completely belong to the computer; thus, computers are generating enormous amount of data which makes handling these data as well as maintaining their privacy an uphill task.

In spite of setting legislation on privacy matters, there should be more points encompassed by ourselves as follows:

1. The website itself provides awareness to its users for collecting and maintaining their data.
2. The privacy policy should be clearly mentioned.
3. The website itself assures to its users that their data will be secured with appropriate policies.
4. The site has to maintain its tools, techniques, and procedures so that they can prevent themselves from unauthorized access and any kind of attacks.
5. The user would be able to insert, review, correct, update, and delete their data on particular websites.

12.3.2 Intellectual Property

Just imagine when we download any new movie from the website, we never think that we are also violating rules that belong to intellectual property law, and if millions of users from the entire world do the same, the company will face a huge loss. The company makes a new product, discusses it with the team, redesigns it, applies different online marketing strategies to permeate across the globe, and opts steps for maximizing the profit from the same business. They take intellectual property right to maintain the ownership of their product so that no other person can access it without their permission.

Intellectual property rights is made for protecting and also enforcing the rights of the owners. These ownerships can be a self-innovation, design, music, movie, writing, and any other materials that are created by an individual who has applied for intellectual property right (Figure 12.1). Broadly, the four categories where we can bifurcate intellectual rights are as follows.

12.3.2.1 Patent Law

Any product, process, or design that is made by an individual or a group of individuals who seek the protection of their innovation can get through patent. Patent law is the way for protecting the invention. It helps in educating people by protecting their invention and

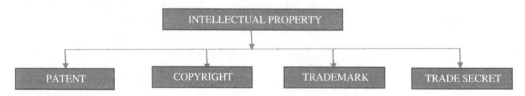

FIGURE 12.1
Category of intellectual property right.

by sharing their contribution to others. It can protect patent owner's designs, processes, and products from accessing, distributing, and importing by other people. It is a branch of intellectual property that protects the right of owner's contribution for a limited period of time.

12.3.2.2 Copyright

Copyright is the law that protects the owner's published materials, arts, entertainment materials, novels, website contents, music composition and its lyrics, and software. It is the legal right of the owner, or we can say it is the right to copy only to an owner. They have an exclusive right to reproduce their product, process, or design. If people access these things by using, presenting, or copying without taking the consent of the owner, they are violating copyright law. This law protects owner's material from unauthorized access, duplication, or copy. These materials have to be in tangible form for applying copyright. It does not protect any ideas, views, concepts, discoveries, logos, brand names, slogans, or title unless otherwise it is in a tangible form. Once it comes in a physical form, it will be eligible for applying it. However, copyright law protection varies from country to country. It is not the same across the globe.

12.3.2.3 Trademark

Trademark is any design, logo, symbol, phrase, or word that is referred by any entity to identify its product. Generally, trademark is used by corporate sectors, business owners, or any legal entity to protect their own marks, symbols, and designs. It makes their identities unique from others. It is a type of intellectual property right that shows that the owner is the first person who registers their mark and have the right to use marks in global market.

12.3.2.4 Trade Secret

A trade secret is one of the types of intellectual property right in which any formula, method, technique, information, or process is made for the economic growth of the creator that is not known to the public. The trade secret is specifically made to provide competitive advantages to the businesses. It is a kind of business practices, designs, and the formulas applied in the businesses to maximize the growth. The owner can utilize their appropriate structure to maintain the confidentiality from outside person. The famous example of trade secret is the method for Coco-Cola and formula for WD-40; it can be a method for manufacturing of product, technical processes like computer program, method of converting raw material into another form, method for making any food dishes, and any chemical formula used in making a product. Like other types of intellectual property right, it also facilitates to protect designs, formulas, and methods from others. However, unlike other types of intellectual property rights, the trade secret is not directly designated by the government agencies. There is no requirement to get registered through the government institution.

12.3.2.5 Comparison of Patent Law, Copyright, Trademark, and Trade Secret

Patent, copyright, and the trademark are frequently used interchangeably; however, there are some differences among them. They provide different forms of protection to the owner for intellectual property. Patents provide protection of designs, processes, and products only for a limited period of time. Patent can be any type of processes, designs, and materials. Copyright protects the owner's published materials, arts, entertainment materials, novels, website contents, music composition and its lyrics, and any software, whereas the trademark distinguishes if the work belongs to the individual or the company with others. Trademark can be a logo, word, symbol, phrase, brand name, or slogan which is not covered by the copyright. Trade secret is completely different from other types of intellectual property. It is made for the internal workability of the organization. The trade secret is not directly designated by the government agencies. There is no requirement to get registered through the government institution.

12.3.3 Contract

Contract is basically a signing agreement in written form that is specifically designed for sales, employment, tenancy, and any other purposes. It is legal, formal, and written documents that govern at least between two parties to ensure that they mutually agree on their rights and duties. It is a legal agreement that meets all requirements sanctioned by the law. In day-to-day activities, all the business organizations use contracts for the operation. For instance, any company that launches its online products and wants to sell them to another institution will have to mutually agree to access it. For the purpose of smooth functioning, both mutually sign on legal agreement.

In another example, most of the top notch IT companies such as Oracle, Cisco, HCL, IBM provides course modules to the students of educational institutions and open online course providers like Coursera, FutureLearn, Lynda, Udacity, Udemy share their courses to the individual learners. These services are based on agreement to the educational institutions. These products are provided as an agreement between the company and the institution for a limited period of time. It may be for 1 year or for the 3 year depending upon the signed agreement. Institutions share the contents of a product to their students once it is approved by both the parties. There is a similarity among all countries in governing contracts, though there are differences in enforcing the contracts as per their private international laws. In case of failing on contract, province or states, or the nation have rules to determine the jurisdiction.

12.3.4 Telecommunication Law

The literal meaning of telecommunication is communication between people staying in long distances where images, data, words, or sounds are transmitted in the form of electronic signals. The governments of all countries regulate communication-related matters as per their norms. The Government is promoting companies to do businesses from the evolution started at time of radio to the modern era. The telecommunication companies must know and follow all regulations set by the government. The users of computer and telecommunication must follow the set norms whether it is related to the bandwidth or the contents shared to others, or the issues related to the market share. The lawyers of computer and communication can easily help to the maven people of the particular industries for understanding all the rules and regulations so that they won't breach them. These lawyers also help them in any litigation and hearings once the violation occurred. The United Nation (UN) agency 'the International Telecommunication Union' situated in Geneva, Switzerland and its operational part 'the International Telegraph and Telephone Consultative Committee' play an important role in standardizing the telecommunication methodology.

12.3.5 Computer Crime

As we have already studied in separate sections of crimes, crimes on computer are any kind of criminal activities that use network and the computer as a tool to proliferate their activities. As it is very widespread, identifying the target is very cumbersome, but many computer crimes target governments and their policies. They may target all the information passed by the government; sometimes, computer crimes may target politicians too. These crimes also target many people for stealing their money by hook and by crook through the Internet and computer networks. For all these kinds of matters, of a computer lawyer can help them get rid of these kinds of frauds. Computer lawyers have to think a step ahead from computer criminals. They utilize all the strategies as per the rules and regulations made to detect and prevent computer crimes. They may work as a prosecutor for clutching computer criminals. The computer lawyers may also defend the person being accused of a computer crime. Computer lawyers play an important role in detecting and preventing computer-related crimes and also in defending a person being accused of a crime.

12.4 Live System

The traditional forensics is generally focused on the collection and the analysis of the data from the damaged system, i.e. a dead file systems. The collection and analysis in traditional ways is only on the read-only basis. In such type of approach, the integration of security-related files is located, reviewed, and verified. In traditional forensics, MAC time analysis is done to reconstruct the events. The drawback of this kind of analysis is that the maven attacker can at any time alter the information. It is difficult to find the clues using the traditional approach when the attacker's intention is unknown. EnCase, SluethKit, The Coroner's toolkit (TCT), and Autopsy forensic browser are the common tools used in traditional forensic analysis.

On the other hand, through live system, the volatile data that can be lost once the power is off are extracted, examined, and preserved. Sometime the investigator may or may not opt some traditional approach to get the data. It is the way to incident response where the investigator simply tries to find if any event has occurred. Live system provides an efficient data collection that can be utilized for further forensic analysis. There are many tool used for the forensic purpose in live system. It can be downloaded freely or through Microsoft's resource kit. It can also be observed through the config file. Some of these tools are drivers.exe, mac.exe, dd.exe, ps.exe, sc.exe, net.exe, now.exe, pstat.exe, uptime.exe, host-time.exe, whoami.exe, etc. The most common forensics response toolkits for live system forensics are incident response collection report (IRCR) and Window Forensic Toolchest (WFT). The live system has certain principles as follows:

- Efficient forensics requires the integrity. It should maintain the integrity.
- It should collect all relative activities too so that the later analysis can be determined if any incident has occurred.
- It requires minimal user interaction.
- It enforces sound data and the collection of an evidence.

The live system analysis is the most powerful activity for the forensic investigation. There are many reasons for analyzing the live window system by a forensics investigator. When we talk about the live system analysis, we consider some perspective through which we can assume the uncertainty level of getting the information tempered in each and every component of the computer. When the expert follows the step to analyze during live scenario, they will have to ensure that all the data are somewhere volatile to some degree. The unaltered data can exist in optical or magnetic media for several seconds, and sometimes it may exist for a longer time and even for years depending upon the quality of the media. Magnetic or optical media are volatile to some extent when the permanent files are stored on it. The level of maximum vulnerability in context of volatility are when the data travels during network transmission across the system bus. In a mean time the data can be existed and captured within a fraction of millisecond and sometimes nanosecond.

Data acquisition and analysis becomes difficult with increasing rate of volatility of the data. Increase in volatility means of more difficulties while capturing the data. There are many factors that can cause difficulties while capturing and analyzing data. All the components of a system are volatile to some extent. Magnetic or optical media, physical media, CPU registers, files, memory, and others are volatile at different levels. Data on a system has a certain order of volatility that is indispensable while collecting the data from the most volatile to least. The memory, swap file, network process, system process, file system information, and raw disk blocks are chronologically volatile. The data will be lost when the system reboots. The last two, i.e., file system information and the data in raw disk blocks, are least volatile compared to the others.

12.4.1 System Activities

The volatility of the different components of the system and their activities as follows:

12.4.1.1 Permanent Files

The data in permanent files remains more than a year. It also hinges upon the life of the media whether it is physical, magnetic, or optical. It also remains in permanent file until it is not deleted by someone. The data remains here for a longer time; hence, the analysis can be done offline.

12.4.1.2 Temporary Files

Most of the application files can create temporary files without the knowledge of users. These files can be obtained for the investigation purposes by experts. It keeps structured data repeatedly in a complete fashion that can be analyzed live. Once the document is closed by the user, the application can clean all the temporary file. The content can be analyzed offline if temporary files remain in the temporary directory before rebooting the computer.

12.4.1.3 Random-Access Memory

As we know, the random-access memory is a volatile memory that keeps their data only for a minute. Here, the experts can get the data that of course not appropriately well structure irrespective of it, they can use these data to find out the searches of words and the phrases. It stores all the information from previously executed programs and currently running programs. In such cases, only the experts can investigate through live analysis.

12.4.1.4 Unallocated Space

The experts use investigation to obtain the information here through unallocated space. Unallocated space is a sector where there is no files reside. This is a place in hard drive where all deleted files, documents, artifacts, and contents reside. Using offline system investigation, the information can be analyzed by the investigator very easily. The life of data on unallocated space is mostly for days.

12.4.1.5 Cache

The experts can perform only live system analysis in CPU cache for on and off cache chips. However, the expert can utilize both live and offline system analyses in case of disk cache. CPU cache carries both instruction and data depending on the size. It can contain more instruction and data if the size is large. In disk cache, a string of data can be obtained for the analysis because it works to improve the time while accessing from the hard disk and writing something to hard disk. The life of the data in CPU cache is a few seconds, whereas the life of the data in dish cache is in hours.

12.4.1.6 CPU Registers

A CPU register contains less amount of information that is not very much helpful for the experts to investigate the forensics. The life expectancy of data in a CPU register is in the range from nanoseconds to milliseconds. So, the experts choose the primary method to obtain the information i.e., only through live system analysis.

12.4.2 Methodology for Live System Analysis

Generally, two methodologies are utilized for performing live window analysis before switching off the system. These are as follows.

12.4.2.1 Implicit or Hidden System Monitoring

Implicit system analysis can be done by observing the system program and the activities of user on computer. The hidden monitoring provides a core action plan for the current and future scenarios. The implicit monitoring performs the following activities:

- It monitors the current network activities that provide the way to collect network-based evidence securely before any acquisition of equipment. It monitors both user and program activities too.
- In keystroke logging, all the key struck is covertly captured that records on keyboard. In such cases, no one can interpret that their action is being monitored by someone. It also monitors the mouse activity too.
- Window administrative tool enables a user to view the system on which they have administrative rights. These tools provides flexibility in managing and later monitoring the network from any location.
- Remote acquisition is also possible for performing remote drive image. For instance, EnCase Enterprise helps to record and analyze the electronic evidences and further helps to prepare a report on data.

12.4.2.2 Explicit System Acquisition

Explicit system analysis can be done on a system either through local connection or remotely. Once the system is secured, the analysis can be done through either command-line interface, windows graphical user interface, or remote command line. The activities of explicit system acquisition are as follows:

- During acquisition, it is indispensable to show any information on the system. This information may be shown from any part of the computer such as memory, current local logins, remote logins, network connection, etc.
- Information can be obtained through current running programs; otherwise, most of the content will also disappear once the power goes off.
- The information is expected to be acquired from the random-access memory before shutting down the system.

12.4.3 Key Elements of Successful Live Analysis

There are chances of getting alteration on data when the analysis takes place during live system acquisition. Certain formulas that can provide a successful live system analysis are as follows:

1. The user must know the reason for performing live analysis and doing live analysis.
2. Once the live analysis starts, each and every step should be documented. It provides the clarity from any deviation in analysis.
3. There should be least modification during the live system analysis. It is obvious that when the analysis starts, there are chances of some alteration on data, but consideration must be given in a least disruptive way.
4. The effect of program that is used for analyzing the live system must be known. It is very important to understand the impact of any alteration too. The analyst thinks about that what amount the memory is alter while running program on system. Next query comes on their mind that will it change the services, may it starts any other service, will it modify the disk, any alteration on file timestamp or is there any chances of releasing network connection etc.
5. There is also the chance of system being already compromised, so the expert has to ensure themselves that they shouldn't rely on any tools while performing live system analysis. These tools can also be compromised and provide wrong decisions.

12.5 Live Computer Analysis

The forensic analysis on system is the most important part for getting results that can help the experts to trace the attacks and the attackers too. It also ensures the recovery of data from the target machines and through the network. In this section, we are focusing on the recovery from systems or target machines. However, when these analysis starts, instead of taking direct analysis on computer, it processed on copy so that the original can't be altered during analysis. Sometimes the data that reside in the original hard drive are copied to one or more hard drives without any alteration. The investigator takes all these hard drives as a source of evidence for the investigation.The transfer of data from suspect's drive to another drive, generally taken as bit stream backup manner. In such cases, bit-by-bit transfer is performed so that there is no chance for any alteration and all deleted files from the suspect's drive can also be swapped. Here, the investigator does not want to permit even a single loophole in tracing the culprit. Bit stream backup process ensures the transfer of contents from the suspect's hard drive that includes all the unallocated space, slack space, bad sector, and swap space.

It is the most important part for the investigator to ensure how the data can be damaged on the drive. The answer of this question definitely provides the exact way for the analysis. The investigator has to think in the following way:

1. There may be a chance that the suspect has overwritten the content on the drive.
2. There might be a possibility that the suspect has applied the degaussing mechanism. Degaussing is a process through which the suspect erases all the contents by changing the magnetic domain where the contents reside.
3. There is also a possibility that the suspect has destroyed all the files before nabbing either physically or erasing all the contents.

The experts analyze systems as per their operating systems. The forensic analysis on Windows and Unix operating systems are as follows.

12.5.1 Windows-Based Forensic Analysis

Windows is the most popular and widely used operating system by the users though it is most prone to get crashed and unreliable compared to other operating systems. It is quite obvious that to retrieve all the deleted files from the Windows operating system must require good knowledge alongside technical skills. The investigator must have knowledge of file allocation and should be familiar with the functionalities of the operating system. When the victim was having Windows operating system, then the investigator may choose umpteen ways to proceed with the investigation. It is quite obvious that the traditional way of live forensic analysis can't be performed when the victim is unable to take out their system from the network due to backup server's inability of swapping its place.

Live response acquisition in Windows ensures whether the incident occurred. The acquisition of data is determined by the nature of the data, i.e., volatile and the nonvolatile data.

Volatile data remain exist until the power is turned off. These information is generally stored in memory, or it may exist in transits. The investigator retrieves these data from the cache, registers, and random-access memory. The traditional method of forensic duplication is unable to trace the volatile data. It may be possible through the live response process that contains information related to running processes, opening files, network connection. So, the investigator may use live response methodology for Windows to retrieve information from there.

When we talk about the nonvolatile data, it's a kind of digital information that is stored within a file system. It resides in some form in the electronic medium. When the power is turned off, it is retained at some specific state. The acquisition of nonvolatile data can be obtained through system event logs, which is available in easy readable format and exists in forensic duplication. Once the machine gets turned off, it would be difficult to receive output in a nice format.

Investigator throws a number of commands for acquisition through live response in Windows operating system. Each command produces information with respect to the given instruction and forwarded to the console. This information further forward for the analysis purpose in forensic investigator's machine rather than hard drive. If the forensic duplication is acquired in future, there is a chance of altered evidence when the data is saved locally to the victim's system. The data can be sent from the victim's drive to the forensic system by netcat command. Network administrators use netcat commands to create Transmission Control Protocol (TCP) channels. Same like telnet client and server, netcat also observes in listening mode. It releases few other commands as follows:

1. Victim system will send the data with following command:

   Command | nc forensic_system_ipadd 2222

   where nc stands for the netcat, and it is necessary to collect information from the victim's system through live response. It is sent over the TCP channel through port on port 2222 that is further saved to the.-+ forensic system in lieu of victim's system.

2. netcat command in forensic workstation:

   nc −v −l −p 2222>command.txt

   where nc refers to the netcat, v stands for verbose mode, l stands for listening mode, and p stands for the port that saves the data on the forensic system through command.

3. Once it finishes by pressing control and c through the keyword, it terminates netcat session. To evaluate the reliability in future:

   md5sum −b command.txt>command.md5

   where MD5 is the checksum that is hash of the content, md5sum stands for the calculation of hash content, and b stands for binary mode.

4. Live Forensic on Window with built-in tools for unusual network entries

   A. displaying the detail information on mapped deices and the drivers

      C :\> net use

   B. It shows all the list of computers, domains, and the resources that are shared by the specific system

      C :\> net session

   C. Command that shows TCP and UDP listening ports and remote IPs.

      C :\> netstat −na

   D. Commands that show TCP and UDP listening ports and remote IPs along with the addition of o that refers PIDS corresponding program and addition of b that refers corresponding exe.

      C :\> netstat −naob

5. Live Forensic on Window with built-in tools for unusual processes.

   A. To check the unknown processes by the users using system end or administrator through GUI

      C :\> taskmgr.exe

   B. To check the unknown processes by the users using system end or administrator through version

      C :\> tasklist –v

   C. To check the unknown processes by the users using system end or administrator with full list starting the service and verbose description

      C :\> wmic process list full

   D. Looking program using PID

      C :\> wmic process where processed=[PID]

   E. To check the running services

      C :\>services.msc for GUI or, C :\> sc query

6. Live Forensic on Window with built-in tools for unusual startup and unusual task.

   A. Registry key along with system startup

      C :\> **reg query [regkey]

   B. Registry key along with system startup using GUI

      C :\> regedit

   C. Registry key along with wmic system startup

      C :\> wmic startup list full

   D. To investigate the scheduled task for GUI

      C :\> taskschd.msc

   E. To investigate the scheduled task for listing specific task

      C :\> schtasks /query / TN task name /v / F0 list

7. Unusual accounts.

   A. Unrecognizable user looks through GUI

      C :\> lusrmgr.msc

   B. Unrecognizable user looks through

      net localgroup administrator or, C :\> net user

12.5.1.1 Tools to Recover Data on Windows

12.5.1.1.1 EnCase

EnCase is a computer forensic tool that is used for recovering data from Windows. This software is utilized to analyze the digital media by network investigations, criminal investigation, civil investigation, and electronic discoveries, and it is also used for the data compliance. All law enforcement companies are effectively utilizing this software to retrieve information from the digital media by indexing, file recovery, file parsing, data acquisition, etc.

12.5.1.1.2 Drivespy

Drivespy is a forensic Disk Operating System (DOS) shell that is specifically designed to emulate the capabilities of DOS. This tool is utilized to examine the DOS and Non-DOS partitions by its hex viewer.

12.5.1.1.3 ILook

ILook is a comprehensive suite of computer forensic tool. This is used for investigation by acquiring and analyzing the digital media on Windows. It gives the details of allocated and unallocated files and works with the compressed file.

12.5.2 Unix-Based Forensic Analysis

Increase in the popularity of Unix-based systems due to its widespread use is forcing for the different investigative ways both in analysis and target platforms. Analysis platform is the one that supports forensic workstations. The target platform is the place where an attacker compromises and makes a criminal violation of policies. As we know, Unix operating system are similar to Disk operating system (DOS) wherein Unix provides directories that are treated as files on the system level. These directories also contain subdirectories or files in lieu of data. I-nodes refer to all files or directories at the system level. An I-node contains a descriptor as name, attributes, authorization, date of creation, last access, modification, user proprietary, group proprietary, position of the file, dimension, etc. The contents are kept in separately i.e., data in the files, and the files in the directories. These files can contain any character in name except for special characters or spaces for carriage return (CR) and the shell. The file extension doesn't contain any certain meaning.

12.5.2.1 Unix Notations

There are some standard Unix notations that show current, parent, home directory, and so on as follows:

- / is the base of the file system that indicates the root.
- /bin/ is the subdirectory in the root for bin that is an arbitrary name. If path begins with '/', it belongs to the absolute path that begin with the root.
- . indicates the current directory.
- bin/ is a subdirectory of 'bin' with respect to the current directory. If path does not begin with '/', it belongs in relation to current directory.
- .. indicates the parent directory.

- ../ bin / shows the subdirectory at par with the current directory. Both subdirectory and the current directory are in the same level.
- ~ shows the home directory of the current user.

The live investigation process on Unix operating system is similar to the live investigation on Windows-based operating system; however, the analysis of Unix provides a different approach compared to Windows. It is a must to know the workability of the investigator before performing the live system analysis. They must have knowledge of how Unix operating system allocates the files and deleted the file to ensure the location of potential hidden files. The view file of Unix is different from Windows. It uses indexing nodes for representing the file. These indexing nodes are a concept of i-nodes. Each and every i-node contains the pointers to the actual data on the disk. These attributes useful for the investigation of the data. It contains read, write, and execute access, permission alongside number of directory links referencing the files, owners id, MAC access time and any medication. it also contains changing on the status such as permission, owner, number of links and the file size. I-node does not contain the file name or we can say the actual data. it is assigned an I-node number contained as in entry directory with the location of actual I-node. The directories of UNIX is a list of associated structure where each of which contain one I-node number and one file name.

12.5.2.2 Live Forensics through Built-Up Tools on Unix

1. Live forensics through unusual processes
   A. list on all running processes

      # ps –aux

   B. list of process specially only one

      # ps –aux | grep [PID]

      It pipes the output ps – aux to the grep. This refers to PID that allow to focus on only one process.
   C. specific process opens all the files

      # lsof -p [PID]

      lsof -p flag along with PID will display all the filed opened by specific process.
2. Live forensics through unusual entries
   A. display the sessions and connection for initial investigation

      # netstat –nap

   B. Display the listening TCP and UDP ports and remote IPs.

      # lsof –i

      The list open file (lsof) provides the comprehensive list of open files
   C. working for the host investigation

      # dmesg | grep –i promisc

      Dmesg piped with grep command to get when machine is set on promiscuous mode. When it is on, it shows that machine is sniffing the network to find the valuable information or to compromise more devices.

3. Live forensics through unusual files that can be an indication of data exfiltration

> find /-uid 0 –perm -4000 –print
> find / -name " " –print
> find / -name ".." –print
> find / -size +10000k –print

From this command we can get the SUID files (Set owner user ID)

4. Live forensics through unusual scheduled task that used through crons that works as a threat actor ensures the malicious activity can be executed again even if the process is killed or found

> crontab –u root –l
> cat /etc/ crontab
> ls / etc / cron

These commands investigate the system-wide cron jobs.

5. Live forensic through unusual accounts

> Sort -nk3 –t: / etc/passwd | less

Herein, / etc/passwd will sort all user by their id

B. To identify those account where the user is deleted earlier and the attacker use these accounts to create it and further to lurk it or deleted again for hiding their malicious traces.

> find / - nouser / -print

12.5.2.3 Phases Involved in Live Forensics on Unix

The process of forensic investigation on Unix platform can be bifurcated into five phases as follows (Figure 12.2).

12.5.2.3.1 Alert

When any automatic devices detect any attacks, it directly raises an alert to a response team. Response team has a work first to provide confirmation of alert whether the attack launched on system or it's a normal activity. These detections can also be done by system administrator through external input.

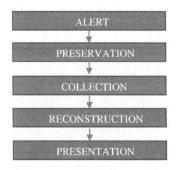

FIGURE 12.2
Phases involved in live forensics.

FIGURE 12.3
Log flow in a Unix platform.

12.5.2.3.2 Preservation

Preservation is an important phase in the incident response (Figure 12.3). Generally while taking an image of crime clues through disk image or any other way, there may be a chance of duplication. The main objective of preservation is to ensure that there is no alteration or modification on crime scene. Imaging the disk under Unix operating system is an indispensable part in this phase. There is a chance of getting common error while making a copy without forensically proven it. Generally, authorize person deals with the original disk however, it is not admissible in interfering on the hard drive. Hence, an image disk is required that is the replica of the original disk. this image disk is a main source of applying all the tools and the methods for analyzing.

In most cases, before delivering incident response, the system is turned off and further cut off from the network as per given criteria and guidelines of preparedness for the imaging copy. The system is turned on by the experts only to keep intact all the information from any kind of unauthorized access. Various tools and techniques create bit-by-bit images to retrieve data. A trusted workstation can be used for the acquisition whether the source disk belongs to the source hard drive or the CD. The external device contains the image of hard drive that include the image of invisible and visible files. It contain the deleted fragments of the file that is not overwritten yet and the details of the directories along with date, dimension, time stamp, file name. In another scenario, reproducing all information can be carried out by creating a clone of another system with the same characteristics. Few additional tools are also required to completely remove the content of hard disk. The wipe tool wipes the disk image destination hard drive. However, this process must be documented on forensic report and must be wiped once the examination phase is completed.

12.5.2.3.3 Collection

In this phase, all digital evidence is stored in a place for further analysis. These collections are used to further examine the scene of the crime and can be utilized for developing hypotheses. These developed hypotheses are investigated with the help of various tools and techniques. This phase also deals with the searching and file recovery. The problem comes during the collection of reconstructed of the data where the chances of data may be deleted or scattered around the file system. In Unix system, few terminologies are completely different from Windows-based operating system. For an instance, there is no mean of slack space in Unix as it stores all the data compactly however it stores optional data in last block. Hence, it also refers that there is no slack in Unix though the unavoidable wastage is stored in the last fragment. Under Unix operating system, the main objective during forensic analysis is to collect evidence and reconstruction of an event.

12.5.2.3.4 Reconstruction

The reconstruction phase reconstructs all the events when a detailed testing has been done to join all components of evidence. In some cases, image files can be examined and gone through in this phase. Reconstruction of an attack is one of the objectives during the forensic analysis. The analysis can be carried out through the analysis of log files. The traces of an attacker can be obtained through the detailed analysis using search of keywords or fragments. The findings through the thorough analysis of log files provides information regarding how the attacker has compromised the system, what changes has been occurred during the attack intervals, and which remote host has participated in it. The experts have to ensure during this phase that there is no alteration of information through the remote attacker which has a high possibility of modification of the data.

In Unix system, there is a command to check the different activities that are following:

A. A command to see where the syslog memorizes the information.

file / etc / syslog.conf

B. While the system set up, there is few log files that required to be examined that are displaying the information during intrusion like removed suspicious IP, logging blocks, etc.

- /var/logs/messages
- /var /adm/messages
- .bash_history
- .sh_history
- Coredumps
- proxy server
- wtmp
- utmp
- secure
- xferlog
- logs/*_log

There are certain tools through which the disk investigation and the analysis can be performed. There are many open-source tools and freeware tools that can be utilized for the analysis in Unix platform under GNU/GPL license.

12.5.2.3.5 Presentation

Presentation is the final phase of live forensic analysis on Unix where all the findings assemble in one place. These collections of findings further send to the investigator or an organization who has approached it.

12.5.2.4 Acquisition Tools

12.5.2.4.1 Sluethkit

Sluethkit is a remote analysis tool that has an HTML browser through which the image of compromised disk can be displayed. All the deleted file in both Unix and Windows platforms can be detected with the support of sluethkit. It also supports to search words and create timeline on the disc activities too. It generates all the files with association of md5 value during the analysis. Wipe is another tool that eliminates all the data on writable support. It sets all the bit with 0 on each disk. It is necessary in forensic analysis to set each bit as 0 for formatting.

12.5.2.4.2 Mac_Robber

Mac_Robber is another tool that is also used in forensic analysis. It helps to retrieve last modification, date of access from file, changes of date on files, etc.

12.5.2.4.3 Test Disk

Test disk also a forensic tool that allows investigators to analyze all the compromised disk. It also helps to analyze the undeleted partitioned. It also supports UFS, BeFS, Netware, ReiserFS, Linux, NTFS, FAT12, FAT16, FAT32, Linux SWAP, etc.

12.5.2.4.4 Tcpdump

TCP Dump is a tool for monitoring the network and debugging protocol, and it is used for acquisition of data. It is a network packet analyzer that supports the network forensic analysis. This tool works on command line. After capturing the logs, it retains network traffic in different output formats. It filters and collects data. It is able to read packets from network card, interface card, or an old saved packet file. The communication of other users or systems (computers) can be intercepted and displayed by using TCPDump.

12.5.2.4.5 FLAG

This tool is specifically made for forensic investigation and analysis of log files. It handles a large volume of data using database as a back end. It is a web-based tool; hence, a number of users can access it by deploying it in the central server in the same time. pyflag is a python implementation on Flag that is rewritten for more robust python programming. This tool helps in network forensics that stores tcpdump traffic within sql database. It performs the complete reconstruction of TCP stream. It also further constructs automatic network diagram in real time. It also allows to log arbitrary files format that easily upload to the database. It supports NTFS, FFS, Ext2, and FAT. It also supports various image file formats including compressed image format.

12.5.2.4.6 Ethereal

Ethereal is a freeware software program that can run in any platform. It supports real-time scanning of FDDI, Ethernet, token ring, and IP over ATM. It also supports loopback interfaces on some machines. Like tcpdump, it can also capture data on live network and can read it from the captured file. Unlike tcpdump, it can read files from a broad range of formats and tools. This tool is also suitable for offline log file analysis. Extensively potential to filter and the extraordinary graphic layout makes this tool more feasible.

12.6 Ethical Issues

The moment computer and its related applications are used in an illegal way, it may start bouncing back to the user in the most undesired manner and it may go up to such an extent of which no one has even dreamed of. Social websites that are used in all over the world such as Facebook, Twitter and many more allows people to communicate with each other but at the same time large number of malicious activities also take place on such social media websites. Facebook dissipated its first viral attack on 10 July 2014. As per the Facebook sources, countries such as India and developed countries from the west are the worst hit by malicious activities on the Internet. In 2002, attackers targeted some large companies like Yahoo, eBay, and Amazon using Distributed Denial of Service. The attackers caused their services interrupted and huge loss to finance. In 2003, an attacker named Clark in Oregon in the US used more than 20,000 zombie computers to launch a DDoS attack against the eBay website. In April 2008, due to its refusal to post a mainland Chinese private game server ad, the Bahamut website suffered a DDoS attack in which it was deluged with hundreds of data packets per second by more than 1,000 computers from all over the globe which paralyzed its services. In August 2009, the social networking site Twitter was also exploited by hackers as a tool to issue Botnet control instruction. After the biggest attack in history on 27 March 2013, we have seen drastic global internal slow downed.

Some unethical activities associated with the computer are as follows.

12.6.1 Piracy

The term piracy refers to unauthorized copying of software (Figure 12.4). This software can be a tool, language, music, antivirus, movie, or any other material that is made after a genuine license is obtained per law. Licensed software are those that are bought from their authorized owners. It is against law to make copies of original software. The following are few types of piracies:

- Online Piracy: the piracy that is related to the accessing illegal files, folders, software, books, etc. from peer-to-peer networks.
- Softlift Piracy: borrow copy of a software from others.
- Counterfeit Piracy: involvement in duplicity, selling copyrights.
- Hard disk loading: selling unauthorized copy of software with popular brand name.

12.6.2 Plagiarism

Plagiarism is a serious ethical offence in the field of academics and industries. Law has not yet set any rules or limitations on plagiarism. According to the oxford, plagiarism means the practice of taking someone else's work or ideas and passing them off as one's own. It is unauthorized use or close imitation of a language or thought of another author and representation of one's own original work. Plagiarism is a wrong practice done by one using others' materials, ideas, expressions, or thoughts. The idea remains problematic with unclear definitions and rules. Plagiarism is considered dishonesty and breach of ethics. Plagiarism is a copyright infringement.

FIGURE 12.4
Piracy.

The University of Illinois at Chicago's Health Informatics Department showed the involvement of students on plagiarism in ten main categories as follows:

- Copying other's work without permission consider as plagiarism.
- If any paragraph of other authors is taken uncited, it will be considered as plagiarism.
- Uncited rewrite of the work will be considered as plagiarism.
- Uncited quotations will be considered as plagiarism.
- Content of different sources will be considered as plagiarism.
- Incomplete citation done on some paragraphs.
- Melding together cited and incited sections of the piece.
- Providing proper citations but failing to change the structure and wording of the borrowed ideas enough.
- Citing not accurately to the source will also be considered as plagiarism.
- Relying too heavily on other peoples' work fails to bring original thought into the text.

In the academic world, plagiarism by students is usually considered a very serious offense that can result in punishments such as a failing grade on the particular assignment, the entire course, or even being expelled from the institution. Generally, the punishment increases as a person enters higher institutions of learning. The seriousness with which academic institutions address student plagiarism may be tempered by recognition that students may not fully understand what plagiarism is.

12.6.3 Privacy

Due to upgradation of computer equipment, people are using these devices for malpractices. For example the use of web cam is for a good purposes but instead of using for good sake, some violates the rules and accessing this in other's private life. Sometimes when we upload our photo, profile, or any information through social-networking sites, it can be retrived for malicious purposes by someone. Some companies are running only for spying others so that they can retrieve maximum information for their own purposes. We should always be alert in public places. Sometimes criminal intentionally involved in the crime to harm other's reputation. for this purpose, they may interact as a friend through social networking sites and, may hurt the person mentally or physically.

12.6.4 Ergonomics

Ergonomics is a field of study that attempts to reduce strain, fatigue, and injuries by improving product design and workspace arrangement. The main aim of ergonomics is to provide a more relaxed and comfortable working environment. Computer ergonomics addresses ways to optimize your computer workstation to reduce the specific risks of computer vision syndrome (CVS), neck and back pain, carpal tunnel syndrome, and other disorders affecting muscles, spine, and joints.

12.6.5 Work Pressure

Work pressure is a serious problem for employees with rapid changes in technology. In cut-throat competitions between companies in launching unique and new products or services, employers make the environment of their employees though. This pressure is just because of escalating consumers' demand toward handy and good products or luxurious services, increasing competition, deadline given by their employer, etc.

Questions

Q.1. What is money laundering? Explain with an example.

Q.2. Explain the difference among patent, copyright, trademark, and trade secret.

Q.3. Which communication body plays an important role in standardizing the tele-communication methods?

Q.4. What do you understand by bit stream backup? Why is it required?

Q.5. How many ways data can be damaged from the hard drive?

Q.6. What do you understand by degaussing? Why is it used?

Q.7. What do you understand by keystroke logging?

Q.8. Explain the role of EnCase tool.

Q.9. Explain the Windows-based forensic analysis.

Q.10. Explain the details of live forensic analysis on a Unix-based system.

Q.11. What are volatile and nonvolatile data?

References

F. Adelstein, "Live Forensics: Diagnosing Your System Without Killing It First," Communications of the ACM, vol. 49, pp. 63–66, 2006.

C. Altheide, "Forensic Analysis of Windows Hosts Using UNIX-Based Tools," Digital Investigation, vol. 1, pp. 197–212, 2004.

R. Dave, N. R. Mistry, and M. S. Dahiya, "Volatile Memory Based Forensic Artifacts & Analysis," International Journal for Research in Applied Science and Engineering Technology, vol. 2, pp. 120–124, 2014.

S. Lee, A. Savoldi, S. Lee, and J. Lim, Windows Pagefile Collection and Analysis for a Live Forensics Context, Future Generation Communication and Networking (FGCN 2007) (pp. 97–101), 2007.

B. J. Nikkel, "Generalizing Sources of Live Network Evidence," Digital Investigation, vol. 2, pp. 193–200, 2005.

P. Singh and A. Singh, "Computer Forensics: An Analysis on Windows and Unix from Data Recovery Perspective," International Research Journal of Engineering and Technology (IRJET), vol. 3, pp. 586–591, 2016.

Index

Note: **Bold** page numbers refer to tables and *italic* page numbers refer to figures.